How To Profit In Contract Design

by Andrew Loebelson

Published by Interior Design Books
A Division of Whitney Communications Corporation
850 Third Avenue
New York, New York 10022

Distributed by Van Nostrand Reinhold Company, Inc.
135 West 50th Street
New York, New York 10020

ISBN 0-943370-02-7

Copyright 1983

All rights reserved under International Pan-American Copyright Convention. No part of this work may be reproduced or used in any form or by any means—graphic, electronic, or mechanical, including photocopying, recording, taping or information storage and retrieval systems—without written permission of the publisher.

Designed by Balukas and Williams Design Group

Marketing and Rights: Lusterman, Grybauskas Inc.

IDB Publication Director: Virginia Evans

IDB Publication Manager: Chris Duffy

Our thanks to the following for their help in providing the photographs and samples used for the jacket design:

Maharam Fabric Corporation; Jack Lenor Larsen, Inc.; American Floor Products; Steelcase; Atelier International, Ltd.; Alma Desk Company; International Contract Furnishings; Neville Lewis Associates, Inc.; Continental Western Life Insurance Company.
Cover and text photograph: David Behl

All firms and people in examples on forms are fictional.

Printed and bound in Japan by Dai Nippon Printing Company through DNP (America), Inc.

Published by Interior Design Books, a division of Whitney Communications Corporation, 850 Third Ave., New York, NY 10022

Distributed by Van Nostrand Reinhold Company, Inc.
135 West 50th Street, New York, NY 10020

16 15 14 13 12 11 10 9 8 7 6 5 4 3 2 1

Library of Congress Cataloging in Publication Data

Loebelson, Andrew.
    How to profit in contract design.

    1. Interior decoration—Economic aspects—United States. 2. Design services—United States—Marketing.
3. Contracts for work and labor—United States.
I. Title.
NK2116.2.L63   1983   729'.2'068   83-12786
ISBN 0-943370-02-7

Contents

To Ruth and Mike for getting me started,
to Deborah for keeping me going,
and to Lester for saying he would make me rich and famous. I'm still waiting.

Introduction

This book is written for all those who hope to be paid for their work in interior design. Students of design should read this book to comprehend the totality of the field of design: It is a business and design is simply part of the overall product a client purchases. Employees of design firms should read this book to understand that the way to get ahead is not simply to increase design skills, but to increase the management skills that are discussed here, both to manage the client and the design team effectively.

Residential designers can discover a new world of design with the possibility of larger commissions and larger fees. They will also be introduced to a more systematized and professional way of practicing interior design than they may be used to, made necessary by those larger commissions. Contract interior designers may find some of the methodologies introduced in this book useful additions to their package of management tools.

Interior designers running their own small business should make use of the information in this book to reexamine their firm and make sure that they are running it at a profit, and not simply for a salary less than they might get working for someone else. Managers of larger firms may find the techniques in this book useful to codify and regularize the production of their professional services — eliminate problems and maximize profits. Architects entering this field should understand the complexity and difficulties which they generally underrate and all too often perform inadequately.

Included in this book are more than three dozen useful forms, checklists, and worksheets. The forms can be used immediately to help you run, or keep track of, some aspect of your office. The checklists are designed to make you aware of the multitude of facets involved in specific, highlighted complex tasks. And the worksheets utilize information you should know about your firm and manipulate that data to produce new information to help you manage better.

That is actually the point of this book, to help you manage the processes, the products, the clients, and the people in Contract Design better.

Good luck.

1 What Is This Business of Contract Design?

This book is called *How to Profit in Contract Design*, and this chapter is entitled "What is this Business of Interior Design?" If you understand those titles, you will understand quite a bit about this field. Let us define some of the terms.

"Profit" is the income left over after paying all the costs of running a business. Those costs include rent, utilities, all the other overhead, salaries for all employees, and a fair draw or salary for the owner. There is no profit in the business if you, as the owner, have not already taken out the true value for your services as designer, manager, and salesperson.

Profit is the value you deserve for conceiving the business, funding it, and running it well. You put in your equity with money, sweat, and worry every day in managing the business. You should earn your profits not from designing, but from running the business. This book is about maximizing the profit from managing the business of contract design, not from designing.

Which leads us to "Business." A business has an economic value of its own. It can be bought and sold. In fact, you should think of it as having a life of its own. It is born, it grows, it can wither and die. It has strengths and weaknesses. It has direction and momentum. It may have obligations, such as contracts and loans, and it has expectations in terms of payments. It has a family of employees who work for it and relatives who use its services. It has resources of capital, stock, experience, methodologies, and employees. It fulfills the needs of both clients and employees. You can earn money from designing, but you earn profits from running a business.

"Contract Design" is interior design work done for another business entity. It is usually done to aid the management in achieving the goals of that business. The design may aid work flow within the organization, control overhead cost by maximizing the rental utility, encourage better communication within the organization, enhance the business's clients' experience, satisfy some personal needs of the employees or management, or enable other business needs of the organization to function better.

Why do so many designers want to work in this area now? The client and design-need may be more rational. The budgets are often much bigger, sometimes in the tens of millions of dollars. Fees can reach the million-dollar level. Businesses may need more continual work than residential clients, require new stores regularly, or periodic reconfiguration as the organization grows.

There may be more visibility in work done for a large organization than in other work.

Architects have indicated that the expertise of interior design is very desirable because it extends their area of design and is much more profitable to them than the architectural portion of their assignment. And the challenge of producing a design which effectively links together thousands of individuals in common goals may be one of the greatest challenges an interior designer or an architect can face.

Why do I consider this book necessary? It is often hard for people in a service profession to consider themselves as a business. It is especially hard in the design field, where so much pleasure is taken in the creative work, to consider the business side more than an unpleasant diversion. This difficulty extends to single practitioners, small firms, and even some large firms.

My students and the professionals who have attended my lectures have made it clear to me that very capable designers may have no concept of the value of their services or how to sell them. When I worked for a large firm, they operated as the extension of the founder's original concept, with few changes allowed for their change in stature, the change in the industry, or the changes in clients.

Too many firms and individuals are "dumb competition," pricing their services at any rate to get work, and then doing a poor job on a low fee, and earning even less. One of my professional goals is to upgrade the general level of client-understanding so we can all have the opportunity to do excellent work at a fair price.

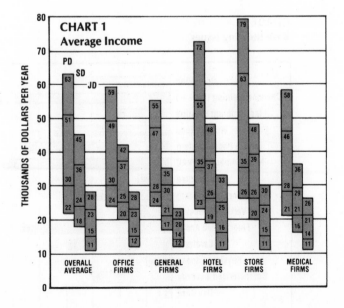

I have seen this "dumb competition" all around since my days in architecture school. When I went back to business school and came out to work in the administration for one of the largest interior design firms in America, the lack of a professional management viewpoint was amazing. I taught "Business Practices for the Design Professional" at the School of Continuing Education at New York University and had dozens of students who were earning decent money managing good size firms, yet many had never considered most of the important issues of running a business. I consult to small design firms who do not know where to go to get advice on business practices. I am a member of an interior design support group, and we share experiences, but there is no codified set of guidelines to help designers try to run their business.

My reasons for producing this book are to help make this industry more professional — not in design services, but in the business of producing those services. This book is written to make us all more aware of what a *business* really is, what the current state of the art of *managing* contract design is, and how to make good money by doing good work.

What is the product of contract design? As in all design problems, we have to start by seeking the real problem the client faces in using his present or future space, defining and analyzing that problem, and producing a space that he can use efficiently and enjoyably.

This profession began with practitioners merely manipulating objects within a space as well as choosing the surface finishes and textures of that space. The goal was purely decorative and its practitioners were decorators.

Then the practitioners began making the spaces function better for their clients by manipulating the non-structural components of the space (walls, windows, doors, and ceilings). They became interior designers.

Now practitioners, especially of contract work where function is of paramount importance, are beginning to have an impact on building shapes, sizes, and

CHART 2
Base Building Issues

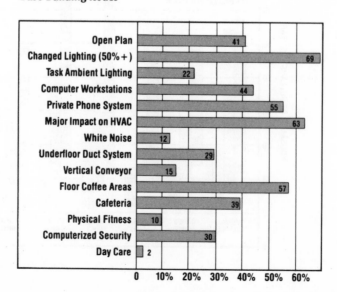

systems. This is entirely appropriate since they tend to know the client's functional requirements better than anyone else. They are becoming interior architects, whether architects like the use of that term or not.

See Chart 2, which shows the impact interior designers had on building systems this year.

Contract Design is an extremely complex sequence of thought, action, interaction, and product. It is easier to discuss if we consider it in phases. While there are many different breakdowns possible, I prefer to deal with the following five phases: programming, design conceptualization, decoration, construction documentation, and supervision. To some extent, each phase can have specialists. The bigger the firm, the more likely they will have specialists.

Phase One: Programming

The programming phase determines what real spatial problems are to be solved by the designer and the client in order to effectively run the client's business. It may, or may not, deal with specific spaces.

The first step is to establish occupancy requirements. Personnel must be interviewed at several levels within the client organization to determine various factors. How many employees are housed at this location? How many different classifications of employees do they recognize? How many different classifications would it make sense to have if each needed a different amount of space or different types of building services? You are trying to determine how many work-space standards there should be and what general amount of space will be required for each.

What is the anticipated organizational growth pattern for the client? Be aware that individual manager's forecasts are usually woefully inadequate. They tend to forecast their past growth ahead for five years, sometimes with some modesty and sometimes with a little empire-building in mind, but they rarely can see change beyond five years. In fact, the organization will continue to grow, and their department might grow, split, and then continue to grow. Or new departments will take over some of their function in a much larger organization. So the sum of department manager's forecasts is the worst forecaster of the future.

The past ten years of an organization is usually a better forecaster. It should be compared with management's business goals to see if they intend to continue in the same manner. Notwithstanding a company's often-stated plan for becoming more efficient in the future, they rarely do so in terms of productivity. They often provide new services, quicker turn-around, or a more personalized product, but they rarely get much more efficient. Therefore, if management claims they want to grow their output, or profit, or earnings-per-share at, say 10 percent per year, then they should plan on their personnel growing at roughly the same rate.

This sounds much too simplistic, but we have found it to be more accurate than low-level manager's forecasts. Banks' personnel, for instance, grow proportionately to the asset base. Increased use of computers has hardly affected this over the last decade. Increased services being offered have affected it more.

Of course you should check out the long term trends in the industry as well. Are changes occurring that should be considered in forecasting growth? Are blue-collar jobs moving offshore, requiring even more management to deal with the increased complexity? Are services becoming available that will eliminate jobs? How are competitors acting? Will a major investment be required by your client to stay with the competition?

How does management feel about your preliminary findings? You must make sure that they deal with real possibilities rather than wishful thinking at this time. In the very preliminary stage, you are functioning almost as management consultants to the firm. Make sure they realize that you are only trying to forecast space requirements and need know nothing more about their plans than their business goals and the acknowledged possible actions they will take to reach them. But make sure they also realize that this is a crucial step in their creating intelligent, cost-effective future real estate strategies.

You have now determined how many people they presently house, how fast they are growing, and how much space each person requires in general. You may now forecast how much space they will have to build or rent for their "move-in requirement." Be aware that no firm should move into space just suitable for the employees they will have when they move in. They must make allowances for growth between the time they move in and the next expected option for more space, or their next phase of building. Given that it is rare to be able to sublet space for less than five years, I recommend to my clients that they move into space that is at the very minimum adequate for at least five years.

You have to determine what special requirements are necessary for the employees to function well. There are numerous factors to be considered at this point. What percentage, for example, of employees will be using CRTs? (The overall average in the country is approaching 50 percent.) Does this organization change frequently? What percentage of employees are moved each year? What percentage of space needs to be reconfigured each year to accommodate these changes? Do any employees need special communication devices? Or storage? Or presentation areas?

What will the company policy be for coffee? Are employees allowed to take it back to their desks, or must they take breaks in specified areas, protecting the carpeting? Is mail a problem? Is copying centralized or dispersed? Which should it be? Is there a record retention program? Are records centralized, dispersed, or is that unknown? Does the company encourage communication or discourage interaction?

Are there special equipment or environmental requirements? Will computers be introduced? Is there a centralized machine area needing special ventilation or chilled water? How will the cabling get in or out of that area? Are mini- or micro- computers proliferating throughout the space? Is there a heat build-up problem? Will there be problems with standard lighting on the screens? Are the printers so noisy that they should be acoustically isolated?

Will a cafeteria be installed? How many people should it be designed to serve? How many turns? Will there be cooking or just warming of pre-cooked foods brought in from outside? Should there be a brown-bag lunch room? Vending machines? Microwave ovens?

Is a trading floor contemplated? Will it require Reuters? Dow Jones? Quotron? Telex? Bunker Ramo? How can you cable it? How much air conditioning will be required? How many people will man it originally? How many eventually?

Are many visitors expected? Is there a need for security? How strict should it be? Should visitors be carefully controlled within one area?

What are the flows within the organization? How does paper flow throughout it? Does that parallel the information flow, or is it different? How do people move in the organization? Who meets with whom regularly? Is that ideal, or simply a result of haphazard adjacencies? Which individuals or groups should be close to other groups or individuals? We normally show these ideal adjacency requirements as "bubble diagrams" at this stage of investigation. When these adjacencies are shown on a cross section of a multiple-story building, they become a "generalized stacking diagram."

What were the shortcomings in the old space that the company had to deal with? Is there time to deal with them effectively in the new space? Do they need a different form of electrical/telephone distribution? Can they use a building standard ceiling or should they get credit for it and install task/ambient lighting? Should they be looking for space with a module size that works better with their space standards?

What are the problems which might become important in the future? Will it become difficult to hire programmers or other special types of employees? Should they upgrade their working conditions in order to have a better chance of recruiting top-notch employees or impressing clients more than they have in the past?

What should the nature of the space be? How would you express its appropriate ambience in a sentence or two? Does management agree with the adjectives you use? How expensive should it be? How long is it supposed to last?

You might be expected to use your findings to do feasability studies or help with lease negotiation. Is a specific space suitable for this organization? How long will it continue to be suitable? What do you expect its real costs of occupancy to be? If the company has to move, will having this space be a benefit or a liability?

If you are helping with lease negotiations, you should determine the true amount of usable space (see the last chapter for definitions) in the proposed premises. You can compare different spaces the client might be looking at. What is the actual value of the space or the work letter? What will the costs of occupancy be? Is the space suitable now? How long will it remain so? Are options available for additional space? Will they be well situated and available at the right time? Are there any other benefits or drawbacks to the space?

When all this has been examined, you have to draw up an appropriate time table for occupancy. The schedule should include dates critical for both your decision-making, the client's decision-making, and the production of documents and space necessary for the client to occupy the space when planned.

The last step in this phase is extremely important. You must produce a report with all the major decision factors for the client to approve. You both must agree on a common basis for continuing the process before you proceed. Otherwise you might end up wasting time and effort on useless work. At the end of each phase, it is absolutely critical that the client approve your progress.

Phase Two: Design Conceptualization

The purpose of this phase is to determine the specific design solutions (basic, not decorative) to the problems defined during the programming phase. This phase should begin with a further refined statement of the desired image, both applied internally to the employees and applied externally to the customers of the business.

Actual office standards should be defined, without the specific furnishings being chosen. That means that a "C" office for a department manager might be defined as a 10-by-15-foot room with a window wall, an internal glass wall on the short side where the door to the access corridor is, furnished with building standard carpeting, a metal desk with matching metal credenza, two cloth upholstered armless visitor chairs, one cloth upholstered executive-level chair, and an optional return or bookcase. Standards should be defined for the president, vice-presidents, managers, supervisors, technicians, secretaries, and clerical workers.

The fewer standards, the better from the standpoint of management and layout. But it is usually difficult to get fewer than three closed office standards and three open work-stations. Privacy, flexibility, efficiency, cost, and previous conditions must be considered in making these choices. From management's point of view, it is a simple managerial decision. But this is the design's most significant impact on the individual employee, and his or her feelings, perceptions, and satisfactions should be carefully considered as well.

The bubble diagrams have to be combined with the actual space to be taken up by each department to create "block allocation plans" overlaying the actual space. "Stacking plans" should show the multiple floor occupancy in some detail.

An overall layout scheme has to be developed at the same time that various other important conceptual solutions are worked out. A lighting concept must be developed that will work well with the module and the office standards.

Acoustical requirements have to be examined in the light of other decisions being made. The electrical/telephone distribution system must be planned to work well with the layout.

Special requirements for floor loading, HVAC, electrical, signal, and acoustical considerations must be specifically delineated. Not only should specific types of furnishings be detailed at this point, but all furniture considered for reuse should be examined, and a general determination of suitability made. This is a necessary step to producing a realistic budget.

Detailed layouts must show people, walls, furnishings, equipment, lighting, and types of materials. With this now available, a preliminary, but accurate, budget should be worked up for construction, furnishings, fixtures, and equipment.

This should be presented to the client, reviewed in detail, modified as required, and then approved in writing. Again, no further steps should be taken without specific, written, approval by the client of the design concept.

Phase Three: Decoration

The decoration phase begins with the design concept statement, budget, and plans and produces the choice of finished items that will meet those criteria.

The reuse items are examined on an individual basis and accepted or rejected. Primary, and perhaps secondary, choices are made for all furnishings. A color scheme is chosen to mesh with the design intent. All surface coverings, materials, textures, colors, finishes, and method of application are chosen. Special lighting is chosen for the special areas. Floor coverings, wall, and window treatments are chosen and specified.

Special cabinetwork is detailed. Necessary graphics are designed. An art program may be developed and individual works chosen. Accessories are selected.

In any particular area, such as systems-furnishings or carpeting, specifications may be drawn up so equivalent systems may be bid against one another. All items should be sent out for estimates. A specific budget is drawn up.

And again the client must review and approve the decorative scheme and budget in writing.

Phase Four: Construction Documentation

The sole purpose of this phase is to produce all the necessary documents so the interior design can be executed exactly as conceived at the lowest possible cost.

The basic document package will consist of furniture plans, layout plans, reflected ceiling plans, electrical/telephone plans, finish plans, door schedules, finish schedules, hardware schedules, cabinet drawings, construction details, and all the specifications and general conditions related to the above.

Purchase order specifications may be required by clients who do their own purchasing (in contract work, many do!). A bid package may be required for either the furnishings or construction part of the package. In other cases, negotiation on behalf of the client may replace the bidding procedure.

The interior design firm may have to prepare and file all plans required with the appropriate authorities in order to obtain the necessary permits and authorizations.

Sometimes an interior design standards manual is prepared, either as part of the basic contract or as an extra cost item. An interiors maintenance manual may also be desired by the client, but-that is always an extra cost item.

If for some reason the final costs differ significantly from the budgeted costs for any part of the project, redesign may be necessary to stay within the overall budget.

Phase Five: Construction Supervision

The prime objective of the construction supervision phase is to maintain budget, quality, and schedule.

Representatives of the design firm must inspect the work in the field on at least a weekly basis. They have to check shop drawings to make sure they correspond closely to the construction documentation and specifications requirements. The design firm must make sure that the contractor corrects problems that occur when field conditions differ significantly from the plans. Work and products are inspected and payments are certified.

The Move-In is planned and coordinated.

A "punch list" listing of substandard work and defective items is created from inspections of all work. The interior designer must work with the contractor to correct these before final payment is made.

Overall management of the project is considered part of this phase as well.

Interior design started out just dealing with the relatively short and simple third phase of "Decoration." You can see how complicated the job has become. It is a difficult job to do an entire project right, and it is expensive. But it is also extremely worthwhile... for your client and for you.

2 Strategic Planning

Strategic planning is a subject far from the minds of most interior designers. That is why this discussion appears early in the book. It is essential that any business, indeed any individual with a real drive to get ahead, should plan carefully his or her moves to the top.

Planning a business's path to success and planning an individual's career path are both similar in timing and scope. The time to start that planning is now. Without a plan, few people know enough about where they stand to truly understand where they want to go. Without a plan, few people know enough, and are lucky enough, to channel all their energies into productive efforts to reach their goals. And without a plan, few people can really learn from their mistakes, and become more effective each year.

In order to plan effectively, any person or business has to conceptualize four things.

The Present Situation — Where you are now.

Measurement Indices — Appropriate measurements of your present situation that are also applicable to your future.

Objectives — Where you want to be in the future.

Strategy — How you get there.

The only other action necessary for success is just that, implementing the plans you have formulated.

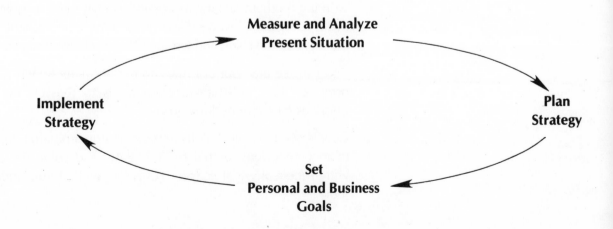

This exercise is not something you can do once, breath a sigh of relief, and get back to solving the problem of the recessed lighting smack dab in the middle of the main air supply duct. You have to cycle through all of these issues at least once a year.

If you do this exercise regularly, you will find that you are far more effective in many aspects of the business. You will be more effective in sales because you will know why that job is perfect for you and why you need it. You will understand what makes you the best candidate for it and how you will use it to get other jobs later on. Your self-confidence and knowledge will communicate itself to the client, making it more likely that you *will* get the job.

You will do better work because you will be more aware of your real strengths and weaknesses. You can compensate for your weakness short-term as you seek to correct them long-term while getting the maximum benefits of those strengths at the same time.

Your whole operation will become more profitable as you learn which jobs you really want and which jobs you would just as soon walk away from. Many clients are drawn to the successful firm that knows enough about itself to turn down work.

Before we start the process of strategic planning for interior design, we should remind ourselves what skills are required for success in this field.

Clients care about five aspects of their interior design solution. They want to solve their space problems, now and for the foreseeable future. They want to correct any functional problems they have now, and make sure no more crop up later. They need to adhere to the budget set by their existing leases or business plans. They want to have no unpleasant surprises in the budgeted cost area by the time the job is complete. And, yes, they do care about the design of their space. But that is often the lowest priority, the least important aspect of the product interior designers offer.

The tendency to concentrate on design is natural and normal. But it is not helpful to your career, your business's health, or some of the prime components of the job now on your boards. We naturally work on the first two problems mentioned, but we want to finish them as quickly as possible. The third and fourth aspects are normally considered pure drudgery, and we delay working on them as long as possible, finish them as quickly as we can, and avoid going back lest we discover something unpleasant. The last problem is the icing on the cake, and we spend as much time as we can on that aspect.

You can see how our priorities do not normally match well with our client's priorities. Part of strategic planning is to reassert the client's important priorities into your outlook on your work.

Clients need excellent skills in problem conceptualization. You must be able to recognize, conceptualize, articulate, and solve the problems they face within their physical spaces. This requires that you understand the client's industry.

You should know the differences between financial, marketing, and energy companies. There are the different personal, professional, and psychological needs of different employees. How do account, media, creative, traffic, and research people differ in an advertising agency? What do people actually do when they work there? Are there different physical needs between a copy writer and an art director? In a bank, what is a "proof" department and how does it function? How different is that from the "trust" department? Who are the clients of your client? Are the visitors to the trust department substantially different from the visitors to the auto loan department? What do they need and what different impression does the bank want to give them?

You often have to understand how your client works better than he does. He may know it so well that he's forgotten it, or he may not be able to explain what actually goes on because the formal lines have broken down through work or environmental factors. You cannot solve his problems until you can articulate them clearly and concisely. Not only do you have to know the ramifications of all your decisions with regard to other components, you should also be aware of the cost extensions, both initially and life cycle.

Only when you have solved these other programming and design-concept problems can you get down to actual design. And, of course, this means using the tools of interior design to solve the problems the client has. Decoration is one of the tools, but as we have seen, it is not the most important one.

In order to effectively solve the client's problem, you still have to get the job produced correctly, on time, and on budget. This requires high documentation skills. This is not simply drafting well and producing high-quality lettering with a carefully maintained chisel point. It also includes scheduling, tight specification writing, and all other means of communicating your desires properly to the people who execute the design.

Project supervision skills are really essential. If you are weak here, your contractor may take advantage, producing a substandard job that will reflect poorly on you, and rightly so. In fact, if you look at what we have been discussing, it would seem that design management skills are at least as important as all the actual skills that go into producing a physical solution.

This section may have seemed like a long diversion, but I have been trying to make the point that a high requirement for success in this field is an excellent understanding of the entire scope of interior design and the complete understanding of all the tools you have to use to produce a high-quality product. A fine decorative skill in contract design may be your least important attribute. If other skills are lacking, the decorative effect will probably suffer anyway. Clients would far rather have bland or mediocre design produced on time and budget than exciting work finished too late for too much money that falls apart too soon after completion.

However, the finest interior design skills, in the broadest and most complete sense will not make your firm a success without high-quality marketing skills. You have to find prospects for your best services — or top-quality services for your best prospects. That requires a fair amount of soul-searching in order to determine what you really do well, as well as some market research to make sure you are providing something people actually need and are willing to pay for.

You should have some skills in public relations to extend the marketing effects of the work that you successfully complete for satisfied clients. Why waste successful work? If it solved someone's problem, other people in similar circumstances will be interested to hear about it and to learn something of the design firm that correctly identified and solved the problem.

You must also clearly recognize and be able to deal with "base-building" issues. Too many interior designers do not even know what this means. The "base-building" includes all items that would normally be built by the base-building contractor. Eighty percent of the cost of a building is in the five systems of structure, external cladding, elevators, mechanical (heating, ventilating, air conditioning), and electrical. Normal "tenant work" consists of non-structural walls, the ceiling and lighting system, electrical and telephone distribution, hardware and finishes. The "Work Letter" describes the number and quality of these items that will be provided to tenants or the cash value that is offered in its stead.

If you know this much, you are ahead of many interior designers. But you should know much more in order to effectively solve your client's problems. Can you change any of the base-building or tenant-work-parameters to help your client? If the distance from the core to the window line of a proposed building is 33 feet and your work station standards are based on a 5-foot module, 3 feet of that depth is likely to be wasted in an 8-foot wide corridor. Will that be useful for this client for file cabinets, or can you save up to 10 percent on the total floor area of the building by shrinking it to a 30-foot depth and still house the same number of people? Will the building standard lighting fixtures work for this client or, since they have an enormous number of CRT's, are you better off getting an allowance and installing a task/ambient system?

You should be able to deal with the conceptual approach to space configuration so as to maximize the building efficiency for your particular client. You should know all the standard approaches to building systems as well as alternatives to them so as to propose cost-effective choices to your client.

You have to be at least equally knowledgable about interior componentry. How well will different types of components work for your particular client? Do they need enclosed offices? Should those offices be demountable partitions for quick inexpensive changes or can the number of standard office types and standard layout around a core eliminate much of the need for change? Is a wire management partitioning system called for, or can you use flat wire? How well do different types of systems work together? Do you need white noise to go with the choice of ceiling system and partition system materials?

What are the ramifications of the decisions you are making? If you decide to put everyone in open plan with task/ambient lighting, does that mean you still have to put registers in the ceiling because the plenum is acting as the return? With no full height walls, are you going to have to core the floor for electrical/ telephone distribution, use power poles up to the ceiling, or install your first flat wire system?

For marketing you should have a consistent image concerning you, your work, and your firm. All paper — drawings, letters, cards, releases, etc. — should appear consistent with the kind of person you are and the type of work your firm does. You are seeking to create an image that people will recognize, and the simpler, more coherent, and more concise it is, the more effective it will become.

If you don't have access to a traditional "old-boy network," and few of us do, you must make your own "old-boy" network through constant "list-building." (We will discuss that later in depth.)

You should have the skills necessary to take knowledge of a potential work opportunity and convert that into a meeting. Sometimes you do that, and sometimes you may hire a marketing person to do that for you. In either case, you should know enough to control that situation well.

You need to keep in touch over long periods of time with potential clients so they do not slip away through your apparent lack of interest.

A separate set of skills you should have, all too often confused with marketing skills, are sales skills. This is the art of converting a known prospect into a client.

You should be able to prepare well, do your homework before a presentation so you know who needs what and on what basis they will make their designer decision.

You should have and project the right image for the client.

You need the incredibly valuable skill of listening well. You can then determine what the client said he needed and offer it to him.

You can price your services correctly for the job *and* the client. But you have to know how much it costs you to produce those services and what the market value of those services might be.

The skills you need for success in this field fall into just a few categories. You have to know your client and his industry. You must understand how buildings are put together. You should understand everything about what goes into an interior. You should have high skills in design. Then you need the production skills to convert design into reality. And you need marketing and sales skills to get the opportunity to demonstrate all those other skills.

With all that in the back of our mind, we can now look at how we should do strategic planning for a firm in the contract design field. You might consider doing the same for yourself as an individual, regardless of whether you are a student, an employee, or a single practitioner. We all should be aware of how we should develop ourselves to meet our goals.

Step One: Analysis of the Present Situation

Considering all the skills critical to your success in this field, what are your present strengths and weaknesses? How well do your skills mesh? Are your capabilities, your image, and your marketing all consistent?

Set down the actual facts that describe you. What is the size of your firm? What size project can you handle? How expensive or complex are your projects? How well does that fit with the size of project you would like to be able to produce? What are your present professional capabilities, personally and firm-wide? What does your present client-base consist of?

How efficient is your organization at producing work?

How do you bill for your services and what are your standard rates? Are those your real rates, or do you bury hours that you think have been unproductive or might have raised the fee beyond what you consider reasonable? What billing rates do other people seem to be getting in your geographical area and market segment? Can you measure meaningfully your market share?

Write down the driving force of your organization. Does that mesh with your personal motivations and those of your staff? Have you considered all aspects of your motivating forces, such as personal, professional, and financial needs? Are they consistent and realistic? How high is overall firm morale?

Describe your firm's financial situation. Can you separate out the value and income of the firm from yourself personally?

How would you define your management style? How well does it seem to work? What is your level of commitment?

In the past, it was impossible to compare many of these answers with industry data because there was no industry data. Now we have data on fees, billing rates, income, production efficiency and much more. The accompanying charts from the "100 Interior Design Giants" provide you with a wealth of data to compare yourself to other designers across the country. Use all of it.

Step Two: Choice and Definition/Redefinition of Goals

You have to set two different types of goals. Long-term goals are set so you always keep in mind what you want to be when you grow up. Short-term goals are chosen so that you take the first, measurable and achievable, steps in that direction. Short-term goals grow out of the long-term goals.

Goals should be set in each of the following categories: personal, professional, organizational, and financial. These goals can be personal recognition, personal or corporate net worth, higher profit margins, raised and maintained billing rates, total fee income, retirement or estate planning, and so on. They can be corrections to, or perceived weaknesses in, your arsenal of skills necessary for success or extensions of strengths that seem underutilized.

These goals should be internally and externally consistent. They must be achievable, visible, and measurable. Short term should be targets achievable in one year. Long-term goals should be rational, consistent, linear arrangements of short-term goals.

One of the easiest ways to figure out your short-term goals is to determine your correct billing multiple. We will discuss that in the next chapter.

Step Three: Strategy Formulation

Now you have to determine what series of actions you will take to achieve your goals. Compare your strengths, weaknesses, and resources. Decide on the tactics that you will use. Usually your tactics will include a financial component. They may very well include a marketing component. They may sometimes include a human resources component. And they will always include a managerial component.

Do you need additional personnel? Perhaps you should be hiring experts in areas you feel a lack, such as marketing, or production, or a target market such as health care facilities. Do you need to add people to your staff overall or do you simply need someone to relieve you of certain responsibilities so you can attend to others?

If you get these new professional skills, will you need more marketing help to sell them? How much would you expect to sell this year?

Are you going to need additional money to hire these new people, or to produce new brochures and do a major mailing? How will you raise that money? Do you need a partner, a backer, or a banker? How will you find them? How much money will you invest in the search?

Can you afford the management time to move in this new direction? Who will take over your old duties? How will you measure their success? Do you need new or improved skills in some area? Where will you get them and how much can you afford to pay in time or money?

What kind of management changes will be necessary to achieve these goals? How will you motivate your staff to strive for goals consistent with yours? Will you use money, or advancement? Is your organizational structure consistent with your goals? How would you change it to better tune the firm to meet those goals?

How will you provide feedback to yourself and your employees so you know how well you are meeting your goals? How often will you provide that feedback? Can you fine-tune your strategy and change your tactics to achieve those goals part way through the year as you start seeing successes and shortfalls?

Write down your goals, strategy, and tactics. Never attempt anything that is not articulated, defined, and measurable. Include appropriate time frames, determine who will be responsible for what actions, and share as much of this with your staff as you can.

Step Four: Implementation

Do it. What are your first steps? How do you follow them? How are you monitoring the process? How are you evaluating the process? Schedule regular meetings to discuss these goals and steps with someone, monthly or quarterly. Use any sounding board you can find. If you practice by yourself, use your lawyer, your accountant, an old professor, or a support group. But force yourself to speak to someone about it, so you can't hide the truth and you can't ignore the need to evaluate it objectively.

Step Five: Analysis of the Present Situation

Start again. Do it at least once a year. Where are you now? Where were you a year ago? Where do you want to be next year? Where do you want to be in five and ten years? How will you get there? What will it take? How will you measure success?

In order to make this process easier, I have drawn up a **Strategic Planning Worksheet**. Let's go through it quickly.

The "total dollar volume of furnishings and construction installed" is the value of all furnishings and construction items that you designed and specified. Thus, in addition to furniture, you might include the ceiling system and lighting which you designed, the non-structural walls constructed to air-conditioning unit you may have specified for the internal conference room.

The "total square footage" figure should be in rentable square feet (RSF). It should be easy to get from the leases. Your fees, number of professionals, and number of employees are all self-explanatory.

You can now determine your operating characteristics. Take your total dollar volume and divide it by your total square footage. This will give you some idea of the relative complexity of the work you are doing compared to other firms in your specialty or size category when you pull that data out of the accompanying charts.

STRATEGIC PLANNING WORKSHEET

Company:	T.I.D.
Date:	1/2/84
Person Completing Worksheet:	A.T.

YEAR END CHARACTERISTICS

Total Dollar Volume of Furnishings and Construction Installed	$ 6,900,000
Total Square Footage of Installations this year	150,000 RSF
Total Fees Earned This Year	$ 325,000
Average Number of Professionals Employed This Year	5
Average Number of All Employees This Year	6

OPERATING STATISTICS

Category	Your Statistics	Your Size Category's Avg	Your Specialty Category's Avg	Differences/Explanations
Avg Vol/RFS	$46/RSF	$50/RSF	$53/RSF	Work with small, cheap, local firms
Fee/Vol as %	4.7%		7.2%	same as above
Vol/Pro	$1,255,000	1,225,000	1,342,000	Quite good, just too many cheap jobs!
Vol/Emp	$986,000	1,035,000	1,098,000	Very good, not too heavy for support
Fee/Pro	$59,100	68,000	76,000	? Can I get these clients to pay more
Fee/Emp	$46,400	57,000	62,000	or do I need better heeled clients?

CURRENT SITUATION

Most work is in: ☑ Office ☐ Hotel ☐ Restaurant ☐ Stores ☐ Medical ☐ Residential ☐ Other

Most Work was brought in by: My contacts - 50/50 new/repeat work

Staff Capabilities are: (category)

Staff Output Quality is: ☐ Excellent ☑ Good ☐ Adequate ☐ Poor ☐ Very Poor

Staff Morale is: ☑ Excellent ☐ Good ☐ Adequate ☐ Poor ☐ Very Poor

Staff Motivation is based on: Medium level salaries, but lots of freedom

Describe firm's current financial situation: Have 4 mo. more work booked already, also 3 mo. payroll in bank - real good shape!

Current firm strengths: Strong client relationships, good contractors, hard working people.

Current firm weaknesses: Pretty dull designs - never published, no high-style images or capability - hard to raise fees.

Last year's goals: Stability - after Dad's retirement

How well did we succeed: Very well - lost no clients

Why: We kept up the quality of our work.

STRATEGIC PLAN

Our long term goals are: Upgrade client expectations - good design - and their willingness to pay for it.

Our strategy to get there is: Get better design - designers - and get published

Our tactics this year will be: Prospect for more style-conscious clients - with deeper pockets! Give staff a taste for it!

We will measure our success by: 1- Getting Published 2- Ultimately raise Vol/RSF + Fee/Emp over national average.

Your fees divided by your volume and expressed as a percentage will indicate to you how highly you are being paid for your services, somewhat determined by the previously stated complexity of work, again vis-a-vis other firms in your specialty or size category.

Volume divided by number of professionals and also divided by total number of employees will give you a good idea of the efficiency of your operation in producing goods and services.

Similarly, the fee divided by the total number of professionals and also by total number of employees will give you some idea of the efficiency of your marketing and sales efforts in producing fees vis-a-vis other firms.

There are no right and wrong answers here. There may be very good reasons why your firm is lower or higher in any area. The important point is to look at these operating characteristics and see if there are areas where improvement is desirable.

You should also take a good, hard look at your current situation. What kind of work do you do and how do you get it? Are you happy with that? How good is your staff, or your own personal professional skills? How would you describe firm motivation and morale? What is the firm's, or your, financial situation?

What do you perceive to be the strengths and weaknesses of the present organization? Rank them in order of importance. (If you run out of room on this form, use another sheet of paper and just put key words here.)

What were last year's goals? How well did you achieve them? Why was that?

Now set down the key parts of your strategic plan for this year. Put down your goals, strategy, tactics, and measurements. Keep this paper handy so that you can look at it from time to time to keep these issues fresh in your mind. Review it at least quarterly and perhaps monthly. Take charge of the process of growing yourself and your company.

And if you are only an employee or a student at this time, it would still make sense for you to do this on a personal basis. You should plan your own life at least as well as you would plan the life of your future company!

3 Determining Your Multiple

The determination of the precise multiple that is right for your firm for the next year is one of the best tools available for short-term strategic planning. The act of filling in the blanks in the single page worksheet provided in this chapter can lead you to think about, and make decisions concerning, all of the controllable expenses and most of the income for the next year.

The **Multiple Worksheet** will make you budget your overhead for the coming year. You have to set your goals for profits in advance, so you know why you are working so hard. It will assist you in setting your fees for any type of work. It will help you to determine how real your marketing plan is and what its chances of success are, since it also forces you to set sales targets. You can use it to determine how many square feet of work you will need in the coming year to meet your sales goals, your employment requirement to meet your production quotas, and whether or not you need to make your people more efficient in producing your design product. You can also use it to schedule your staff.

The way to determine the multiple is fairly simple in concept. First you have to decide what your income goal should be for the coming year. That income goal is the sum of all the salaries you pay, total fringe benefits, budgeted overhead, miscellaneous costs, plus your desired profit.

Then you determine the amount of salary or direct personnel expense (the DPE is the salary plus related fringe benefits) that you expect will be expended on tasks billed to the client over the course of the entire year.

Dividing the first number, the income goal, by the second number, the billable salary, will give you the multiple on salary. Dividing the income goal by the DPE will give you the multiple on direct personnel expense.

There is a sneaky reason for doing it both ways. Because the DPE is a larger number, consisting as it does of salaries plus fringes, the number derived by the division will be smaller. Thus, it will be far easier to quote to a client. It can be used for public consumption.

If we divide the income goal by the billable salary, we end up with a larger multiple number. The result of multiplying the smaller salary number by the larger salary multiple is always *exactly equal* to the result of multiplying the larger direct personnel expense number by the smaller multiple. However it is usually easier to deal internally with salary, which is easily known, rather than adding fringes to make the direct personnel expense.

If all this seems as clear as the assembly diagram for a two-circuit wire management system panel, I will make it much easier to understand by stepping through the worksheet line by line. The left side is used to determine total budgeted (planned in advance) expenses for the year. Let us go through it carefully.

Line 1

Fill in the total amount of salaries you are planning to pay during the year. Include a reasonable salary or "draw" for the owner. This should be equal to the cost of a replacement person, if the owner is forced by reasons of health, or otherwise, to withdraw from active participation in the firm. Only in this manner can we make sure that we are planning on getting profits, and not making up uncounted salary demands when the year is finished. Also include the pro-rated salary increases you will be giving during the year as well as the salaries of anyone you expect to hire.

At the same time remember *not* to include any wages or salaries for overtime. You want to plan your year so that you achieve your profit goals without the use of overtime (which, it so happens, is incredibly profitable to a business, and will be discussed later). This will also allow more management leeway throughout the year because it becomes an option, not a prerequisite for meeting the planned goals.

Lines 2 through 13

These are the standard fringe benefits that most firms offer. The first three are normally required by law, although some firms hire only consultants to avoid some of these payroll taxes. Holidays, vacations, and sick leave are additional costs for the firm for each hourly worker, but add no additional cost for salaried workers. The pension plan cost is the amount your accountant demands you set aside for the future liabilities you are creating in such a plan. The insurance plans all cost some specific amount which is easy to ascertain. Other possible fringes include paying for educational courses, lunches, and so on. Typical costs of fringe benefits in terms of their percentage of payroll are shown in the accompanying chart.

Direct Personnel Expenses

Typical Fringes	Per Cost of Payroll
Holidays (7)	3.7
Half Days (4)	1.1
Sick Leave	1.9
Vacation	4.8
Unemployment Taxes	1.8
F.I.C.A.	6.7
Workmen's Compensation	0.1
Medical Insurance	3.7
Group Life Insurance	1.6
Pension Plan	0.5
Dental Insurance	0.0
Total	25.9%

MULTIPLE WORKSHEET

Company:	T.I.D.
Date:	1/3/84
Person Completing Worksheet:	A.T.

YEARLY BUDGETED EXPENSES

1	$ 170,000	Total Salaries, Total Fringes	
2		FICA $	12,000
3		Workman's Comp	1,000
4		Unemployment Ins	4,000
5		Hrly. Holidays	6,000
6		Hrly. Vacations	8,500
7		Hrly. Sick Leave	3,400
8		Pension Plan	1,700
9		Medical Ins.	7,000
10		Life Ins.	3,500
11		Dental Ins.	—
12		Education	1,000
13		Other	1,000
14	$ 49,100	Add Total Fringes $	49,100
15	20,000	Independent Contract Salaries	
16	35,000	Rent	
17	3,000	Utilities	
18	3,500	Telephone Equipment Rental	
19	4,000	Long Distance (non-reimbursed)	
20	6,000	Reproduction (non-reimbursed)	
21	500	Postage/Express (non-reimbursed)	
22	250	Messenger Service	
23	1,200	Office Equipment Rental	
24	1,500	Service Contracts	
25	5,000	Office Supplies	
26	1,500	Capital Improvements or	
27	—	Depreciation	
28	5,000	Insurance—Errors & Omission	
29	5,000	Insurance—Fire & Theft	
30	3,000	Legal Representation	
31	2,000	External Accounting Services	
32	1,000	Agency Hiring Fees	
33	2,500	Bad Debts (1.5% of total income)	
34	$ 1,000	Professional Fees, Periodicals, Promotion	
35		Travel, Promotion $	5,000
36		Entertainment	5,000
37		Photography	2,000
38		Printing/Brochures	1,000
39		Special Mailings	500
40		External PR Svcs	—
41		Other	
42		Other	
43	$ 14,000	Add Total Promotion $	14,000

44	$ 1,000	Local Travel
45	(5,000)	Interest (Positive or Negative) :
46	—	Other
47	—	Other
48	297,550	Equals Total Budgeted Yearly Expenses

YEARLY PROFIT TOTAL

49		Profit by Recipient Taxes (for the Government) $	23,000
50		Retained Earnings (for the Company)	15,000
51		Dividends (for Owners)	20,000
52		Profit Sharing (for Employees)	17,000
53	$ 75,000	Add Total Profit Goal $	75,000

YEARLY INCOME GOAL

54	$ 298,000	Yearly Expenses (Line 48) PLUS
55	75,000	Yearly Profit Goal (Line 53)
56	$ 373,000	Equals Yearly Income Goal

YEARLY BILLABLE SALARIES

57	$ 170,000	Yearly Payroll
58	25,000	Support Staff Payroll (Subtract)
59	12,000	Professional Salaries for vacations, holidays, sick leave, half-days before holidays, etc. (Subtract)
60	19,000	Normal Unbillable Professional Salaries (Subtract 14%)
61	10,000	Extra Unbillable Principal's Salary/Draw (Subtract)
62	$ 104,000	Equals Yearly Billable Salaries

YEARLY BILLABLE DIRECT PERSONNEL EXPENSE

63	$ 49,000	Total Yearly Fringes (Line 11 Divided by)
64	170,000	Total Yearly Payroll (Line 1 Equals)
65	29	% Fringes as a per cent of Payroll Multiply By
66	104,000	Billable Salaries (Line 62 Equals)
67	30,200	Billable Fringes (Add Lines 66 and 67)
68	$ 134,000	Equals Yearly Billable Direct Personnel Expense (DPE)

THE SALARY MULTIPLE AND THE DIRECT PERSONNEL EXPENSE (DPE) MULTIPLE

69	$ 373,000	Yearly Income Goal (Line 56)
70	104,000	divided by Yearly Billable Salaries (Line 62)
71	3.6	equals the MULTIPLE ON SALARIES
72	373,000	Yearly Income Goal (Line 56)
73	134,000	divided by Yearly Billable Direct Personnel Expense (Line 68)
74	2.8	Equals the MULTIPLE ON DIRECT PERSONNEL EXPENSES

Don't forget to add in the fringes for new employees or salary increases. Bonuses and profit-sharing are not fringe benefits because they are contingent on profits and are taken out only when there are some profits.

Line 14   The total cost of fringe benefits is the sum of lines 2 through 13.

Line 15   Independent contract salaries are the consultants mentioned before. Most firms use them when work peaks to avoid hiring people for whom there is no work foreseen beyond the present. Other firms use them almost exclusively. These folks normally earn quite good hourly wages to make up for the fringes they don't get and the security they don't have.

Lines 16 through 18   These categories should be self-explanatory, but do not forget to include expected rate raises during the year as well as other incidentals such as holiday gratuities, unreimbursed repairs, etc.

Lines 19 and 22   These communication costs are getting more expensive all the time, especially as deadlines force the use of extensive long distance calls for telecopying and express mail services and the inevitable messenger services. While much can, and should, be billed back to the client, some has to be paid by the firm. Include a reasonable budgeted amount.

Lines 23 through 27   These expenses are all for running your office. Remember that some capital improvements can be expensed (charged off in full in the year acquired) and some should be depreciated (a percentage charged off each year). Include appropriate amounts in either category, but don't double-count. Service contracts are getting more and more expensive, since we are also getting more and more electronics in the office. Include hardware cost, software costs, and service costs when you budget micro-computer purchases.

Line 28   Errors and Omissions Insurance for major projects can usually be passed along back to the client, especially if they request it. But you can get some on your own. ASID makes some available to their members at reasonable cost. Having such insurance may even be a bit of a marketing tool.

Line 29   Fire and Theft Insurance is self-explanatory, however there are other worthwhile forms of insurance also available. One, for instance, will protect you from loss if original documents are destroyed. Include whatever seems appropriate.

Line 30   The costs for legal help may require both a retainer cost and fees. Be generous if you are starting out and need to use your attorney for frequent advice or if you do a lot of work for other attorneys. America has become suit crazy and you should be prepared.

Line 31   Assuming you don't have a CPA (certified public accountant) on your staff, include a generous fee for accounting help. If he has a decent allowance you won't feel guilty about calling and asking for advice. Also, if you get serious about managing your firm, as I suggest you do, your accountant will be doing some extra numbers work this year. You may have to give him a raise.

Line 32   If you do plan on hiring anyone this year, and there is a possibility that you might hire them through an agency, remember that agencies charge as much as 20 percent of the first year's salary in fee. If you don't use an agency, you might include some advertising costs here.

Line 33	Bad debts occur in various ways in this business. One client may not accept a piece of furniture and you have to resell it at a loss. Another may not accept a design, even after it was approved earlier, and force you to redesign at no charge. Or some clients might just not pay for some part of the design effort which they did not like. In any case, the common rule of thumb for small businesses is to set aside 1.5 percent of gross income for bad debts. I would suggest that is appropriate here as well.
Line 34	Firms often pay the yearly dues for professional organizations for staff members. They also subscribe to a lot of expensive magazines.
Lines 35 through 43	The marketing and promotion budget should be carefully thought out in advance. If you are planning on getting some jobs photographed this year, you should realize that the better photographers charge upwards of $1,000 per day and you are lucky to get six photographs (but the right ones) for that price. Printing can add up quickly, especially if you go for four-color work. Even the better black and white work can add up, what with double-dot halftones and such.

Mailing is extremely expensive, not just for stamps, but you may well need special envelopes and the time to stuff them. Other possible promotional expenses might include hiring a PR specialist, advertising, small gifts, etc. Travel and entertainment should be a realistic appraisal either of what you expect to spend or a budget to keep your perks within. Some people have said that about 2 percent of your yearly budget ought to be devoted to the hard costs of marketing (that is, not including your, or other employees', salary), but I think that is a minimum sum for a small visual business. We will discuss this subject in much more depth in a later chapter, but include a reasonable allowance here now.

Line 44	Often local travel is not reimbursed so plan on some expense here. Usually the principal is too rushed to take public transportation in cities and therefore takes cabs, while the lower paid employees can't afford taxis on their own time and take them on company time as one of their few perks. If you work in a big city, be generous here.
Line 45	Interest can either be a positive or negative number depending on whether you borrowed money or had profits to invest. Remember, we are adding up expenses here, so any interest or dividends income you get will be a negative number.
Lines 46 through 47	Other possible expenses include company automobile expenses (include garage, repairs, gas, in addition to basic ownership or leasing), parties, liquor, flowers, and whatever else turns you on and you can afford. You may also be more secure if you put some contingency in here. But the list is quite complete, and you should have been generous in any area where you were not too sure, so any contingency you add can be small.

Line 48   This is the total budget for all expenses that you can foresee for the next year.

Profits are not simply what is left over from income after you pay your expenses. You must consider that profits serve four separate groups of entities. You should carefully consider what each deserves and needs and target that amount.

Line 49   Obviously Uncle Sam comes in for his share first, as do his cousins at the state and city level.

Line 50   The company deserves some of the profits. These retained earnings can be put aside for bad times, used in good times for expansion, or just kept around to better the company's credit. If you are incorporated, these also serve as a tax shelter. Retained earnings are very important to the stability of a company and should be allocated right after taxes.

Line 51   The owners deserve some return on the risk they take for investing in this company. They partake in the profits through dividends in a corporation or just taking out a part of the profits in a partnership or sole proprietorship.

Line 52   The employees certainly deserve a share of the profits of a successful company. They should probably take out about a share equal to the owners since their efforts can make or break the efforts of the owners to have a successful business. And their continuity within a firm can make management easier and the product more consistent and effective.

Line 53   If you add up the needs of all four groups who share in the profits, you have the profit goal for the year. In most companies, the goal for profit before taxes is about 20 percent of total income. However there is no reason that it should be limited to that in a field as individualistic as interior design.

Lines 54 through 56   If you add up the total budgeted yearly expenses and the yearly profit goal, you get the yearly income goal. This is your target for sales for the year.

Lines 57 through 62   The yearly billable salaries are determined by starting off with the total salaries and subtracting the salaries for people who are never billed and part of the salaries for others equivalent to the percentage of time that they probably won't bill. Of course, all support staff should be subtracted. You would never bill out your bookkeeper or receptionist. Most secretaries are not billed out. In some cases you might have them bill out the time they spend specifically on one project, such as typing fifty pages of specifications. But even in those cases, they would probably not bill out over 50 percent of their time. Remember *not* to budget any overtime.

Even professionals cannot bill out all of their time. The average loss factor is about one seventh or 14 percent for time spent filing or working on sales presentations. Principals probably bill out even less of their time, since much time is spent on marketing, sales, and general management.

Lines 63 through 68   Direct Personnel Expense (DPE) is a commonly used term to denote the total cost to a firm of employing an individual. This includes both salaries and fringes. In these lines we are simply finding out the average percentage of salaries that fringes equal for your particular firm and adding that amount to the billable salaries to get the billable DPE. As we discussed earlier, there will be slightly different management uses for each multiple.

Lines 69 through 71   The multiple for salaries is derived very simply by dividing the yearly income goal by the yearly billable salaries. This is the simpler number to deal with internally because you can just relate it to an employee's hourly, weekly, or yearly salary. Unfortunately because it is a larger number than a client may be used to seeing in a competitive situation, you shouldn't use it externally.

Lines 72 through 74   The multiple for direct personnel expense is derived in an analogous fashion by just dividing the yearly income goal by the yearly billable DPE. Since this is always smaller than the Multiple on Salary, this is what we let the client see, if it suits us. The industry average is uniform at 2.5 for this figure, although a few firms are charging 2.75 and occasionally even 3.0. We will discuss the various ways you can use this just a little further along.

This rather exhaustive worksheet has taken us through every monetary activity you might perform throughout the year, except for one. We have not considered any time spent on purchasing or any income from resale at a mark-up. I feel quite strongly that *professional* designers should be compensated for the time they use their professional knowledge and skills on behalf of the client, and not on the same basis as a retailer mechanically marking up furniture. I would even assert that it is unprofessional, since an incentive is created to purchase more expensive items than might be necessary. There is also a disincentive built in to the system toward saving the client money that usually involves more, not less, design time. The bigger the job or client, the less likely it is that resale will be any part of the process, especially in contract work.

On the other hand, a lot of business is still done on a resale basis. I would suggest, if that is how you work, that you consider your business to have two separate profit centers, the design services (billed out by the hour or square foot) and the purchasing services (billed out as a percentage mark-up). That is the best of both worlds. You never waste five hours looking for an ash tray and you still get compensated for putting your money at risk for ordering a chartreuse lacquered end table. The common mark-ups in contract work range from 10 percent to 15 percent, although one firm in the "Top 100" charges 33 percent.

Uses Of The Multiple

You can use the multiple internally in many ways. You can set individual billing rates for each of your employees by taking their hourly salary or DPE and multiplying it by the appropriate multiple. If you have several employees in total or in each category, you can average their billing rates derived with the multiple and use that as a categoric billing rate, i.e., drafters, $30/hour; designers, $50/hour; and principals; $75/hour.

Remember that the client has no need to actually know the multiple, just the rate. You can use any rate greater than, or equal to, the average. And remember, if you can just keep your people about as busy as you planned when you figured out the multiple, you will make the profit goals you set *automatically*.

At the same time, the multiple is extremely useful working backwards. Suppose you have gotten a job for a certain fee. If you divide that fee by your salary multiple, you will have the dollars in salary you can spend on this project and make your 20 percent profit. If you divide that total salary by the average hourly wage in your firm, or the wages of the people who will be working on the project, you will know exactly how many hours it should take to complete this project profitably.

Given that design is a never-ending process, as we all discover whenever we design something for our personal use, this information is incredibly valuable. Now each of your people will know exactly what amount of time is budgeted for solving this design problem. Even better, you've solved part of the scheduling problem as well. Both of these subjects will be dealt with much more later on, but consider just how neatly this system ties all the management issues of design together.

One other use of the multiple should be discussed at this time. It can be used to check if the production of professional services is in balance with the national averages for efficiency in volume produced or fees received as shown in the Production Efficiency Worksheet. If you divide your income goal by your total number of employees and also by your total number of professionals, you will get the average fee income per employee and average fee per professional. By looking at the data provided by my annual January Survey in *Interior Design* of the Top 100 Design Firms and in July of the Second 100 Interior Design Firms, you can see if you are aiming high or low. Since you can compare with size

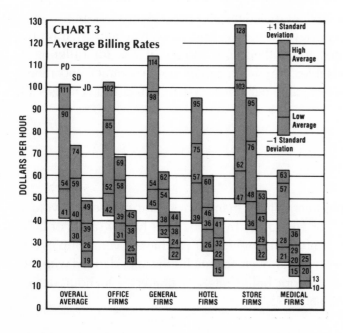

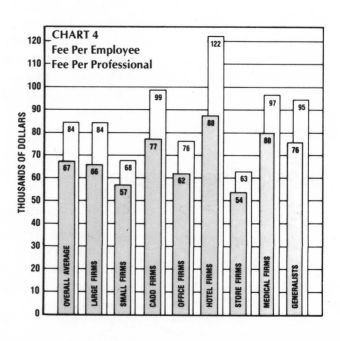

PRODUCTION OPERATION ANALYSIS WORKSHEET

Company Name:	T.I.D.
Date:	1/4/84
Person Completing Worksheet:	A.T.

Your Income Goal:	$373,000	$623/Emp	= Avg Fee/Employee Assumed in the Multiple Worksheet
Divided By	7		
No. of All Employees:			
How you compare: We will still be lower than the nat'l average		$57/Emp	= Average Fee/Employee of Your Size Firm in the "Top 100"
Why: Half are clients are repeat - can not change them		$62/Emp	= Average Fee/Employee of Your Type Firm in the "Top 100"

Your income goal:	$373K	$67.8/Emp	= Avg Fee/Professional Assumed in the Multiple Worksheet
Divided By	5.5		
No. of Professionals			
How you compare: We're still below average but catching up		$68/Emp	= Avg Fee/Professional of Your Size Firm in the "Top 100"
Why: Just to get up to avg. is a big step for us		$76/Emp	= Avg Fee/Professional of Your Type Firm in the "Top 100"

Your Income Goal:	$373K	173K SF	= Marketing Goal in Square feet
Divided By:	$2.16/sf	$50/SF	Multiplied by Avg Cost of Furn. & Construction per Sq Ft
Your Avg Fee/Sq Ft:		$8,650K	Equal Anticipated Volume for the Year

Anticipated Volume:	$8,650K	$1,236/Emp	= Avg Volume/Employee Assumed in the Multiple Worksheet
Divided By	7		
No. of Employees			
How you compare: 20% higher!		$1,035/Emp	= Avg Volume/Employee of Your Size Firm
Why: Perhaps we work more efficiently since our jobs are all (too!) similar		$1,096/Emp	= Avg Volume/Employee of Your Type Firm

Anticipated Volume:	$8,650	$1,573/Prof	= Avg Volume/Professional Assumed in the Multiple Worksheet
Divided By	5.5		
No. of Professionals			
How you compare: Some 25% higher!		$1,225/Prof	= Avg Volume/Professional for Your Size Firm
Why: Same as above - but we also have low level of support - good!		$1,342/Prof	= Avg Volume/Professional for Your Type Firm

category and specialty category, you should be able to get a pretty good picture of how you compare in income with other professionals.

If you take your income goal and divide it by the average fee per square foot shown in those articles for your category, you will have an idea of your sales goal for the year in square feet. If you take that square footage figure and multiply it by the average cost of furnishings and construction for the work you are doing, you will know how much *volume*, as I call it, you are aiming to produce next year. If you divide that number by your number of employees and also by your number of professionals, you will see how efficiently they should be producing. You can also compare those numbers to the average for the industry to see if your firm is an efficient producer of services or not. A **Production Operation Analysis Worksheet** is included to help you know your firm better.

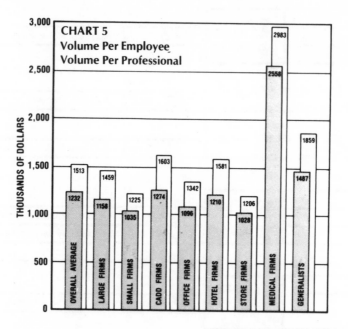

Once you become familiar with your operating characteristics, you can easily interrelate all these operating numbers. It is very important that you be able to do so. Your company lives and dies on the basis of these numbers. You have to see what each project or person does to your firm's operating characteristics.

Then it is up to you to make it more efficient, if that seems necessary. The act of discovering this information is the first step. The rest of this book should help with other steps on the road to efficiency.

4 Setting The Right Fee

The choice of the fee you plan on charging a client for any particular job has three important related components that imply conflicting courses of action. The client may base all or part of his purchase decision on the size of the fee you choose. This marketing component suggests the lower the fee, the better your chances are of getting the contract.

If you are chosen, the amount of effort you can afford to put into finding the correct solution for the client will be determined by the amount of time you can fund from the total fee. This project management component would suggest that the higher the fee, within reason, the better the job you could do.

And, of course, your profits will consist of what remains of the fee after you pay your expenses of design. The profit motive would suggest that the higher the fee, the more benefits you will ultimately enjoy. You have to balance these three sets of needs — marketing, project management, and profit motive — in order to choose the right fee. And having done so, you can relax about the outcome. If someone gets the job for less, you know that you would either not have done as good a job as it deserves or you would not have received the profits you should get for a good job.

I would suggest three well-developed approaches to setting a fair fee for a job, and two quick checks. The three well-accepted methods of fee determination are by the square foot, by the expected man hours, and as a percentage of total cost. One way to check the accuracy of these is to establish average costs for a drawing, and apply that to the job. Another quick check is to decide how long the job will take, how many staff people you would keep on the job, and multiply your average salary by the people, by the months.

But before you start any of these approaches to setting fees, you must take time out to find out as much as you can about the prospective client, the potential assignment, and the way the contract will be handled.

The Information Checklist in this chapter can help you make sure that you have tried to get the minimum information necessary to intelligently set fees.

The first area of inquiry should be the space the client occupies. How much space is there? How many people occupy it? How fast has the organization grown over the last several years? Is there a formal set of office standards? How many? Are they modular? How many people are in enclosed offices? How many in systems furniture/bank screen areas? How many in pure open plan?

Are they planning on changing any of that? What is the apparent corporate level of taste in furnishings? Do they know of any particular problems they wish solved at this time?

Next you should try to discover as much as you can about their new location. Have they chosen one yet? Do they need help with feasability studies or lease negotiation? How much space are they planning on moving into? Do they have good drawings of the space? Can you believe it if they say they do? Is the space truly modular? Are they planning on reusing any of their existing furnishings? How much, and is that a certainty? What is the expected budget for the move? Tenant improvements (construction)? Furnishings, fixtures, and equipment (F, F&E)? What is the value of their work letter?

What special areas will be required and how much space will they take? Executive dining? Employee dining? Coffee areas? Boardroom? Special communication areas? Presentation rooms with special audio/visual capabilities? Trading desks? High security areas? Vaults? Computer rooms? What percentage of workstations will have terminals? Will reproduction be centralized, dispersed, or both?

The final area of inquiry should be how they intend to manage the project. Do you have an experienced, competent single contact to work with? A committee? Who will make the decisions? How accessible are they? How accessible and interested is top management, if they will not be handling the day-to-day decision-making? What is your level of confidence in your answers in this last area?

Now you may have gathered enough information to figure out the appropriate fees for this client. Probably the most accurate method of determining fees is to estimate the person-months it will take to complete the project. I call this the time method. The positive benefits of this exercise lie in the detailed information you are using. You can assign individuals, budget their time over the course of the project, and complete your manpower planning and most of your scheduling at the same time.

By the same token, if you don't know enough about either the project or the design process to forecast well, you may lead yourself down the garden path to a very wrong estimate. This method does not rely on any national averages or other information to protect you from poor judgment or oversight. You should, therefore, always figure your fees out at least two different ways, to double check on your assumptions and make sure as little as possible is left to chance.

If you look at the **Fee Estimation Worksheet-Time Method**, you will see that it already includes several concepts you should know well by now, the five phases of interior design and the multiple. The work is broken down into the phases we've discussed earlier: programming, design conceptualization, decoration, construction documentation, and supervision/management.

You may prefer to use different phases according to the way you run your practice, but these are well known and well understood by most practitioners

Company:	Mary Kay Cosmetics
Contact Name:	I. Epstein
Person Completing Checklist:	A.T.
Date:	1/5/84

FEE ESTIMATION INFORMATION CHECKLIST

1. How much space are they presently occupying?	14,000	RSF

2. How many people now occupy their space?	67	
What percent are in enclosed offices now?	40	%
What percent are in systems furniture/bank screens now	0	%
What percent are in the open now?	60	%
Will that change? *Yes* Why? They wish to upgrade to "systems" furniture	30	%

3. Why are they moving? What problems will they solve?	Out of Space	
4. What is the corporate level of taste in furnishings? (high for exec's + public)	Very High	
5. Have they chosen their new space yet? Two blocks down Post Road	Yes	
6. Do they have a lease yet? (Realtor introduced us)	Yes	
7. How much space do they plan to move in to?	18,000	RSF
8. How many people will ultimately occupy their new space?	80 (?)	
9. Do they have good drawings of their new space?	No	
10. Is the new space truly modular?	No - Old Bldg	

11. What is the expected budget for F,F&E? They don't know — assume	$25	/RSF
12. How much of their existing furniture do they expect to to reuse?	0	%

12. How much will their Work Letter be worth? Just a guess	$10	/RSF

13. What special areas will be required and how much of each?	0	RSF
Executive Dining?	0	RSF
Employee Dining? "Brown Bag" room	150	RSF
Board Room? Yes - very important	450	RSF
Special Communication Areas? Just Telex	—	RSF
Special A/V Rooms? Yes - but same as Bd. Rm.	450	RSF
Trading Desks? No	—	RSF
Secure Areas? President's art collection	?	RSF
Vaults? No	—	RSF
Computer Rooms? No — But CRT's (CPU + WP) at 1:4 ratio	—	
Central Reproduction? No	—	RSF

14. What percentage of their workstations will have CRT's? %	25 %
15. How soon is their expected move-in? 6 mos. — NO EXTENSIONS	
16. Do you have an experienced, competent single contact to interface with? NO	
17. Is senior management interested and accessible? Yes - deal directly w/ CEO - great!	

and clients. Within each of those phases, I have shown six different skill/wage levels: principal, project director, senior designer, junior designer, drafter, and other billable support. You may also have different classifications and should modify this form accordingly.

All you have to do is take the average salary for each category, multiply that by the number of people in that category assigned in this phase, multiply that by the percentage of their time that they will allot to the project during that time, multiply again by the number of months in the phase, and finally multiply by the multiple on salaries that you determined in the last chapter.

That produces the fee you must receive for that category of employee in that phase in this project to complete the work and make your profit (which is built into the multiple, as you remember). Doing the same thing for each category in each phase will produce the fee you need to get for the entire project and, again, make your profit goal.

As mentioned before, the nice thing about this method is that you have now determined both a manpower budget and a schedule to produce the job. For instance, you should now be able to tell two designers they should finish their work in programming this project by devoting half of their time for three weeks, and so on.

The second method, the square footage method, is a more abstract way of deriving the fee. It also responds more directly to the method most often used for billing large contract jobs, which is billing by the hour, times a multiple, up to a guaranteed maximum price based on a dollar-per-square-foot figure.

In 1982, according to the "Top 100" survey, the "fair fee" for "average" office work was about $2.46 per rentable square foot. That was an average across the country and for all size jobs. You should determine what the fee should be for your company doing an absolutely normal job.

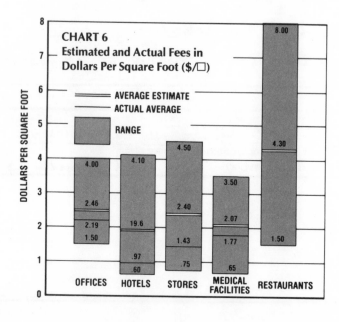

CHART 6
Estimated and Actual Fees in Dollars Per Square Foot ($/□)

FEE ESTIMATION WORKSHEET
Time Method

Client:	Mon Diey Cosmetics
Date:	1/6/84
Person Completing Worksheet:	A. T.

Months to Move-In:	Average fee and billing rate information is published annually in the January issue of interior Design in the "100 Design Giants" story.
6	

PHASE & NAME	CATEGORY	Average Salary Per Month	X	Number of Personnel Assigned	X	Months in this Phase	X	Total % of Time Req'd This Phase	X	Multiple on Salaries	=	Fee Required
Programming	Principal	$ 4,165	X	1	X	1	X	20 %	X	3.6	=$	3,000
	Pjt. Dir.	$ 3,333	X	1	X		X	20 %	X		=$	3,400
	Sr. Designer	$ 2,500	X		X		X	%	X		=$	
	Jr. Designer	$ 1,666	X	1	X		X	33 %	X		=$	1,800
	Draftsman	$ 1,250	X		X		X	%	X		=$	
	Bill'ble Support	$ 1,250	X		X	1	X	%	X	3.6	=$	
Design	Principal	$ 4,165	X	1	X		X	20 %	X	3.6	=$	3,000
	Pjt. Dir.	$ 3,333	X	1	X		X	20 %	X		=$	3,400
	Jr. Designer	$ 2,500	X	1	X		X	40 %	X		=$	3,600
	Jr. Designer	$ 1,666	X		X		X	%	X		=$	
	Draftsman	$ 1,250	X	1	X		X	20 %	X		=$	900
	Bill'ble Support	$ 1,250	X		X	1	X	%	X	3.6	=$	
Decoration	Principal	$ 4,165	X	1	X	1	X	10 %	X	3.6	=$	1,500
	Pjt. Dir.	$ 3,333	X	1	X		X	20 %	X		=$	2,400
	Sr. Designer	$ 2,500	X	1	X		X	50 %	X		=$	4,500
	Jr. Designer	$ 1,666	X	1	X		X	30 %	X		=$	1,800
	Draftsman	$ 1,250	X	1	X		X	20 %	X		=$	900
	Bill'ble Support	$ 1,250	X	1	X	1	X	10 %	X	3.6	=$	900
Construction Documentat'n	Principal	$ 4,165	X	1	X	1	X	5 %	X	3.6	=$	750
	Pjt. Dir.	$ 3,333	X	1	X		X	25 %	X		=$	3,000
	Sr. Designer	$ 2,500	X	1	X		X	40 %	X		=$	3,600
	Jr. Designer	$ 1,666	X	1	X		X	25 %	X		=$	4,500
	Draftsman	$ 1,250	X	1	X		X	50 %	X		=$	4,500
	Bill'ble Support	$ 1,250	X		X	1	X	%	X	3.6	=$	
Supervision	Principal	$ 4,165	X	1	X	1	X	5 %	X	3.6	=$	750
	Pjt. Dir.	$ 3,333	X	1	X		X	20 %	X		=$	2,400
	Sr. Designer	$ 2,500	X	1	X		X	20 %	X		=$	1,800
	Jr. Designer	$ 1,666	X	1	X		X	10 %	X		=$	600
	Draftsman	$ 1,250	X	1	X		X	10 %	X		=$	450
	Bill'ble Support	$ 1,250	X		X	1	X	%	X	3.6	=$	

Total Fee Required =	$ 48,450

We have also discussed that contract work can be defined in five phases. In my experience at one large company, the actual fee breakdown was as follows:

Phase 1   Programming 14%

Phase 2   Design Conceptualization 20%

Phase 3   Decoration 24%

Phase 4   Construction Documentation 28%

Phase 5   Supervision/Management 14%

If we apply the average fee to those percentages, we get the following square footage costs by phase:

Phase 1   Programming $0.34

Phase 2   Design conceptualization 0.49

Phase 3   Decoration 0.59

Phase 4   Construction Documentation 0.69

Phase 5   Supervision/Management 0.34

$2.45

Now we can look at a prospective job, examine the phases, see if they are simpler or more difficult than an average job, apply a correction factor, and come up with a new fee. This is precisely how we use the **Fee Estimation Worksheet-Square Footage Method**.

The first step is to decide what your own average "fair fee" should be. If you are not sure, it would probably not be too far wrong to use the national average of $2.46 per rentable square foot. Remember, this is a fairly easy number to defend to a client.

Next, you should make any overall judgments about this particular job versus the average job. I would say that the average job is between 5,000 and 50,000 rentable square feet. A significantly smaller job is probably some 10 percent or so more expensive just because the project management overhead, start-up, and other incidental costs are spread out over a smaller base. A significantly larger job might be 10 percent or so less because of certain efficiencies in design you can create. A very large job is not much less, because its size creates other inefficiencies. For instance a two-million-square-foot job may require second sourcing and coordination of carpet mills.

Another overall factor would be the timing necessary to get the client in on time. Is it critical? Is the required move-in date closer than would normally be comfortable? How much closer?

Now take your fee for this size job and correct it for possible problems or

FEE ESTIMATION WORKSHEET
Square Footage Method

(Average fee data available in January Interior Design Magazine)

Client:	MonDieu Cosmetics
Date:	1/7/84
Person Completing This Worksheet:	A.T.

Area of New Location   18,000 RSF

Our overall average fee for this type of work is	$ 2.16 /RSF
Because of its size, we should correct that by a factor of (+ or −)	___ %
We expect the style of management to require a correction of (+ or −)	___ %

Average fee for this size of job and management type	$ 2.16 /RSF

PHASE	NAME	PERCENTAGE OF FEE	AVERAGE FEE FOR THIS SIZE & TYPE	AVERAGE PHASE COST	CORRECTION FACTOR	PHASE FEE	CORRECTION RATIONALE
1	Programming	14%	X $ 2.16	= $ 0.30	X —	= $ 0.30 /RSF	No hard programmatic problems
	Does the client already know what their space problems really are? Has a lease been negotiated? Do they have standards? Do they need a long range plan to deal with their real estate?						
2	Design Concept	20% 2.16	X $ 2.16	= $ 0.43	X 1.2	= $ 0.54 /RSF	High style concept for exec. areas
	Is anything special required? Is the space easy to work in? Will it be a high style/expensive space? Or reused furniture? Is the client very interested? Is his wife helping the designer?						
3	Decoration	24%	X $ 2.16	= $ 0.52	X 1.5	= $ 0.78 /RSF	Much custom work expected. Entire exec. area
	Is there a board room involved? Individual executive offices? Will it be a high style/expensive space? Or reused furniture? Is the client very interested? Is his wife helping the design?						
4	Contract Documentation	28%	X $ 2.16	= $ 0.60	X 1.2	= $ 0.72 /RSF	Great deal of cabinet work / custom mill work
	Are there good drawings of the space? Are there any complex problems? Is there much custom work? Will the job be bid? Is there any fancy equipment in the space? Many consultants?						
5	Mgmt. Supr'n	14%	X $ 2.16	= $ 0.30	X 1.1	L= $ 0.33 /RSF	More details to go wrong
	Can you use one of your contractors or does the client or the building require one of theirs? Is there much built in? Is there enough time to do the job properly? How good is mgmt?						

Adding all five Phases equals the Total Fee Per Square Foot =	$ 2.65 /RSF
Multipled by the Total Square Footage =	X 18,000 RSF

Equals the Total Fee for this job =	$ 47,700

efficiencies in the programming phase. Are you going to be involved with feasability studies or lease negotiations? Does the client have space standards? Are they the right ones? Do they understand their space problems? Really? Is their organization structure firm, or are they going through changes? Will everyone be available to answer your programming questions?

The correction factor should be something like .9 for a simpler job or 1.05 for a slightly more difficult job. You take the percentage of fee for this phase, multiply it times the average fee that you just figured out above, to derive the average phase cost. You then multiply that by the correction factor to get the Phase Fee. This is much easier than it sounds, especially if you use the attached form.

The same process should be repeated for each phase. In the design conceptualization phase you should ask a variety of questions. Does the new space appear easy to work in? Is very little, or quite a bit, of special work required? Is it modular space? Will it be highly stylized space? Are many tenant improvements required? Will they be using the building standard fit up, or will you develop a special one for them?

The decoration phase is one where the correction factor could easily be doubled or tripled. Is there a board room involved? Will you be doing private offices for top executive officers? Is that a significant proportion of the project? Will it be high style, expensive space? Is the client very interested in design? Will he be very involved? Will there be much custom cabinetry?

In the contract documentation phase, it helps to start with good architectural drawings of the space. Do they have them? Are there any complex problems? Computer areas? Trading areas? Vaults? Kitchens? Is there a lot of fancy equipment involved? Are many other consultants involved? Will this job be bid?

Management supervision is usually easier when you can use a contractor you know and respect, and harder when you have to use a building's contractor or, possibly, another contractor the client is tied to. Can you choose the contractor? Will there be much built-in furniture? Is there any reason to suspect possible union problems? Is there enough time?

Since this category also includes nonspecific management time, you have to decide if this client will be easy to deal with. Do they pay their bills on time? Is there good communication between different levels of their management team? Do you have access to the people you will need for decision-making?

If you follow through this form, you should end up with a fee per square foot somewhere between $1.50 and $4.00, unless it is a very unusual space.

One advantage of this method, is that if they decide to take more space, you will automatically be paid for it. Another advantage, mentioned before, is that you are starting out with a recognized standard cost, which you can then defend to the client. If you have not been in business for very long, this method offers you a data base that you will not generate for yourself for some years. It also forces you to think about how you will do the job before you start it.

You can convert this information back into scheduling information by dividing by the multiple to get back to salary available to complete each phase.

The only disadvantage to this method is that you might guess incorrectly about the personality of the client firm or the client project manager. But at least you have thought about it. And next time you'll be older and wiser.

A third method of figuring fees is based on a percentage of cost. I believe it has significant disadvantages. It is just not done very much in contract work. Many firms have their own in-house purchasing departments. What do you do when they reuse their furniture? How do you get paid when work is cancelled? And how do you overcome the suspicion of fee-bloating if you recommend a more expensive item over a less expensive item?

Also, I hear from some firms that they like to charge on a straight 15 percent commission on all purchases, construction, and services. But no firm actually does that well. In fact, the national average percentage actually received, according to the "Top 100" survey is 7.2 percent, far less than the average "fair fee," as a percentage, which is considered to be about 12 percent.

Since no one does that well, I have to assume that the actual base figure is often applied exclusively to the furniture, fixtures, and equipment. The F, F&E commonly runs about $20 per square foot, times the average 7.2 percent fee, equals $1.44. If we add in work letter items above and below the ceiling, which averaged about $13.08 last year, the fee would increase to $2.38, which is very close to the national average.

That suggests that a fair fee would be about 7.5 percent of the costs of all new furniture, furnishings, and equipment plus the cost of work letter items, which include the ceiling, lightings, internal walls, doors, bucks, outlets, etc.

Since most firms do charge between 10 percent and 15 percent for purchasing, it reconfirms the fact that many clients reuse some or all of their furniture. The

CHART 7
Estimated and Actual Fees as a
Percentage of Volume

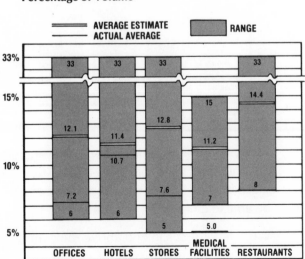

unknowns make this a very difficult method of figuring fees. I would suggest that you just think through the process for most jobs and see if it makes sense.

On the other hand, in the real world some firms do charge 15 percent on everything. Since their average is so much less in fee than the $4.50 this would bring in, we have to suppose much of the fee is lost to reuse, internal purchasing, etc. Since there is so much "fat" in a contract written on this basis, firms can take those losses from their fee base and still do well.

Notwithstanding all the objections I have just raised to this method of billing, if you really want to go ahead with it, I have provided a **Fee Estimation Worksheet-Cost Method**. You can actually estimate your fee in two ways. The first is based on cost per square foot and the second is based on the cost per work station.

There are four different components of the overall cost for tenant space: furnishings, fixtures, and equipment; work letter items below the ceiling, work letter items in and above the ceiling, and other tenant improvements.

The average cost nationally, according to the most recent "Top 100" survey, is $19.97 per square foot for furnishings, fixtures, and equipment. You should modify that figure by the taste/cost level of your client, the amount of expected reuse of existing furniture, and whether all such items will pass through your documentation so you can charge for them. The resulting figure, when multiplied by the square footage, will give you the total cost for this area.

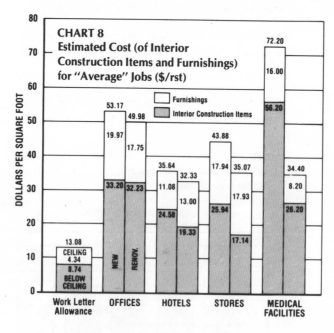

Work letter items below the ceiling include walls, doors, paint, hardware, electrical and telephone outlets, carpeting, and so on. The national average for these items is $8.74. You must adjust that by the percentage you actually will be able to charge for in your agreement.

Work letter items in and above the ceiling include the ceiling itself, standard office lighting, registers, returns, and so on. Some of those items you might be

Client:	*M.D.C.*	
Date:	*1/8/84*	
Person Completing Worksheet:		*A.T.*

FEE ESTIMATION WORKSHEET
Cost Method

COST PER SQUARE FOOT ANALYSIS

Cost of Furnishings, Fixtures & Equipment for this job (The average cost of F,F&E nationally is $19.97.*)	$ *25* /RSF	
Multiplied times the area of this assignment	*18,000* RSF	
Total expected expenditure for F,F&E in our documentation	=	$ *450,000*

Cost of Work Letter below the ceiling for this job (The average cost nationally is $8.74.*)	$ *9* /RSF	
Multiplied times the area of this assignment	*18,000* RSF	
Total expected expenditure for these items in our documentation		$ *162,000*

Cost of Work Letter above the ceiling for this job (The average cost nationally is $4.34.*)	$ *3* /RSF	
Multiplied times the area of this assignment	*18,000* RSF	
Total expected expenditure for these items in our documentation		$ *54,000*

Cost of Tenant Improvements expected for this job (The average cost is $33.20 for new and $32.23 for renovation work.*)	$ *30* /RSF	
Multiplied times the area of this assignment	*18,000* RSF	
Total expected expenditure for these items in our documentation		$ *540,000*

Total Expected Expenditures For All Items In Your Documentation	$ *1,206,000*
Multiplied By Your Fee Percentage	× *4.7* %

TOTAL FEE	$ *56,600*

COST PER WORK STATION ANALYSIS

Area of assignment	*18,000* RSF
Likely cost of enclosed offices	$ *10,000*
Number of employees in enclosed offices	*32*
Total cost of office furnishings and enclosures	$ *320,000*

Likely cost of low walled workspaces	[partition systems]	$ *6,000*
Number of employees in low walled workspaces		*2.4*
Total cost of low walled work stations		$ *144,000*

Likely cost of open work stations	$ *2,000*
Number of employees in open space	*24*
Total cost of open work stations	$ *48,000*

Total cost of other tenant improvements	$ *500,000*

Total Expected Expenditures For All Items In Your Documentation	$ *1,012,000*
Multiplied By Your Fee Percentage	× *4.7* %

TOTAL FEE	$ *47,500*

* Average costs available in January issues of *Interior Design*.

able to charge a fee for and some probably won't get into your fee base. Both of these cost areas should be multiplied by the area to derive total costs.

The last area is tenant improvements. This includes special and decorative lighting; all walls, doors, and hardware above building standard; all structural changes such as internal stairs, vaults, or vertical conveyors; and mechanical additions such as package air conditioning units for internal conference rooms, venting for kitchens, etc. The costs for these improvements average $33.20 for new spaces and $32.23 for renovated spaces. You have to decide how much you will actually get to charge for and include that amount times the area for a total cost factor.

If you sum these four costs and multiply the result by your billing percentage, you will have a projected fee. You must make it clear that any work you do specifying items is the same as ordering them. That way your fee should be based on all your work and not just that which you purchase.

Another method of creating the projected cost data for billing on a percentage basis is to use the costs per work station analysis, which is also on the worksheet.

First consider the client and answer some basic questions. How much furniture will be purchased new and how much do you expect to reuse? Will they be using enclosed offices of demountable partitions or built-in stud and drywall? Will the low-wall types of work stations be systems furniture or regular desks surrounded with bank screens? What will the taste level and cost level of furnishings be? Will they use metal or wooden desks, etc.

If you consider all these questions carefully, you should be able to come up with a projected cost for enclosed offices, low-walled work stations, and open plan work stations. Multiplying these average prices by the number of work stations to be provided (not just for present employees, but including expansion spaces) will give a budget cost for much of the job.

You should still add an allowance for other tenant improvements, as you did above, but you might include extra cost furnishings for top executive offices, board room complex, or other extraordinary furnishings as well. Multiplied by your percentage, this will give you another check of your fee basis.

I still consider this the least professional method of charging for design services. And when I represent a client, I will not permit them to sign a design contract based on a percentage of purchases. On the other hand, there is nothing wrong with charging 10 percent to 15 percent for actually purchasing furniture for a client. In most cases, you only purchase a very small percentage of the cost of the job to accommodate clients who don't wish to purchase certain decorative items themselves. It can be a good profit center. Just don't base your entire design fee on this.

One more method of figuring fees is a quick and dirty way an architecture firm I used to work for employed. We used to estimate that it took an average of 100 man hours to complete a 30" × 46" drawing. A presentation board required about a quarter of that time. Multiply the total number of hours by the average billing rate for the firm and you have the fee.

Of course, you should figure out your own averages for your particular firm. Look at old jobs, take out the drawings, and figure out the costs. The results will be rough at best.

But this method may jog you to think of different aspects of the job. You may think of additional boards for complicated areas, additional details for complex cabinetry, or combined drawings for smaller jobs. It should just be one more check on your proposed fee.

The last method of estimating fees is to see how long the job will last, estimate how many staff people you will need on the job full time from start to finish, and using your average salary for the entire firm, multiply the months times the people times the average salary for the estimated fee.

The better you know your business, the easier it will be to look at it from several different angles. And this is certainly one area where familiarity breeds competence.

The only way to do this really well is to have kept good records of previous jobs and to use that information to build up a data base. Some old timers carry that data base around in their head. Most of us don't, and need to do the hard work to look smart. There is a form provided later in this book called the Project Analysis Form which you should use for every project you work on. This will provide you with the basis for intelligent fee setting in the future.

We have not discussed the marketing aspects of pricing. I believe that, in most cases, you should be able to sell your services at a fair price, without resorting to price-cutting. If you sell at lower prices than you feel the job will cost, then you will either take a loss, presumably because you will make it back later (but you rarely do . . . clients recognize pricing weakness and keep you at that disadvantage), or you will have to produce an inferior job within the budget you set, or you will have to go back for more fee creating a bad impression and a lack of desire to use your services again.

Don't be dumb competition underselling yourself . . . and everyone else in the profession trying to do good work at a fair price. Sell the services the job deserves at the price that allows them to be performed well.

5 Marketing

Marketing consists of plans and actions designed to get you in a position to make a sale. It is not selling. Marketing should result in your knowing who the prospects are and their knowing who you are. Sales will convert those prospects into clients. In this chapter we will concentrate on marketing. Please hold off making any sales until the next chapter!

I think of marketing as five different tasks. The first task is to determine where the interior design work actually is. This is not the same as determining where you want to work. Finding out where clients are and what they actually need is vital. This is called "*market research*."

The next step is to make yourself presentable to these newly located potential clients. This has to be done on many levels: organizationally, on paper, and physically. You should have a distinctive competence. You must know your competition and look at least noticeably different. At the same time, clients usually feel somewhat comfortable with familiar settings and personnel, so you want to appear somewhat similar to them. Overall, this is "*image-building*."

Having developed your image, you must now make it known to the general public. You should be able to use newspapers, magazines, trade shows, parties, and many other means. This is "*public relations*."

You will also want to build a file of actual potential clients from whom you are seeking work. You should be able to use your own public relations efforts, formal and informal networks you join, purchased sources, and more. In this "*list-building*" phase you are looking for names of people, not just companies.

Finally, you want to make yourself known personally to all the names on your lists. You will need to send written material, make telephone calls, go to see them, and then keep in touch with them. This is "*making contact*" and it is the immediate precursor to actually making a sale.

These steps—*market research, image-building, public relations, list-building, and making contact*—take a large amount of time, effort, and money. Many of us hate the idea of doing the personal-contact parts of the effort such as telephone calls and cold calls. But if you do not make the effort today, there may be no need to try tomorrow since your company may not be there. Firms in this field come and go quickly. They don't fail because of poor work.

Usually they fail because of poor management and unsuccessful marketing.

Marketing costs both time and money. Some experts have suggested that you should spend about 2 percent of your income in hard costs for brochures, newsletters, reprint mailings, and so on. About twice that will probably be spent in time, both of the principal and support staff. In the small business of interior design, especially in a start-up situation, you might end up spending much more than that. Marketing requires a real commitment on your part. Don't stint on it, because this is the lifeblood of your company.

Marketing also does not happen by chance. It requires much thought and the formulation of an entire marketing strategy. You should do this in the same manner as you do strategic planning for the firm in general. Each year analyze where you are and what you are. Set some marketing and sales goals and objectives. Determine your tactics, the steps required, and assign responsibility for each. Implement and measure the results. Check progress at least quarterly. And do the whole thing again, and again.

Marketing is a slow, difficult task. For every new client, you may have made your pitch to five. To get to those five, you may have contacted twenty-five or fifty. These are good averages. The important thing to remember is that everyone gets rejected. A lot. So don't lose heart and give up.

Step 1: Market Research, or, Targeting Your Efforts

You can greatly improve your sales success rate by targeting your efforts. You should look at the situation from several points of view, but always asking the same one question: where is the work? A **Market Research Worksheet** is provided to help you think through this process.

Design work is needed wherever new construction is taking place or where renovation work is being done. Geographically, you should look for where such work is happening. This can be on a national, state, or local basis. Is there a section of your city that is being gentrified? Are businesses moving back into part of downtown? Are professionals taking over another section and converting old buildings to small offices for all those "P.C.'s" (Professional Corporations) for doctors and lawyers.

Is there an intersection or state road outside of town where many new small speculative office buildings or office parks are springing up? Is the area around the city or the state capital showing signs of expansion? Is the financial service industry taking over the downtown of your city? Is the state university taking over another ten acres? Is the medical center taking over another city block and doctors' offices taking over even more around that?

It is easier to try to make an impression on fairly limited market segments. Geographically, you should know whether you are trying to become known within the city, or trying for suburban work. You should not discount all other areas, but allow your decision to help prioritize your efforts.

It may seem silly for you to look at the national trends when you are just a little firm in a small field. The reason for doing so, however, is that the trends are well reported on a national basis. That way you can observe some of these trends in the bigger areas and see if they are also happening in your small corner of the world. If computers are taking over our lives, and the largest computer chain store now has 400 stores internationally, does that help focus some of your thoughts in your town?

Simultaneously, you should look at the industrial base of your surroundings and see if one or more industries are worth targeting. Which industries are healthy in your overall area? Are discount brokerage offices springing up all over? Are small, storefront clinics becoming popular? Are restaurants having a resurgence for the two-income families in the newly gentrified section of town? Is government a growth business, needing more and more office space? Are lobbyists and other governmental adjuncts filling up the offices around the government center?

Speaking of government, what is it supporting these days? Is it education, health care, day care, or energy businesses? Is there a high-tech industry in your area? How many telephone stores are there in your city? How many more will there be next year?

Another area to consider is the building type that might be proliferating around your town. Are miniature shopping centers becoming popular? Small office parks? Suburban office condominiums? Do you think you could work well with the builders? The big builders or the little ones? Are there new up-and-coming builders you should meet? Are there downtown builders and ones who concentrate more in the suburbs?

The last area to look for work is in the various segments of the real estate industry. Do you want to meet the people who are renovating downtown or moving to the suburbs? Some brokers concentrate on large offices, small offices, retail establishments, new buildings, or older buildings.

So the first part of market research is to discover where the work is so you can concentrate your efforts by geographic, industry, building, and realtor segment. It will also help to examine yourself now to see what your own strengths and weaknesses are.

Your strengths could include qualities such as roots in the community, many years of practice there, good connections into abc industry, good connections with xyz building company, a long series of practical designs, a strong shop, an ability to turn out work very quickly, or do great custom work, or an extremely fine traditional (modern) design sense. Maybe you won a prize, or got published, or got a very big contract. Just look at yourself and your operation and be fair.

Also be fair about your weaknesses. Perhaps you have a new business, a small shop, no track record, not much back-up, practical but bland design skills, and so on. Write them down.

Company:	Top Interior Design
Date:	1/9/89
Person Completing Worksheet:	A.T.

			Target
ACTIVE GEOGRAPHIC AREAS:	Locally:	Near I-95 / I-84	Try to break out of county to cover STATE.
	County Wide:	In the Capital	
	State Wide:	~~Hartford~~, Stamford, Greenwich	
	Nationally:	— not for us — — YET !	
GROWING INDUSTRIES	Locally:	Insurance, Banks	the Financial Industries
	County Wide:	same	
	State Wide:	All financial services + Computers	
	Nationally:	Financial Services, Computers	
PROLIFERATING BUILDING TYPES:	Locally:	Small office condo's	Go for small office condo's for job + refferals
	County Wide:	same	
	State Wide:	"Professional" office bldgs	
	Nationally:	National Headquarters	
ACTIVE REALTORS:	Locally:	Century 22, Heisenberg + Sons, C.B.	Heisenberg knows this market.
	County Wide:	same	
	State Wide:	C.B. + C.W.	
	Nationally:	C.B. + C.W.	
STRENGTHS:	Personal:	Graduated State U — where are those guys?	
	Professional:	27 year business — lots of satisfied clients.	
	Firm-wide:	Proj. Dir. been practicing 34 yrs - Sr. Des. now arch.	
WEAKNESSES:	Personal:	Don't give mgmt. enough time - I like DESIGNING.	
	Professional:	No real design pizazz / Almost too competent.	
	Firm-wide:	Little experience w/ clients wanting good design!	
COMPETITION:	By Location:	We're #5 by size in town	
	By Specialty Industry:	Same, but we're tops for small law firms.	
	By Building Type:	none	
	By Realtor Preference	We have NO realtor contacts	
OPPORTUNITIES:	Internal:	Can we use our new arch? F. Dealer contacts.	
	External:	Can we meet those realtors?	
THREATS:	Internal:	My staff seems to be getting bored.	
	External:	No marketing force, image, or presence.	
GOALS:	Long Term:	Get some exciting work - top executive offices - maybe local offices of national firms?	
	Short Term:	- Get to know som realtors — Get some interesting non-legal jobs - Get published!	

Look around at the competition you may have in each of the areas I have discussed. It may not make much sense to go after a large but stagnant market that has lots of competitors. You want to find an area where you can establish some credentials before other firms discover it or become well entrenched.

Consider what opportunities you now have. Don't ignore factors such as your spouse having lots of contacts now that he or she has been elected president of the sisterhood, the congregation, the professional association, or the PTA. Don't forget your friends who might have an office that many clients come to, or who are converting an old house to doctors' offices.

Note what threats you might be facing. There might not be any growing area in your county. Business is terrible for everyone. A new and large furniture store may have opened nearby that is giving away design services. You may have only one month's capital before you have to fold your tent. At this point you have some work, but no new prospects. Perhaps a big interior design firm has just opened a branch in your area.

Look at all the information you have gathered on the Market Research Worksheet and formulate some targets. You are looking for a healthy industry that may be relatively concentrated geographically and also, perhaps, in a particular building type. There should be fairly good access to it through some means, such as a few builders and/or realtors. It would be best if there were no well-established competition or if it was such that you could compete effectively.

Your target markets should also be reasonable for a firm of your own particular strengths and weaknesses. If your company consists of one person, you should be looking for a target market that would respond well to personal service, such as new lawyers, proliferating Chinese restaurants, or nail sculpture studios. Ideally, you are looking for the kind of market that leads to other assignments because it gives you good exposure. Just doing the lobbies of new speculative office buildings may make your name known to prospective tenants.

You might establish some long-term goals, such as being a recognized expert in a particular kind of industry or building type or being an important designer in a particular geographic area.

You must establish short-term goals as well. Actual sales could be included, but that is not a necessity. If you are trying to break into a new field, you might simply have a goal of being able to make five presentations to office managers in that field. Or you may want to meet the major brokers in your area. Or you may wish to get something published in one or more of the journals that serve the industries you have targeted.

Don't do this in a vacuum. Talk to people, especially prospective clients, if you can. If you don't know anyone else, talk to your lawyer and a banker. Buy them lunch and make it clear that you are not pitching business, but merely seeking advice. Check that your expectations are realistic and see if they have any other leads. If you know you are not seeking their business (now) and they know it, you may be able to relax and have an excellent discussion. Keep them informed as you proceed.

As we go through the other steps of marketing, this particular phase will undoubtedly become more defined. Marketing demands great consistency to be effective, so make sure your targets and your other marketing efforts are all coordinated, or refine each phase until they are well coordinated.

Step 2: Image-Building

Now that you have chosen one or more target markets, you have to try to tailor your image appropriately to those potential clients. Your image is made up of your physical appearance, the standard written documents you use to communicate, and the brochures, portfolios, and presentations you use in face-to-face meetings.

To a large extent, all of us prefer dealing with people who seem to imply the least risk. Business people usually like dealing with mirror images of themselves. If you are planning on dealing with brokers and bankers, you will probably dress differently than you would if you were trying to get work from hair-styling establishments. The top names of all the big interior design firms dress in banker-type pin stripe suits.

That is the safest approach. Be conservative in your dress. Men should wear suits and women should also wear tailored, fitted, conservative cuts. Obviously you should be well groomed, have a decent haircut, and so on. The best way to approach the question of personal appearance is to ask yourself what you would wear to your prospect's office if you were interviewing for an entry-level job in his firm which is, after all, what you are doing.

Some people feel that it is necessary to look like a "designer," whatever that looks like. While you might dress slightly more stylishly, it has not been my experience that successful designers dress significantly differently than their clients. They should look successful and current. The people they hire for positions of lesser responsibility may dress more informally. The heads of companies, no matter how small, tend to dress conservatively and well.

Try to have an office as soon as you can afford one. It doesn't matter how small or cheap it is. Designers can work out of nearly any space and make it look decent and presentable. But make sure the rest of the organization fits your desired image.

Never use an answering machine. It makes you look like an amateur. A good answering service can give you the appearance of a staff even when there is none. If you do have staff, make sure they have good telephone technique. If they don't, teach them to answer in a carefully modulated, low, pleasant voice and learn to take the name and company of the caller. Make them practice if necessary. Anyone with client contact should look and dress the part.

Your written material should also be appropriate. There should be an identifiable design and feel to all your written documents based on design, typography, logo, ink, and paper. Designers, more than other business people, feel the need to design everything. Too often they over-design their written documents.

Start with your letterhead. Keep it simple. You don't need lots of rules, boxes, or dots to indicate that the stationery was "designed." A simple, straightforward approach may be more memorable. Then add *one* item to make it distinctive. That item could be a rule, an off-center piece of data, the placement of address at the bottom, etc. Just don't do everything at once.

Many designers use a logo. Make sure yours is sufficiently different to be worthwhile. In New York, there are design firms known as GHK, GK, GN, HOK, HLW, and so on. Seriously question whether the use of initials will simplify or complicate your quest for visibility.

Designers often tend to use strange typefaces to enhance the feeling of "design." Too many typefaces look forced and will be difficult to match in the future. Souvenir had its two years in the sun, and is now a cliche. Other "fashion" typefaces die just as quickly. Stick to the basics: Helvetica, Futura, Optima, Univers, Baskerville, Bodoni, Garamond, Memphis. Avoid all script, novelty, and calligraphic type styles. Think how they will look both on the typed page and on a drawing.

Don't use strange-colored inks, either. Basic black is always in, and the press does not require an extra cost clean-up before they run your job. Grays and sepias look very nice, but you may find it hard to keep matching the colors. If you use a brown ink and then get a brown typewriter ribbon, it looks nice, but forced. And you know you will run out of those ribbons on the day you're typing your biggest proposal. Also consider the effect the ink color has on photocopied documents. If you send someone a copy, will your letterhead look trashy?

Your paper stock should be of high quality. The client touches this, and recognizes it instinctively. Watermarked, name-brand paper is worth it if you are not well established, but want to look as if you are.

You can print in several different ways. Engraved printing is always the best, the most expensive, and what you want to do if you can afford it. Many printers do *thermography*, which is a funny method of melting granulated ink onto the paper to create raised lettering. It is also shiny, and I think it looks as cheap or cheaper than good quality metal plate offset, the third standard method of printing, and the cheapest.

When you have your basic design set out, you have to consider how many different items you should have printed. You need letterhead, second sheets, envelopes, mailing labels, transmittals, purchase orders, specifications, time sheets, expense reports, and cards. Only the letterhead and the business cards should be as high a quality as you can prudently afford. But all your other standard business documents should share the same design, the same image. That is another reason to avoid colored inks, paper, and so on in your original design.

Your business card deserves a little more discussion. It should be standard size. Big ones are noticed more, in a negative fashion, as the recipient mutilates it while stuffing it into his wallet. It won't fit in card files, and thus might get deposited in the round file. Remember that the card should be your image, so if you wear silver lame jumpsuits, by all means print it on silver foil. Be conservative, but make it well designed.

By the way, we in the interior design profession have a tendency to think that we can design anything. Sometimes our printed documentation disproves that. If you have to, hire a decent graphic designer to do this for you. No one need ever know.

Be practical in your approach to this whole subject. Aside from your card and mailing label, everything else you do is probably going to be photocopied. So make transmittals, time sheets and expense reports on normal 8½-by-11-inch paper. Blind embossing costs a great deal, and disappears in copies. Is it worth it? Always have your name, address, and telephone number on any document you hand out.

If you choose a typewriter typeface to go with your letterhead, and you should, is it easily available? The common business typefaces of Letter Gothic (sans serif) and Courier 10 (serif) are usually available wherever you are. My reports have been saved more than once by last minute changes in the client's office with their typewriters. Don't make that impossible for yourself by choosing the most esoteric typeface you can find.

I have provided a checklist for you to go by in determining your documentation requirements. For many of these uses, I have provided sample forms in this volume. All you should do is modify the actual printing so it looks like the rest of your format, and print them up on an inexpensive offset press. Good design, planned for that kind of reproduction, will look quite presentable.

Another category of written document that requires a great deal of your thought is your brochure. The problem with most brochures I see, is that they try to say too much. Your brochure should state clearly and succinctly:

- Who you are
- What you do
- How you do it
- Who your clients are
- Your staff and their qualifications

- What your distinctive competence is
- Some sense of history, longevity, or track record

This does not have to be very large, glitzy, or four color. Just a few of the right photos should suffice to show what you do and how you solved someone's space-related problems through design. Black and white photos can often do this as well as, or better than, colored photos. If the photos are well chosen, *and explained*, you can make your point.

The brochure must be well designed. Its graphic identity should match your other documents in color, type, and so on. You can make simple one-page brochures aimed at different market segment targets, or you can make a more complex one that can be customized through inserts into pockets or different bindings. But do make sure you know to whom you are speaking and what you want to say.

Nine out of ten brochures end up in file folders. Make sure yours fits by being the standard 8½-by-11-inch or smaller.

A **Brochure Checklist** is provided so you can make sure your document is as successful as possible. The questions should not each be answered individually. You should write a paragraph or two in simple, straightforward prose stating what you can do for this particular type of client and why he would find your service valuable. Make sure that this is understandable and valid. And remember, for most clients *design* is the least important aspect of your service. They wish to know how you will solve their space-related problems.

Some jargon from the advertising profession will help us to consider the brochure, the portfolio, and much of public relations as "advertising." In advertising, you always seek to stress the "client benefit" your product offers and the "USP," or "unique selling proposition," which states why you can provide that benefit better than anyone else. Your written material should stress these concepts, the benefit you offer the client and why you can perform better than any other designer.

Another major means of telling potential clients about yourself is the portfolio or slideshow. The basic concept behind this and the brochure are very similar. The portfolio/slideshow simply allows you more time and images to make your points.

And that is critical to remember. You are trying to get the viewer to remember specific points, the client benefits and the USP, not just images of pretty spaces. If you can't tell a story about each picture, what the problems were, and how they were solved, the image should probably not be in your collection. Doesn't "and this is a pretty picture..." sound weak as a sales tool?

You should use sequences of photos to emphasize the client benefits. They should also be used to vary the pace of the presentation and to keep the prospect interested. It helps to mix in graphics such as charts, schedules, drawings, perspectives, or graphics done specifically for the presentation to

Company:
Date:
Person Completing Checklist:

Paper	Normal Size for Function Good Weight Good Quality/Watermarked for Client Contact
Ink	Normal Color Should Photocopy well Should look good with normal typewriter ribbons
Typeface	High Quality Classic Typeface Sans Serif—Helvetic, Futura, Optima, Univers, etc. Serif—Baskerville, Bodoni, Garamond, etc.
Design	Same Throughout, including blind embossing, rules, logos, margins, etc.
Information	Always have name, address, and phone number on every document you produce.

You Should Have the Following Documents to Run a Design Firm:

	Size	Design, Ink, Typeface	Paper Quality	Name, Address Tel. Number
☐ **Business Card**	2.25" × 3.5"	Matching	Excellent	Included
☐ **Letterhead**	8.5" × 11"	Matching	Excellent	Included
☐ **Second Sheet**	8.5" × 11"	Matching	Excellent	Included
☐ **Envelope**	No. 10	Matching	Excellent	Included
☐ **Brochure**	8.5" × 11"	Matching	Excellent	Included
☐ **Purchase Order**	8.5" × 11"	Close	Good	Included
☐ **Specification**	8.5" × 11"	Close	Good	Included
☐ **Schedule**	8.5" × 11"	Close	Good	Included
☐ **Minute**	8.5" × 11"	Close	Good	Included
☐ **Memo**	8.5" × 11"	Close	Good	Included
☐ **Mailing Label**	4" × 6"	Close	Good	Included
☐ **Transmittal**	8.5" × 11"	Close	Acceptable	Included
☐ **Expense Report**	8.5" × 11"	Close	Acceptable	Included
☐ **Time Sheet**	8.5" × 11"	Close	Acceptable	Included

control the flow and make certain points. If you think about the graphics, you can make them emphasize your USP.

Like any good story, yours should end on a high note. Run through the entire sequence and practice it for friends, relatives, and advisers to make sure it works.

Physically, if you are using a portfolio, buy a good quality binder. Try to get the best photographs you can. Of course, good professional photographers cost about $1,000 per day which will net you five or so photographs of one job. Even poor photographs can be greatly improved by cropping to emphasize what you want to show. If you have only small and/or poor photographs, try grouping them on one page to increase their importance. You can also have photostat reductions of plans, sections, and perspectives made to swell a small portfolio.

(If you take your own photographs and know a little about photography, here are a few simple hints. Use a tripod. You're best off with a wide angle lens, preferably 28mm or wider. If you are using color film, try to photograph during daylight hours and turn off all artificial lighting. Use "daylight" film and open up at least four stops any time a window is in the field of vision. An alternative is to use "tungsten" film at night and only turn on regular bulbs while keeping all fluorescents turned off, if that will illuminate your space sufficiently well. You can also buy photofloods of either kind to light the space for you, but that gets much more complex. Filters are available to correct for the awful blue-green coloration of anything illuminated by fluorescents, but it is very chancy as there are four types of fluorescents, which all change color as they age.)

Another alternative is to use obviously amateur snapshots of the space, but create a small presentation board for each project in your portfolio so the prospect can see your real choices of fabric, material, and finishes while viewing the color-distorted, but actual space.

Have short descriptions of the client, the space, the problems, and the solutions typed up and made part of the portfolio. It is far better to describe how you solved the problem than what your sources and materials were. Just a few coherent stories are much better than many random pictures. And, again, try to group them to create the flow of thought you wish your client to follow.

Any reprints of stories about you, even from the Sunday Shopper, will provide some credibility. Letters from clients satisfied by your work will also add to your credibility and act as references.

Read over all your written material. Is it aimed at clients or designers? Does it speak to clients in their own language? Does it stress the client benefits? Is it logical and internally consistent? Does your USP come across? Ask a friend in the client area to review it and offer criticism.

If you plan on doing a slideshow instead of a portfolio, be aware that it is a clumsier method and requires more specific physical arrangements. There are self-contained rear screen projectors that are no bigger than a shopping bag,

Company:	*Top Interior Design*
Date:	*1/11/84*
Person Completing Checklist:	*A.T.*

For this brochure, *#1*, my target audience is:	*Branch offices of national firms*
The primary benefit we offer this client is:	*Lots of local experience, good contractor/ supplier relationships — — ON TIME — ON BUDGET —*
How meaningful is this benefit to this target audience?	*Very, for managers reporting long distance to their superiors*
The reasons our services provide that benefit is:	*DAD was here for 25 years, establishing our reputation*
Is this a unique service in some manner, from any other available?	*The service is not unique, but our longevity is.*
Is this message stated in language the target audience understands?	*We keep it clean and simple — and our client list is enormous!*
Is this a distinctive competence of our firm?	*Our competence is not distinctive — but our longevity is.*
Should this brochure be modified for other audiences?	*We need a more exciting brochure — but we still need more exciting jobs.*
Do we have other brochures for this audience?	*No — should we print some older looking brochures for a sense of history...probably not, but its a thought.*
A secondary benefit for clients of our services is:	*Are our long term contacts with suppliers, lawyers, etc. of value?*
Do your illustrations explicitly support the benefits and reasons expressed?	*GOOD DULL OFFICES — But we can show a converted warehouse... and some funny old buildings which now function well.*
Does this brochure differentiate us from our competition?	*We stress the 27 year / 2 generation business with long list of repeat clients*
Does this brochure have the usual qualifying items?	☑ Who you are ☑ What you do? *} new graphics* ☑ How you do it ☐ Your Client List *Very long + impressive* ☑ Your staff ☑ Your distinctive competences ☑ Your history
Does this document suggest the proper and usual image of your firm?	☐ Design/Logo/Typeface/Ink *Simple Bodoni* ☑ Paper Quality ☐ Size *8½" x 11"* ☑ Name, Address, Telephone

but are still awkward to set up. I would suggest you save the slide show for when you have been asked to make a formal presentation. But if you insist on it as a marketing tool, follow all the same guidelines discussed for the portfolio. I will discuss slide show presentations further in the next chapter.

Above all, for either portfolios or slideshows, remember the old adage, KISS. That stands for *Keep It Simple, Stupid!* Don't bombard the prospect with brilliance, or baffle them with bull. Just *talk* with them.

Step 3: Public Relations

Public relations is the art of making yourself known to your potential clients. You can do it by making news through personal appearances, newspaper stories, published work, and your own mailings. The goal is to make many people *who might have work* aware of your name, what you do, and how they can contact you.

Getting your work published in the trade magazines is the most common public relations goal of designers. But, if you think about it, you will be speaking primarily to your peers and not to potential clients. At best, publication in the trade press acts as a third-party recommendation for your talent, but you still have to get that message to your potential clients yourself.

In order to get your work published in the design press, you need good quality transparencies, the bigger than 35mm, the better. The more popular magazines are quite particular about the quality of the photographs they will use, and to get them will cost you, as mentioned before, upward of $1,000. If you are considering spending that kind of money, read an issue or two and note which photographers names appear more than once. These are the photographers whose work the editors like, and using them will double or triple the chances of your work being accepted.

To get published, you should also have a story. What was the problem you were called in to solve? Why was it so difficult that they needed your expertise? How did you triumphantly solve it? All stories should answer the old newspaper questions: Who? Did What? Where? When? Why? And How?

You should also have data on the client, the sources, plans, a photo of yourself, and, if you want the package back, a stamped, self-addressed envelope.

A **Public Relations Checklist** is provided to make sure you have everything you should. Also provided is a **Publications Checklist** so you can get those submissions out quickly and accurately.

Even after you get published in one of these magazines, you will probably have to buy lots of reprints (at $1 – $3 each) to distribute to your potential clients. If you want to reach them directly, you are better off going to their trade publications instead of your own. If you go to the public library, you will find a volume called the *Standard Periodical Directory* published by Oxbridge Communica-

Company:	
Date:	1/12/84
Person Completing Checklist:	A.T.

For this portfolio/slide show, my target audience is: office managers & local office managers of national firms

The primary benefit we offer to the audience is: On time + On budget

How is this benefit meaningful to the target audience: Show cheap offices - especially & Temporary offices which don't look it.

Is there a cogent reason why our service will provide that benefit: Long experience, plus good trade contacts

Is this message simply and clearly stated in images and language? Yes - plus we show four offices for the same firm as it grew.

Does each image:
- ☐ Reinforce your message?
- ☐ Have a story to it?
- ☐ Show a problem solved?
- ☐ Have a good client name?

Is each image:
- ☐ Of good photographic quality? Some could be better
- ☐ Cropped properly?
- ☐ Lit correctly?

Does the portfolio/slideshow have a flow to it for greater interest and to create a more powerful message? We have integrated graphics to show HOW a job gets done.

Does it logically build support for your message? Yes - a job from start to move-in

Does it have sequences to vary the pace and build stronger supporting points? We use before photos, graphics, humorous cartoons (just 3), forms, schedules, etc.

Does it mix graphics and photos for emphasis and pacing? Yes - and our in-house worksheets

Does it list the usual qualifying factors?
- ☑ Who you are
- ☑ What you do
- ☑ How you do it
- ☑ Your Client List
- ☑ Your staff
- ☑ Your distinctive competences
- ☑ Your history/staying power
- ☑ Your address & telephone no.

Can it be varied for different types of clients? NOT YET, but I hope we can soon.

Is this message simply and clearly stated in language the target audience understands? Yes

Does the portfolio/slideshow match the graphic image of other written material? Yes

tions, Inc. This lists all the periodicals published in the United States by subject. Thus, if you wanted to reach bankers, you would find *The American Banker, Bank Administration Monthly,* and about a dozen more. State law journals are also usually interested in free stories.

For these types of periodicals, you can provide two different types of stories. The first is a design job you did for a client in that particular industry. The second is a story about a subject of interest to the periodical's readers, such as lease negotiation, the value of work letters, or how you measure how big a space actually is.

To get a design job published, you need a magazine that does that sort of story. Or you can try to place it in the facility managers' magazines such as *Modern Office Procedures,* or *Today's Office.* You need the same sort of material mentioned before, except that 35mm slides are acceptable. You should realize that the problem you solved and how you solved it is even more important than the pictures.

To get the informative sort of story published, all you have to do is write an intelligent, informative, well-written piece and send it around. Double space your story and write the source on each page. These magazines are always looking for material to publish, and they are usually quite pleased to find someone who will do it for them for nothing.

To reach local people and industries, you apply similar techniques to get stories into the local newspapers, you can use similar techniques, substituting only black and white glossy photos for the slides.

If you don't yet have a story, create one. Do some research about something in the design field that will be important to your target market. Offer to speak about it, for nothing, at a trade association dinner, the Rotary Club, your church or temple, or any other place you think clients might be present. Make sure the message is for them, not for other designers. Talk about all the old chestnut topics, such as the office of the future, new information storage technologies, adoptive reuse of old structures, data processing needs in today's offices and how to physically accommodate them, and so on.

Always have something to leave with them. It could summarize your talk, or even better, promise more information if they write in and ask for it. The handout should be low key, have your name and address, and a summary paragraph of your qualifications. It should, of course, match the rest of your graphic image.

Now, if you have given a talk somewhere, you now have a story to write about for the local paper and the trade press. You always have to make your own breaks, and it is a surprisingly easy task to create your own news.

By the way, assuming you have built up some useful information for these stories or talks, you also have a good mailing piece. I normally trash every piece I get touting a firm, but I keep those little handouts that neatly summarize human proportions, work station standards, current costs, square footage conversions, and so on.

If you have something to say but can't find a place to say it, volunteer to serve on boards or organizations. Join the American Management Association. Take a real estate course, get your salesperson license, and join the local real estate association. Serve on your church or school board. People who do volunteer work are often just the sort of people who can either help you out or know people who can.

If you enter a competition and win, place, or show, write a story. If you make a speech, write a story. If you are published in a trade magazine, write a story for the local press. You can get stories written about you by calling publications, asking what they are interested in, and whom to contact. Write a release (just the facts) and a pre-written story (most editors are lazy). Send it in and follow up at weekly intervals. You would be surprised how easy it is to get something published.

If you can't do this yourself, you might hire a PR person. There are three kinds of PR people. The first know a lot about this industry. They are good, and expensive, and you probably can't afford them if you are starting out. The second may be good in general, but know little about this industry, so you have to manage them closely. They may write better than you do, but you know better what you want to say and to whom. Also, you will care about it much more than they do.

The third kind are useless or worse. Even if they are just hacks, they can do you more harm than good. An excellent way of telling the three kinds of public relations practitioners apart is to ask people of the press; design or local. They know who is good, mediocre, or a turn-off to them, which is terrible for you. Use the press as your reference board.

So make sure that the PR person you hire does for you all the things previously discussed. Don't assume that they will do so without your interest and supervision. Get regular reports on their progress and gauge that against their costs.

Keep your name in front of the public. Put your name in the windows of space you are designing. Don't be shy. Make it into a little game and maybe you can even enjoy it. If you are good, and have something to say, people deserve to know about it.

Step 4: List Building

In this phase, the intent is to build up lists of potential clients. You want to get the names of companies in your target area and the names of the people within those companies who handle the interior design work. They often have the title of Director of Facility Management or Office Manager. It could also be something totally different. Are they the real decision-makers for the purchase of new services? Who else might decide about new work? You should know the names of the top people in the company, what real estate they presently

occupy, who did their last interior design work, how they like it, and when they might need new work again.

A **Client Call Report** is provided for you to organize this data in a file system. There is space provided for you to note what happened each time you called and what your next step should be. By using one of those cute little "flag" clip-ons at the top, you can make sure you contact these people regularly, like every quarter, to make sure you don't miss anything.

Alphabetize this file by company name and key each contact sheet in to a master photocopying mailing label sheet. This is a sheet with names and addresses of the contacts arranged in a grid that can then be xeroxed onto a Dennison label sheet, an 8½-by-11-inch page with about two dozen peel off labels. By xeroxing one page of master mailing addresses onto this other page, you can peel off all the labels and address dozens of letters in five minutes or so. By cross-coding the contact sheet with the mailing label sheet, when a change occurs, you can easily locate and change the mailing label.

(This whole area is perfect for the use of a Data Base Management System on any small computer, which I will discuss in a later chapter.)

You build up your list from a group of fellow travelers who can all mutually benefit from the trading of information. You want to create your own network from firms in your immediate field such as architects, engineers, contractors, furniture dealers, records management consultants, audio-visual consultants, marketing consultants, and management consultants. This network can feed names of prospects to you, assuming you will do the same for them, since you can work as a team. Given that aspect, you wish to keep the quality level of your network as high as possible.

Next you look to your local sources, starting with your existing clients who are usually surprisingly helpful about people in their fellow industry. Try to get information from the local real estate associations such as BOMA (Building Owners and Managers Association), NACORE (the National Association of Real Estate Executives), and REBNY (the Real Estate Board of New York). Read *Real Estate Forum, Real Estate Review,* and the *Real Estate Investor* for additional leads.

Talk with the city and county Directors of Economic Development, local Chambers of Commerce, Industrial Development Corporations, and city, county, and state business groups to get leads and names for your list.

Go to corporate sources as well. The directors of area development for the local utility companies often know who is expanding. Banks are excellent sources of knowledge about area business. Talk to the senior real estate and construction loan officers. And institutional investors such as insurance companies and investment/mortgage brokerage houses often know what is happening in the construction field.

Keep all these people in your network, because you all should be able to

contact next in month

CLIENT CALL REPORT FORM

Client Firm Name:	PUBLIC SERVICE		
Client Contact Name:	KAY TYKE	Tel:	(337) 492-2485 X 314

Information on Firm:

President:	Fred Elloate
Location:	MAIN ST, HOTFORD
Size of present facilities:	50,000 RSF
Current Employment:	250 ±
Lease(s) end:	1989 (35,000), 1993 (15,000)
Who does work for them now:	FR/PJ and some in-house
Other Information:	1930's style interiors

Information on client contact:

Title:	Director, Facilities Management
Years in job:	18
Background	Draftsman, moved up gradually

Personal Background (family names, dates, etc.): Wife - Helen, Sons Joe (17) John (15) Likes to fly-fish

CONTACT HISTORY

Date:	Contact:	Remarks:
5/82	Ray T.	Took him to lunch at P&A, told him about T.I.D.
7/83	Ray T.	Asked for some help on stds - sent 8/1/83 - Who's his boss?

mutually benefit from information about new projects in various stages of development. Enlightened self-interest can keep a good network functioning well.

Finally, if you have time, read *Businessweek, Forbes, Fortune, Dunn's Review, Barrons*. The more like your clients you are, the more they trust you. You can buy listings of new jobs from *The Dodge Reports* (McGraw Hill, 1221 Avenue of the Americas, New York, NY 10020) and *Standard & Poors* (751 Main Street, Waltham, MA 02154).

Keep any business card you are ever given. Each contains enough information so that the person will probably accept a call. Note on the back when and where you got it.

Once you build up your list, make sure you contact people regularly through calls and mailings. Mix them up, so you don't appear too much of a pest. Calls should be made no more than once a month, and probably once a quarter unless a job is in the offing. Mailings should be as often as you have something worthwhile to say, but no less than once a quarter. Don't waste much money on something they will quickly throw out. Try to find something worthwhile to send.

Whenever you call a contact, update your Client Call Report Form and change the tab to set up your next call. Rank and prioritize your contacts. We all have too little time to do everything.

Step 5: Making Contact

This phase consists of getting your firm and face known to the prospect, before a job is known to be available. It is easiest if you follow three steps. First, write and say you will call. Then call, keep it brief, and arrange an appointment. Lastly, have your meeting and promise to keep in touch.

Of course this whole process will be wasted if you are not trying to see the decision-maker. One way to find out is to call the president of the company. He, or his secretary, may brush you off to the appropriate person. If you are lucky, you will have gotten the brush-off from the president. That way, when you call the decision-maker you were trying to reach and say that the president suggested you call, he will tend to be more receptive.

Of course, his secretary might not be as receptive. If she truly tries to guard him from salesmen like you, there are a couple of techniques to get through the barrier.

But first, assuming you have the name of someone, send a letter stressing the value of good interior design services, the fact that you do work in this area already, your distinctive competence, your high quality of service and adherence to budget and schedule, and say that you will call soon. Keep it to one page with the simplest of brochures or inserts.

PUBLICATIONS CHECKLIST

Design Publications

Architectural Digest 5900 Wilshire Boulevard Los Angeles, CA 90036 att: Paige Rense, Editor in Chief	Architectural Record 1221 Avenue of the Americas New York, NY 10020 att: Charles Gandee, Associate Editor	Contract 1515 Broadway New York, NY 10036 att: Len Corlin, Publisher
The Designer 192 Lexington Avenue New York, NY 10016 att: Muriel Chess, ASID Editor	Designers West 8564 Melrose Avenue Los Angeles, CA 90069 att: Carol Soucek King, Editor	Florida Designers Quarterly 4510 N.E. 2nd Avenue Miami, FL 33137 att: Gloria Blake, Editor in Chief
Interior Design 850 Third Avenue New York, NY 10022 att: Stanley Abercrombie, Editor in Chief	Interiors 1515 Broadway New York, NY 10036 att: Beverly Russell, Editor in Chief	Interiorscape P.O. Drawer 77 Elm Grove, WI 53122 att: Jeffrey A. Morey, Editor
Metropolis 177 East 87th Street New York, NY 10028 att: Sharon Ryder, Editor	New York's Inside Design 127 East 31st Street New York, NY 10016 att: Suzanne Sapia, Editor	Progressive Architecture 600 Summer St., PO Box 1361 Stamford, CT 06904 att: Pilar Viladas, Interior Design Editor

Consumer/Shelter Magazines

Better Homes and Gardens Locust at 17th Des Moines, IO 50336 att: Shirley Van Zante Design Editor	Holiday Homes International 51 Weaver Street Greenwich, CT 06830 att: Helene Nichols, Managing Director	House Beautiful 1700 Broadway New York, NY 10036 att: Joanne Barwick, Editor in Chief
House and Garden 350 Madison Avenue New York, NY 10022 att: Jacqueline Sonnet, Decorating Editor	Metropolitan Home 750 Third Avenue New York, NY 10017 att: Dorothy Kalins, Editor	The New York Times 229 West 43rd Street New York, NY 10036 att: Susan Slesin, Home Section

Client Oriented Magazines

Corporate Design Magazine 850 Third Avenue New York, NY 10022 att: Roger Yee, Editor	Facilities Design & Mgmt 1515 Broadway New York, NY 10036 att: Anne Fallucchi, Editor	Hotel and Motel Management 141 East 13th Street New York, NY 10003 att: John Gamrecki, Editor
Modern Office Procedures 11 Chester Avenue Cleveland, OH 44114 att: Victoria E. Jackson, Senior Editor	The Office 1200 Summer Street Stamford, CT 06904 att: William Schulhof, Editor	Today's Office 645 Stewart Avenue Garden City, NY 11530 att: Eileen Tunison, Editorial Director

Prepare for your telephone call. Know exactly what you want to say in advance. Have good telephone manners. Sit up. Speak from the chest and not the throat. Your voice will sound stronger, more pleasant, and more competent. Use facial expressions. People can actually hear a smile in your voice.

If you have a great deal of difficulty trying to get past the telephone guardian, try using the following techniques (courtesy of Paul Mills and Bernie Roberts, who produce training programs, such as *Mastering and Maintaining Successful Client Relations for Interior Designers,* available through *Interior Design*.)

When faced with a secretarial *objection,* respond with a *sympathetic statement,* continue by *stressing the benefit,* and *ask for the appointment.* Follow this conversation:

Objection:	"Mr. Big is too busy right now to speak with you."
Sympathetic Statement:	"I understand. I wasn't expecting that he could speak with me just when I called."
Stress Benefit:	"But I've helped a lot of firms in his situation. I'm sure he would like to see me."
Ask For Appointment:	"Can you set an appointment for me next Tuesday morning or Wednesday afternoon?"
Objection:	"Just why did you wish to speak with Mr. Big?"
Sympathetic Statement:	"I'm glad you asked. I understand he handles design and space decisions for your company. That is why I would like to speak with him."
Stress Benefit:	"As a good executive, I'm sure he would like to compare our services to others."
Ask For Appointment:	"Which day next week will be best for him?"
Objection:	"Could you leave your number and he will get back to you?"
Sympathetic Statement:	"I wish I could, but I am out so much it would be very difficult to reach me."
Stress Benefit:	"I'm sure Mr. Big would like to see how we have solved his problems for other companies."
Ask For Appointment:	"When may I call him for an appointment? Or can you set one up...is Tuesday or Wednesday better?"

The odds are that you will have worn down the "gate keeper" by this time. If not, try calling at lunch hour, when the secretary is likely to be at lunch, and perhaps "Mr. Big" will pick up his own phone.

Think about this conversation with Mr. Big in advance and plan it. Always try to control the conversation, without appearing to do so. Establish a rapport with a friendly comment, but don't be familiar. Don't use his first name unless invited to do so. Never, ever, use his nickname. If you can find something in common, like the mutual friend who gave you his name, use it.

Stimulate his pride with a little "stroking." Make an interesting comment leading up to your pitch, like "did you know we have saved an average of 5 percent of our clients space per person in the last five jobs we've done?" Stress the client benefit. You should have saved money, space, or someone's business.

Allow the person you are calling to make some connections. Ask for help — most people love to help. Ask who, what, where, why, when, and how questions. These are soft, non-threatening sounding words that elicit further responses from the person you are calling. They also avoid any "yes" or "no" responses when you are not ready for them.

Be a good listener. That is difficult and requires conscious effort. Ask questions. Verify answers. Make reflective, positive sounds, such as, "yes," "uh-huh," "I see," "And?," "So," "Tell me more...," "I don't yet understand...." Echo words to lead him on, such as "...need more information?"

This sounds longer than the entire conversation should take. You are trying to get an appointment, not make a sale over the telephone. Leave something for the meeting. Control the answers to get ones you want by forcing a choice between equally desirable alternatives from your point of view. This is what you just did with the secretary, above.

Follow the same format of overcoming objections by using a sympathetic statement bridging to stressing a benefit and winding up by asking for that same old appointment. Follow this conversation, with more thanks to Paul Mills and Bernie Roberts for example:

Objection:	"I'm not interested."
Sympathetic Statement:	"I understand, Mr. Big. It would be unrealistic to expect that you might be interested in something that hasn't yet been explained."
Stress Benefit:	"It will take me less than 14 minutes to explain how our services can directly benefit you. Then you will be able to make a decision from a position of strength."
Ask for Appointment:	"Is Tuesday at 10 or Wednesday at 3 better for you?"
Objection:	"I don't have the time right now."
Sympathetic Statement:	"Of course, Mr. Big, I realize you are working on a very tough schedule."
Stress Benefit:	"But I've got some ideas that will result in real benefits for you."
Ask for Appointment:	"I'll be glad to set up an appointment at your convenience. Would before 9 be better than later in the day? Would tomorrow be better than the day after? Which do you prefer, a bagel or a donut?"
Objection:	"We have no money in the budget for design."
Sympathetic Statement;	"That's okay, Mr. Big, these days we all have to watch our costs."

Stress Benefit:	''That's why I would like to talk to you about how we have helped other companies like yours reduce their housing costs.''
Ask for Appointment:	''Would late in the day be better than before lunch tomorrow?''

This whole conversation control technique can be rather abrasive and make you come across like the Electrolux salesman. I would suggest that you master it by calling up the building department and trying to get a C. of O. (Certificate of Occupancy) for raw space, getting your car registration a week after the deadline, and so on. Then go easy with it. The technique will come back when you need it in a more subtle way, and be even more effective.

Given all that effort, I am sure you have gotten an appointment. This is not a sales meeting. We are assuming that you simply wish to convert the non-impression this person has of you into one of competence and interest in his problems. By the same token, you are meeting with him to find out as much as possible for future use in possible later sales situations.

In an interview, you want to handle yourself as professionally as possible. Be on time and dressed conservatively. Give Mr. Big a firm handshake, and look him straight in the eye as you introduce yourself. Try to make eye contact about half the time. Too little eye contact leaves the impression that you are untrustworthy, too much is overly intense and forward.

Ask, don't tell. Listen as much as possible, speak as little as you can. The more the client speaks, the more he respects your own conversation. Reinforce with little nods, yes's, and soft, reflective, positive sounds. Try to find some commonality so that you can create a personal relationship rather than a business relationship.

Know in advance what impression and knowledge you want to impart to him through the interview. But do it subtly. You want to just drop facts and figures that he will hear without your making a point of telling him directly. Plan those five or ten facts in advance and wait for the right moment to use them, perhaps as part of question. For instance, to let him know you are right up with the latest in technology, you might say something like, ''We've had some interesting results with flat-wired CRT's. What has your experience been?''

If you are obviously looking for information and not trying to make a sale, the client will know it and relax. Try to leave with something you can do for him.

Ask ''good questions.'' These are questions that are *open-ended,* such as ''What have you heard about...,'' instead of closed, yes-no questions such as ''Have you heard....'' Don't ask pointed questions such as ''What's wrong with...,'' but ask *open* questions such as ''How do you feel about....'' Avoid pointed questions, such as ''Do you like this scheme...,'' and ask instead *less direct* questions, such as ''What type of scheme were you thinking of?'' Ask questions with only one point, rather than compound questions with two or more related answers. And be mildly humorous, if you think you can do so properly. Don't overdo it.

PUBLIC RELATIONS CHECKLIST

Company: *TID* Date: *1/15/84*

Client Name: *J+M, Attorneys At Law*

Person Completing This Checklist: *A.T.*

Company Address: *14285 Post Road*
Tertiary, CT
05432

Client Address: *857 River Road*
S. Hartford, CT
04523

Story:	Lead Paragraph:
☑ Who? *T.I.D. / J+M*	*Johnson & Murphy, a law firm forced to vacate their previous quarters when dioxin was discovered in their atrium, moved into a brand new office in a converted warehouse on River Road last Friday. Top Interior Design, located in Tertiary, CT, converted an old Studebaker warehouse into offices for the 35 person law firm in just four weeks. Arnold Top, partner in charge of the project credits great local manufacturers for producing furniture so quickly.*
☑ Did What? *converted warehouse for 35 ppl in 4 wks*	
☑ Where? *S. Hartford*	
☑ When? *Occupied last week*	
☑ Why? *Moved in a rush 'cause of dioxin.*	
☑ How? *Made most furnishings locally*	

Other points to be brought out:

Release Requirements:	Trade Magazines	Shelter Magazines	Newspapers	Client Trade Press
Final Photographs	Large Transparencies Highest Quality	Anything to catch their interest—They take them if accepted	Black/White glossies	35 mm slides are OK
"Before" Photos	Not necessary	Include	Include	Include
Story/Facts	Include Fact Sheet	Double-spaced story	Most Important—Tell	completely
Client Information	Not Necessary	Not Necessary	Include	Include
Sources	Include	Include	Not Necessary	Not Necessary
Plans	Include	Include	Include	Not Necessary
Your Photo	Include	Include	Include	Not Necessary
Biography	Not Necessary	Not Necessary	Include	Include
Self-Addressed Stamped Envelope	Include	Include	Include	Include
Follow-up Call	Two Weeks After Mailing	Two Weeks After Mailing	Two Weeks After Mailing	Two Weeks After Mailing

Control the conversation to learn the following information. Do they have a problem? How do they live now? Do they have a formal facilities program now? What budget or building information is available?

Who is the decision-maker (confirmation)? How do they choose their design services? Who have they used in the past to solve their space problems? Were they satisfied? How do they solve their problems now? Can you find out typical fees they're paying now? Do they face any special housing issues now?

Are any projects now being considered. Who might be in the running? Could you be considered?

While all this is going on, you should be slipping in those preplanned qualifications, connections, and concerns. Make sure you leave him with the impression you planned to.

Speaking of leaving, do so reasonably quickly. Part of the impression you are trying to create is that of a busy, successful, efficient administrator.

Try to tour the space if you can do so, without appearing pushy.

Go back to your desk and update the call report right away. Let any member of your network who helped set up the meeting know how it went. Feed any good information you may have gotten back into the network for other people's usage. Try to get back to the person you interviewed quickly with some follow-up, especially if you left with some small thing to do for him. If not, schedule your next contact now, and put it on the call report. And try to keep a constant impression and direction for each contact.

Stay in there looking for the ultimate job. A former student just told me that she got a job after seven years of contact with someone. Lots of big firms, like insurance companies, like to "second source" their services and are always looking for new, good firms. So keep up the efforts.

Company:	*T.I.D.*
Date:	*1/16/84*
Person Completing Checklist:	*A.T.*

Form Your Own Network

Professionals

- ☐ Architects:
- ☐ Engineers:
- ☐ Contractors:
- ☐ Builders:
- ☐ Realtors:

We have worked with dozens of local firms — but we find out they have work too late — If we give our work to a few more firms, perhaps they will give us more work! We have to get to know the local branches of National Firms.

Consultants

- ☑ Acoustical:
- ☐ Art:
- ☐ Audio-visual:
- ☑ Lighting:
- ☑ Records Management:
- ☑ Security:

We have never used these consultants, but perhaps if we did, they would tell us when jobs were imminent. And they probably know many of the professionals listed above!

- ☐ Furniture Dealers: *We know, and work well with these folks already*
- ☐ Furniture Distributors: *We use 2 now — should we split our business 4 ways?*
- ☐ Classmates: *Where are they? Got to give Alumni Records my current address.*
- ☐ Your Lawyer (and others): *We use a small, old, tiny firm — who's up & coming?*
- ☐ Your Accountant (and others): *Can we give a talk to the CPA association?*
- ☐ Your Banker (and others): *We should let him know what we're doing.*
- ☐ Friends: *Must see if SAM S., JIM K., or Deirdre know any one.*
- ☐ Relatives: *My second cousin works for a NYC architect — who does he know?*
- ☐ Other:

Join Local Networks

- ☑ Facilities Management Association: *They're forming one now — should I get in on grd. flr.?*
- ☑ American Management Association: *Their programs are quite good — and maybe I can give one.*
- ☐ Local "Booster" associations: *My brother-in-law is a rotarian*
- ☐ School/Church/Synagogue associations:
- ☐ Local Real Estate Associations: *Shall I get a R.E. Salesperson license to join?*
  - ☐ BOMA   ☐ NACORE   ☐ REBNY
- ☐ The Chamber of Commerce: *I'll call them*
- ☐ City Business Leaders Groups: *There's a new one to re-use the old Mills*
- ☐ County Business Leaders Groups:
- ☐ Other: *I'll call the Reporters who cover local business for lunch.*

Local and Corporate Sources of Names

Local

- ☐ Existing Client Base: *If I tell our lawyer base, they work on leases for clients....*
- ☐ Co-relative Firms with your Clients: *and who are their clients?*
- ☐ City Director of Economic Development:
- ☐ County Director of Economic Development: *take to lunch — our lawyer should know them*
- ☐ Industrial Development Corporations:

Corporate

- ☐ Utilities, Directors of Area Development:
- ☐ Banks, Senior Real Estate Loan Officers:
- ☐ Banks, Senior Construction Loan Officers:
- ☐ Insurance Companies, Real Estate Investment Depts:
- ☐ Investment Firms, Real Estate Investment Dept:
- ☐ Other:

Got to find some names and take them to lunch — I better join a health club to work off all these lunches!

6 Sales

The art of selling can be broken down into four separate tasks: preparation, presentation and interviewing, negotiating and closing, and reviewing your success or failure.

You may not believe this, but the truly critical skill in sales is preparation. This is good news for most of us, because it means we don't have to be born with honied tones and a good line of blarney. If you prepare carefully and completely, you have an excellent chance of making a sale regardless of how fine a public speaker you are.

In the last chapter we discussed the first phase of your preparation. You should have found out who the decision-maker is for this particular company and what his problems actually are. At that time you were, subtly, "qualifying" yourself, proving yourself capable of doing his work and creating the desire on his part to consider you when work is next needed.

At the same time as you were "qualifying" yourself to work for him, you should have been "qualifying" him. Is he likely to be worth the effort to keep in touch? Or, more precisely, how much effort should you spend to keep a high profile with him?

If you find out that real work is likely to be done in the near future, much more preparation is required. You should learn as much as you can about the company and its industry. The public library has many useful volumes. *Standard & Poors* and *Dun & Bradstreet* offer capsule summaries of the status of many firms, including all publicly held companies. The *Readers Guide to Periodical Literature* will show any mentions of the company in most popular magazines. The *New York Times Index* will list when and where any mention of the company appeared in the *Times*.

Your network might be able to tell you more about the company, the personalities of the major officers, and the kind of work they are contemplating.

Try to learn as much about the job as you can. How much work is being contemplated? How many square feet and how extensive a design job will be required? What special kinds of areas will be involved? What part of the company is being redone or moved and who will be in charge of the project? What tasks are required and when will they have to be finished? Are there any other team members in this effort and have they been chosen? Is there a budget? Is this the first phase of a larger project or is this complete in itself?

Try to tour the client's space, either in the qualifying interview or after you've been asked to pitch some specific work. You want to get a feel for the organization and the way the employees work. You should also be looking at the style and budget of their existing space to get a feel for what they are comfortable with.

Find out as much as you can about the presentation or interview. How many people from the client side will be there? How much time will you have to make your presentation? How many firms are they interviewing? Who are they? Who will make the hiring decision and when will it be made? Does it have to be approved by anyone else?

Where will the interview or presentation take place? How many people does the room seat and in what pattern? Will there be a projector and screen or should you bring your own? Are there windows and can they be closed off? Will there be presentation easels? Are there map rails? Chalk boards? Tack boards?

What times are available for making your presentation? Do you have a choice? (If you do have a choice of time to present, my opinion from the client-side of the best times to present, in order of desirability are: last, just before the lunch break, first, all other times, and right after lunch.)

Learn more about your competition. How busy are they? What do they usually charge? What do they do best? What do they do most poorly?

Study yourself, vis-a-vis the job. What are your strengths for this type of job? Where are your weaknesses in performing this type of work? Who should be part of the team from your office?

In order to make this information-gathering process a little more organized, a **Sales Preparation Interview Checklist** is provided.

Your presentation material will be of three different types, written, visual, and oral. Each emphasizes a different part of the total impression you are seeking to create. The written part emphasizes the business-like component of your services. The visual material accentuates the artistic portion of your product. And the oral presentation emphasizes your firm's personality, the personal service, and the interactive aspects of the process. Each part can, and should, reinforce the other. But each, by its very nature, carries a slightly different message about a different part of the complicated process we call interior design.

Since the written submittal will express your competence at the business components of the assignment, you should make absolutely sure that there are no typos, no corrections, and no mistakes. It should be neat, clean, and extremely well organized. Your writing should be succinct and concise.

If you are sent a request for a proposal (known in this industry as an RFP), make sure that you answer every question asked. It is permissible, however, to customize it to tell the story you want. Make it easy for the client to read: keep it as short and to the point as possible.

The RFP probably asks for (and if it doesn't, you should include) your firm's history; its current ownership; your qualifications, including client list and references; your methodology for completing a project similar to theirs; the personnel you will have working on this project, including their roles, responsibilities, and qualifications; your proposed schedule for this project; and, if they have requested them, a budget and your proposed fee, including the method of payment.

Make sure this document looks good. It should match your graphic identity and have high-quality special graphics (for the schedule, for instance). It need not be costly, nor need it be expensively or extensively customized. A xerox or blue line of the company logo might make it seem a little more specific, but spending a great deal to have a custom vinyl cover produced is probably money wasted.

You should show some actual thought about the project you are being considered for. But don't go too far, since it is easy to make a mistake concerning matters you have not yet been informed about. And, again, there should be no mistakes in this submittal. Go over it as many times as it takes, retype any page that looks less than totally professional, and hand in a perfect document. Double check to make sure that you have answered all the questions asked.

Call to make sure you know to whom it should be delivered and where he or she is. Make sure it gets in on time. And call to make sure he or she got it.

Call and determine how they will view the visual portion of your presentation. Are you going to give a slide show to four people, or see one person in his office? Is a slide show appropriate or would you feel better going over your portfolio one-on-one with the client? If you are presenting to several people, you need to know where, what the room offers for presentations — screen or wall, projector, light control, easles, chart rails, tack boards, and chalk boards. As mentioned before, how many people will be there and how will they be sitting?

While the visuals will qualify your design ability, remember that they are also reinforcing your graphic image and personality. I think it helps to reuse some of the illustrations from the proposal as well as, of course, the usual graphic image items to reinforce important concepts, such as budgeting, scheduling, and the organizational structure you are going to bring to this project. Every image should reinforce one of your positive qualities.

Like your brochure, each image or series of images should illustrate how you solved someone's problem. Show just one or two pictures of each of the types of work, or types of spaces, you have designed. Don't bore people with your slides. Make sure that they look as good as you think they look. Use series of images, graphics, and before/after pictures to vary the pace and keep people interested. Use graphics to change the pace and keep the viewers more alert. Let both graphics and series of slides create sequences that stress the points you want people to remember.

Client:	*Mon Dieu*
Contact Name:	*I.E.* Date: *1/17/84*
Person Completing Checklist:	*A.T.*

1. Who will be interviewing interior designers?	*Isaac Epstein, Pres.*
Where will the interview take place?	*His office*
When will it take place?	*Tuesday, 2/12 @ 3PM*
How do you get there?	*Post Road*
Who will make the actual decision?	*He will*
When?	*He says 1 week —*
2. Who is the competition?	*3 other local firms AMM/PBI/CRF*
Have any worked for this company before?	*No*
How busy are they?	*Not very*
What are their strengths and weaknesses?	*All have more pizazz / less longevity than T.I.P.*
3. How long will you have?	*1 hr*
Will you make a presentation or be interviewed?	*A PRESENTATION was requested*
If interviewed, where?	*his office.*
What facilities are available?	*A carousel/screen/easal*
4. How much do you know about the firm?	*Too little — they are new and hot — make jeans*
What business are they in?	*Fancy blue-jeans + cosmetics*
Who are the owners?	*Epstein — 100%*
What other locations do they have?	*Just mfg.*
How big are they in total?	*67 ppl in HQ*

5. How much do you know about the job?	*A new building*		
How much space are they presently occupying?	*14000 RSF*	*14000*	RSF
Have they chosen their new space yet?	*Yes*		
How much space do they plan to move in to?	*18000 RSF*	*18000*	RSF
Is the new space truly modular?	*sort of - new spec bldg*		
How many people now occupy their space?	*67*		
What percent are in enclosed offices now?	*40%*	*40*	%
Will that change? Y/N Why?	*Half of open plan to be upgraded to systems*		
How many people will ultimately occupy their new space?	*80*		
What is the corporate level of taste in furnishings?	*High — I.E. has famous art collection*		
What is the expected budget for F,F&E?		$ *25*	/RSF
How much of their existing furniture do they expect to reuse?	*None —*		
How much will their work letter be worth?		$ *12*	/RSF
What special areas will be required and how much of each?			
☐ Executive Dining:			RSF
☑ Employee Dining:	*Brown bag room*	*150*	RSF
☑ Board Room:		*450*	RSF
☑ Special Communication Areas:	*Just Telex*		RSF
☑ Special A/V Rooms:	*in Board Rm*		RSF
☐ Trading Desks:			RSF
☑ Secure Areas: *?*	*Art Collection?*		RSF
☐ Vaults:			RSF
☐ Computer Rooms:			RSF
☐ Central Reproduction:			RSF
What percentage of their workstations will have CRT's?		*10*	%
How soon is their expected move-in?		*6 mos.*	
Do you have an experienced, competent single contact to interface with	*— Don't know —*		
Is senior management interested and accessible?		*YES*	

As I mentioned before, if all you can say about a slide is that the design is beautiful, dump that slide. Make sure you have a story about each. Never use a canned presentation. No matter how honied the tones of the professional narrator, the client wants to meet and hear you. If you can't speak for yourself, how can he expect you to present your work later on?

One very successful salesman for interior design services, Dave Mayfield, says that all slides look alike, and he prefers to just walk in and talk with the client. He does it very well, but he also has dozens of expensive reprints that he can leave with the client. If you can do something like that and feel more comfortable making a similar kind of pitch, try it. It sets you apart and makes you much more memorable.

I will vouch for the fact that most slide presentations I see consist of similar-looking slides of boardrooms showing a sea of beautiful wood, a modern top executive's office, a traditional top executive's office with Hitchcock chairs and real moldings, the conference room, the trading floor, the sea of open plan, the law office, and the glass entrance doors with the client's logo showing through.

But, by the same token, most designers are not inspired hawkers of their wares, and the slides act as the best crutch they have. Poor speakers often become quite eloquent as they describe the jobs they are showing and relax enough to let their personalities shine through.

The moral of the story is to use the techniques you feel most comfortable with and that work best for you. The two are always the same.

The oral presentation should mesh with the written and visual presentations. And it should be given by the team that will do the work. Many firms have marketing people who have done most of the marketing effort. But when we get down to brass tacks, the client wants to hear from the principal who will be in charge, the project director, and the senior designer. The "marketeer" is welcome as a coordinator of the meeting, to make sure things flow smoothly and the designers answer all the questions put to them, but he or she should not take a major role as an actual presenter.

The design team should never bring more than four people to a presentation. It tends to look clumsy and overwhelming. In fact I think they really should not bring more than the number of people the client will have, unless that will be only one. In that case the principal and one senior member of the staff should probably go, but you might ask the client whom he would like to meet.

Of course most interior design firms consist of fewer than four people. There is nothing wrong with that, but bring them so the client knows that there is back-up. You can also stress, with conviction, that with such a small firm, you will be giving him the best personal service which he could never get from a bigger office.

If you have a one person office, it is best to have a string of "part-times" whom you hire by the hour to handle emergencies and overloads. These people can also be included as part of your team, to show your back-up.

Rehearse what each member of the team is going to say. Make sure that everyone knows his or her role, who is in charge, how much and how little to speak, the overall impression you want to make, and the points you want the client to remember. Also make sure everyone is clear on timing.

If you, or a junior member of your staff, find it difficult to speak in public, try this method. Have them write out their speech word by word. Go over it until it is a well written piece. Practice reading the speech aloud several times. Then copy the key words of key points onto a file card. Tear up the longer written document. Having practiced from it and having the key phrases handy will help make the talk both natural, since it will be spoken and not read, and easier, given all the practice repeating all the original words. Practice giving the speech from the cards, if possible, in the room where the presentation will be held.

Just one more suggestion about a presentation. If you can, and if you have an office, it is worth trying to hold it there. You will have more time with the client and you can expose him to much more of your work.

Make sure your office is properly prepared for a client tour. Have lots of different jobs, current or not, tacked on the walls. Have presentation boards, schedules, details, all sorts of different items obviously being worked on.

If the client is coming, prepare your receptionist. Dave Mayfield, who always thinks of every detail, makes sure his receptionist says "Good morning, Mr. Big. You're expected. I'll let Mr. Mayfield know you are here." That little phrase does a lot. It lets the client know you've planned well and the entire staff knows about him. He feels important. He can also relax, since you have things well in hand.

Make sure your people are around. There is something slightly demoralizing for a client to walk into an empty office. He doesn't know if you really have any employees or not. If you are having a client in at lunch time, buy pizza or deli for the staff so they are present and animated. It makes a much better impression.

There is not too much more to the actual presentation. With luck, you got your choice of either first or last slot. Come with an agenda stating who is there, their title, and what part of the presentation they will be giving. Plan on leaving at least ten minutes and as much as half of the presentation to questions and discussion.

Start with a quick introduction, telling the client who is here from your group and what you will be showing them.

Every good presentation has the following points made. And no matter how hackneyed they sound, you too should make them.

- This job is extremely important to us because....

- It fits right into our schedule because....

- We just happen to have the perfect team available, consisting of....

- We need you as a happy, satisfied client so we can....

The client has to feel that his will be your most important project so he will have confidence that he will get the best people, his work will come first, and he can count on your best efforts.

The client is always worried about whether you will be able to devote the right people, and the number of people, to his project. He wants to hear that another job of the same size or bigger is just winding down and you are now ready to take on another project of this size and scope.

He certainly doesn't want to get the third team. Whoever you bring has to be the finest in each of their categories. Even if they are independent contractors, they are part of your team, and you were lucky to get them.

The reason you need this client as a satisfied client is just reinforcement of the first point. Perhaps you are breaking into a new area and you need this as the first example of the fine work you can do for others in this area or field. Or you have a long string of successes for firms similar to his and you can not afford to blow it now.

The discussion and question time at the end is extremely important. After the rehearsed spiel is finished, you can finally talk naturally to one another. I've seen it happen time and again that, at this point, everyone relaxes and real communication starts to happen. Now the interviewers can ask you what is really on their mind and you can respond simply and easily.

Sometimes, though, the discussion period starts with an uneasy silence. You should break the ice by asking questions about the job. Find out about budget and schedule. See how many special areas there will be and how extensive they are.

This nuts-and-bolts kind of conversation has three great advantages. It cannot fail to break the ice and get you talking. You will be talking about an area where your competence and expertise shine through. And you will be, in effect, already working on the project. The client can begin to feel comfortable with your experience in this give-and-take portion. And you will have started the project. So make sure you leave time for this type of conversation in the presentation.

Leave on time. You wish to appear considerate and in control. Before you go, sum up what you have said...especially the four major points mentioned before. Leave something with them, so they have your name and a physical reminder of your presence. An ideal item to leave behind is a reprint or one page brochure that repeats some of the visuals they have just seen, so you

SALES PRESENTATION CHECKLIST

Client:	MonDieu	Date:	1/18/84
Contact Name:	I. Epstein	Tel:	493-2405
Person Completing Checklist:			A.T.

Where will the interview take place?	The President's office — 1715 Post Road
How do you get there?	Main St → 1st St → Post Road (20 min. max)
At what time will you present?	3 PM

How long will you have?	1 hr
Will you make a presentation or be interviewed?	Presentation
How many will be at the presentation?	2 (I.E. plus his Ad. Asst.)
What is the room like?	exec. office — poor light control
What A/V facilities will be available?	carousel/ screen/ easal

Is your slide show appropriate for this specific presentation?	yes
Have you used the Brochure/Slideshow Checklist?	yes

Who will be interviewing interior designers?	Epstein/President
Who will make the actual decision?	he will
When?	1 week

What is an appropriate range of fees for this job?	$2.25 – 3.25 / RSF
What is the lowest fee you would do this job for?	2.00 – to get one flashy office to show

Who is the competition?	3 locals
Have any worked for this company before?	no
What are their strengths and weaknesses?	good design — higher priced — less "history"

How much do you know about the firm?	Not enough — 3 yrs old, burgeoning, entrepreneurial
What business are they in?	fashion + cosmetics — jeans and lipsticks
What image do they have of themselves?	Very flashy — go getters — up + coming FAST
Who are the owners?	Just "Ike"
What other locations do they have?	none
How big are they in total?	67 in HQ, rest imported or from mills.

Who will be presenting?	T.I.D. A.T.-Principal, R.D.-Proj.Dir, F.M.-Sr.Des.
What will each say?	A.T.- Intro, history, wrap-up and moderate slides R.D.- Project Methodology F.M.- Design Approach.
Why is this job so important to you?	It's work! Also need to expand in this area — you are excellent choice and showcase.
How does it fit into your workload schedule?	Perfect — J+M is just wrapping up
Why is your team perfect for this job?	F.M. did some store design before joining T.I.D. - w/ our office experience is perfect match
Why do we need this project to be so successful?	Want to get in on ground floor w/ new successful co. Also need high style exposure of our existing capabilities.
What further information will you ask for?	Do they need help negotiating lease? Do they have real plans? Is the move-in fixed?
Do you have an agenda prepared?	Yes.
Do you have something to leave behind?	Yes.

provide instant recall in their later deliberations. Thank them for the opportunity to appear.

We have not mentioned price at all, and if you are lucky, you won't have to either. Often you can talk about a range given all the unknowns in the job. Discuss the details of the job and offer to send a full proposal in the next day. You are trying to get them to choose you on the basis of merit, not price, so you can't be sandbagged by firms pricing their services at a "loss leader" level.

If that is unacceptable and they won't let you out without a price, get into the detailed discussion of what the job actually consists of, as we discussed before. And then give them your best shot. As you remember, my chapter on pricing preceded this chapter, which suggests that you should have some idea of the right price in advance. Of course the more you know, the more accurately you can price your services. Hold off as long as possible and then give the fairest price you can...and read the following section on trying to close the sale.

If you have an interview you should prepare almost exactly as you would for a presentation. The major differences are that you will probably be meeting with only one person and you might have a chance to close the sale then and there.

If you have not had the opportunity before, tour the client's space now. Say intelligent things about the space, never disparage it, and look for hints of client budget, taste, style, and management type.

Your actual presentation of visual and verbal material will be similar to the larger presentation. In this case, you might use a portfolio or one of the self-contained rear screen projectors to make the presentation more personal. You should be able to control the conversation far better with one person than with many.

There are some additional conversational control techniques that you should be aware of, in addition to the ones mentioned before.

Get the client used to saying "yes." *Encyclopaedia Britannica* salespeople are trained in a special selling technique that is worth knowing about. They present to the individual with visual aids which have many of the important points to be made written out in their entirety, in addition to the pretty pictures. The salesperson is supposed to read these points exactly, underlining the words with his finger as he says them. This captures the client's attention and forces him to keep the same pace as the salesperson, reading in his mind as the salesperson reads aloud.

There are seven points in the course of the presentation where the salesperson asks a direct question to the client. These are always questions where the answer should be yes. An equivalent question in this field might be, "Don't you agree, Mr. Big, that your employees will be happier in new, neat, organized space than they are now in your present overcrowded conditions?" The encyclopedia salesman can't continue until the client actually says "yes." A nod will not do.

After the salesman has proceeded through six of these questions in the course of the fifteen minute presentation, and gotten six positive "yes's," the last question selling the actual service has over a 90-percent success rate.

The point here is that you want to get the prospect used to saying the word "yes." Never ask yes-no questions you don't know the answers to in advance.

Paul Mills teaches some more conversational control techniques. Use "negative word question forms," such as *"Won't* you save money with professional guidance, Mr. Big?" to get positive responses.

Use "positive statements with negative word questions," such as, "Starting right now will get you in earlier, *won't it?"* to get more positive responses.

If you see your prospect is desperate to be negative, allow him to vent those negative feelings in a manner you control by using a "negative word question," but with a "positive word question phrase," such as, "We can't afford to make a mistake here, *can we?"*

If the client is not responding well, start with "helping words," such as *"Do* you want to see some of our designs first, or *do* you want to see our client list?" Or you can use those "soft W words" such as, who, what, where, when, why and how: *"When* are you considering starting the project, Mr. Big?"

Pay very close attention to your prospect and read what he is saying. If he is in *agreement,* he will be agreeing both in body language (nodding, leaning forward) and in verbal language ("yes," "true," "that seems right"). His *attitude* will either be *wondering* (leaning back, looking around, hearing every telephone ring, eyes following people walking by his door) or *attentive* (eyes wide open, leaning forward, nodding, smiling).

Listen for where his interests are. He might be asking *operating* questions, such as, "How can we change this format?" Or he might be asking *service* questions, such as "When will you provide us with the budgetary information we need?"

He might be showing interest in the *terms* by asking, "What kind of contract do you work with?" He might be interested in *guarantees* and ask, "How can we be sure it will be on time?" He could be asking for more data on *particulars,* such as, "where would we go for..." or be asking for more reassurances by using phrases like "I really shouldn't...," "I hadn't planned on...," and "I didn't have this in mind when I...."

These are all decision signals that you should pick up on and respond to.

You overcome a prospect's objections with a five-step process. First *listen* with your eyes, ears, and most importantly, your mind. Second, *probe* for any additional reasons behind the stated objection. Third, mentally formulate your *answer* for use later, not right away. Fourth, *sympathize,* but don't agree or disagree. And fifth, ask a *question* designed to get the prospect to provide the answer you have already formulated.

Listen:	"I don't feel we should spend so much."
Probe:	"You feel that you can't afford it?"
Answer:	"This is actually the quality you need and just within your budget."
Sympathize:	"I realize that it seems more than you may have expected."
Question:	"How has your experience been with buying cheaper tools for your manufacturing process?"
Listen:	"My wife can handle it."
Probe:	"Oh? She's done this type of work before?"
Answer:	"Without real contract experience, she'll never be able to produce such a large job on time and budget."
Sympathize:	"I'm sure she has outstanding residential taste."
Question:	"We would normally assign three people to this job. How many people will she have to assist her?"

Another excellent conversational control technique is to get the client verbally into a position where he is already enjoying the advantages of your skills. Start with the *benefit* or satisfaction to the client. Continue with a *description* of what you will actually do. And finally ask for an *evaluation* by the client of receiving the benefits described.

Benefit:	"You will save a great deal of maintenance time with this new furniture system."
Description:	"Three men can move an entire station in less than an hour."
Evaluation:	"How much do you think you will save a year if you continue to move a dozen stations every month?"
Benefit:	"With better lighting, there will be far less glare on the CRT screens and your operators will make fewer errors.
Description:	"The indirect lighting provides uniform ceiling illumination so there won't be any ceiling light sources to reflect on the screen."
Benefit:	"How much will you save if each operator makes just 10 percent fewer errors?"

Now that you have your prospect seeing the benefits of your proposals, saying yes on request, and you have overcome all of his articulated and non-articulated objections, it is time to close the sale.

You should have had a range of costs in your head when you came into the interview. As you spoke, you probably narrowed that range. If you have to provide a single number, make sure you leave bargaining room. Many of the prospects you will face are used to haggling. You will want to allow them to

Client:	MOLE' COMPUTERS
Date:	1/19/84
Person Completing Form:	A.T.

Job location:	I-95 / I-84				
Job size:	300,000 RSF	$ 600,000	Fee	$ 15,000,000	Construction Budget
Firm which won contract:	FR/PS				
Winning bid:	$580,000				

Official reason we lost:

Cost - but really lack of big job experience

Believable?   No - we're just too small

How do we think our presentation went: Very Well

How did each member of the team present:

A.T. - OK, I guess
R.D. - Didn't have his heart in it
P.M. - Really great - she was up for this one

Did the client seem interested?   Yes - they asked all the right questions

Were they interested in anything in particular: Unfortunately, all about the largest jobs we have done to date

Is that worth stressing in other interviews: We have to get some better answers - lumping phased work into one area measurement.

What was well received?   They did like our methodology, checklists, etc.

What was poorly received: they saw through our smokescreen about large job experience.

Should that be eliminated from other presentations: Can't be. But we can make better answers.

How did they say the presentation went: They liked it.

How could we improve it:

1. Get a big job under our belts
2. Get some different looking photos. The same photographer makes all our work look similar.

Is this client worth keeping in touch with: Yes - they will grow continually

When should we call next: 6 mos. after move-in

"beat you down" to the number you wanted all along. They are probably pretty good at it, so don't make it easy. If they sense the ploy, they will truly beat you down to a lower price than you planned on.

Use some of the techniques you learned before and try the following time-honored closings.

Summarize: "From what you have told me, these are the services you need.... That's correct, isn't it?" (positive statement with negative word question phrase to elicit a positive response)

Assume the Commitment: "Don't you agree that we can't get your furniture in on time if we don't start right away?" (negative word question to elicit a positive response)

Offer Positive Alternatives: "Shall we start right now or bright and early tomorrow?" (control of options)

Ask Directly: "Here is a copy of our normal contract with an attached list of services. Please read it and tell me if it is satisfactory."

Conditional: "If we can commit those people, will you accept our proposal now?" (if-question)

Minor Decision: "Why not start off on an hourly basis until we firm up the true scope of the project?" (W-word question)

Special Conditions: "Why not take advantage of the time we have available and the good lease option you have now? We don't want to lose those advantages, do we?" (W word question plus a negative word statement with a positive word question phrase to elicit a positive response)

Notwithstanding all of the above, you might be screaming "no" inside. Your own impressions are very important. It is healthy to be afraid of a new kind of work, or a job larger than any you've ever done. But sometimes your instincts are right when they say you should avoid this client. Maybe it is because they expect far too much and they are willing to pay far too little. Perhaps you just know it will be impossible to work with this group. First impressions and personality count for a lot. Sometimes no client is far better than a bad client. If you have truly strong negative feelings, consider turning the assignment down.

Win, lose, or rain cancellation, you should analyze your sales attempt. How well do you think you performed? What have you learned? How would you improve upon it next time? Write it down on the **Lost Job Evaluation Form**. Make sure you learn from every attempt.

And keep in touch. Today's lost client may be back for better services next year. Tell your network what happened, so they can pitch their business to the winner. They will appreciate your thoughts and reciprocate in the future.

On the other hand, if you got the job, celebrate and turn to the next chapter to brush up on writing a good contract.

7 Contracts

"Congratulations, you got the job!" is always a welcome sound. But it ushers in one of the trickier aspects of running a business. You have to draw up a good contract *and* get it signed.

A word about the latter first. You should never, NEVER work without a contract. All too often we are led down the garden path by some client who is enthusiastic about starting the project but less than enthusiastic about signing the contract. The delay is blamed on the "legal department," or some such thing.

Danger signals should go off all over your body. This fellow is not going to worry about your fee... he will probably avoid paying some of it. Reimbursables, revisions, and all sorts of other items will be unacceptable. Payments will be late. The more in arrears he is, the more you are trapped since you have no contract to fall back on.

It is hard to refuse to start work before a contract is signed since we are always in a rush and, besides, we tend to find dealing in money matters somewhat distasteful. Conquer that fear and distaste. The only thing standing between you and the poorhouse is a series of *signed* contracts.

Sometimes, even though no signed contract has been returned, we bill the client and he pays the bill. We feel relieved, but we shouldn't. The reimbursables, the revisions, and the all-important last payment may never be paid. Legally, if a payment is made on the basis of an unsigned contract, the contract becomes valid. On the other hand, the client probably has a lawyer on retainer, you probably don't (although you should!), and the cost in legal fees will more than eat up the moneys in question.

The moral? Submit the contract as soon as you can, certainly within the first week. Expect it to be signed within the first month. If it isn t, offer to stop work until it is signed. By that time you should know some of the other members of the client organization, have been around enough for them to know you, and have made some progress in the actual work. You should then have enough power to get your contract signed. The power is not to cause difficulty for your contact, just some embarrassment. If you can't, maybe this is not the client for you.

A proper contract includes all of the following:

Who will be doing the work? Who are they working for? Who will be representing the client? Can the contact legally represent the client? (Normally only an officer of a corporation, a vice president, secretary, treasurer or president, can commit a firm to a contract.)

When does this contract begin? What is included? Here you have to describe the various aspects of a job. This includes the premises, the tasks to be performed, and those tasks specifically excluded from this contract.

First, you want to clearly spell out the area involved. The premises should be located by address, square footage (rentable square feet are usually part of the lease documents and, therefore, are well defined), occupants, and the borders of the space.

For example, you might be working on the Credit Card Department at 1 Broadway, the 24th floor and the northeast quadrant of the 25th floor, totalling approximately 32,000 rentable square feet (BOMA standard). It does not take long to define it that way, but you have now clarified that the Proof Department, located next to the Credit Card Department, is not part of the assignment, and you deserve extra fees for doing work in that area.

You will also want to clearly show what work you expect to do for the client as part of this assignment. While most firms do this by writing three to thirty pages of description, some firms do so with a checklist of tasks. Ken Walker, who has built up a good size firm, once said his list of services runs all of three pages.

I think that is a neater way of defining the work and serves several other purposes as well. You are clearly checking off tasks that are in the assignment, and just as importantly, showing which are not. You can also check off those assignments which would be, or will be, extra cost services. You will also check off those that are to be provided by other contractors, hired either by the designer or the client, but paid for by the client. A short narrative should also be included, describing how you perform your services. This may clarify some procedures in the client's mind. It will also come in handy when you define *his* responsibilities.

This can be a marketing tool when you sit the client down and go through the list including some and excluding others. He will know all the things you are doing and may see some that you are excluding that he had not thought of before, but would want done. He may add those to the assignment, increasing your fee.

You should state quite specifically the areas that are not covered by the quoted fee. The first such area is revisions in any work already approved by the client, which should not be unreasonably withheld. Far too many designers leave this out and end up spending large amounts of free time for clients who have reorganized a section, department, or even the entire company after you've already designed their space.

A simple sentence such as, ''Additional work resulting from changes requested and authorized by you after our previous work has been approved will be

SCHEDULE OF POSSIBLE SERVICES

Client: **M.D.C**

Date: **1/20/84**

Person Completing Schedule: **A.T.**

N ☐ Normal part of our services
E ☐ Extra service to be provided for this job at additional cost
C ☐ Service provided by other consultants reporting to designer

PHASE 1: PROGRAMMING

N E C

Scheduling

N	E	C	
☐	☑	☐	Determine design schedule
☑	☐	☐	Determine work schedule

Determine Functional/Organizational Req'ts.

N	E	C	
☑	☐	☐	Personnel growth rate
☑	☐	☐	Individual space requirements
☑	☐	☐	Map operating procedures
☑	☐	☐	Note Visitor Requirements
☐	☐	☐	Business equipment requirements
☐	☑	☐	Specials equipment requirements
☑	☐	☐	Lighting needs
☐	☐	☐	Security needs
☐	☑	☐	Record retention requirements
☑	☑	☐	Audio/visual requirements
☑	☐	☐	Acoustical requirements
☐	☑	☐	Special environmental needs
☑	☑	☐	Heavy floor loading areas
☑	☐	☐	Special HVAC requirements

Feasibility Studies

N	E	C	
☑	☐	☐	Evaluate existing space
☑	☐	☐	Evaluate proposed space
☐	☐	☐	Financial feasibility studies
☐	☐	☐	Lease negotiation assistance
☐	☐	☐	Long term strategy formulation
☐	☐	☐	Inventory/eval. exist. furniture

Establish Program

N	E	C	
☑	☐	☑	Establish office standards
☑	☐	☑	Establish furniture type standards
☑	☐	☐	Special structural requirements
☑	☐	☐	Communications requirements
☐	☐	☑	Mechanical/electrical requirements
☑	☐	☐	Departmental relationship matrix
☑	☐	☐	Funct'l relations'p bubble diagram
☐	☐	☐	Stacking diagram

PHASE 2: DESIGN CONCEPT

N E C

N	E	C	
☑	☐	☐	Allocation plans
☑	☐	☐	Layout plans
☑	☐	☐	Detail (walls, doors, furn) plans
☑	☐	☐	Preliminary design concept furniture, equipment, colors, finishes, qualities, etc.
☑	☐	☐	Preliminary budget
☑	☐	☐	Special furniture & equipment
☑	☐	☐	Concept presentation plans, rough models, drawings
☐	☐	☐	Presentation models
☐	☐	☐	Presentation renderings
☐	☑	☐	Corporate identity programs

PHASE 3: DECORATION

Design Scheme

N	E	C	
☑	☐	☐	Furniture
☑	☐	☐	Finishes
☑	☐	☐	Materials
☑	☐	☐	Decorative Budget
☐	☐	☐	Art Program
☑	☐	☐	Presentation boards
☑	☐	☐	Accessories
☑	☐	☐	Specifications
☑	☐	☐	Cabinet Drawings

PHASE 4: CONTRACT DOCUMENTATION

N E C

N	E	C	
☑	☐	☐	Floor plans
☑	☐	☐	Furniture plans
☑	☐	☐	Reflected ceiling plans
☑	☐	☐	Electrical/telephone plans
☑	☐	☐	Sections
☑	☐	☐	Finish schedule
☑	☐	☐	Hardware schedule
☑	☐	☐	Door/window schedule
☑	☐	☐	Special conditions
☑	☐	☐	HVAC/Engineering plans where req'd
☑	☐	☐	Purchase Orders
☐	☐	☐	Bidding
☑	☐	☐	Negotiation

PHASE 5: CONTRACT ADMINISTRATION

☑	☐	☐	Coordination
☑	☐	☐	Scheduling
☑	☐	☐	Quality/quantity inspection
☑	☐	☐	Payment authorization/Clerk of Wks
☑	☐	☐	Contract document interpretation
☑	☐	☐	Review/approval of shop drawings
☑	☐	☐	Handling of change orders
☑	☐	☐	Coordinate with other consultants
☐	☑	☐	Revisions as necessary
☑	☐	☐	Coordinate/oversee move-in
☑	☐	☐	Handle punch-list

Other Services

☐	☑	☐	Provide "as built" reproduceables
☑	☐	☐	Provide facility standards manual
☐	☑	☐	Provide maintenance manual
☐	☐	☐	Post occupancy audit
☐	☐	☐	Yearly facility audit
☑	☐	☐	*custom furniture for I.E.*
☐	☐	☐	
☐	☐	☐	
☐	☐	☐	
☐	☐	☐	
☐	☐	☐	

undertaken, if requested, on an hourly basis at our standard billing rates," will suffice.

Other areas that should fall into the same category of additional work would be work in spaces outside of the boundaries described in the contract and work made necessary by the default or defective work of a contractor.

Other costs that are never part of the fee are expenses undertaken on behalf of the client. These include postage, messengers, long-distance telephone, reproduction, travel and sustenance, governmental permit fees for the project, and additional liability insurance taken for the benefit of this particular project. These charges also include the costs of presentation models, renderings, and photographs.

Any other responsibilities of the designer, besides professional services, should be spelled out. These might include tasks such as monthly status reports. Having spelled out some of your responsibilities, you should spell out the responsibilities of the client. The primary responsibility they have is to make timely decisions so that you can make your schedule. That means a rough schedule should probably be part of your contract.

A contract schedule can have just a few dates to be effective. You should have dates for:

- Start-Up

- Survey Information Approval

- Layout Approval

- Preliminary Budget Approval

- Design Concept Approval

- Final Design and Budget Approval

- Purchase Order Approval

- Construction Documents Issue

- Start of Construction

- Move-In

(These are all shown on the **Project Analysis Form** in the chapter on Scheduling.)

You should decide with the client whether they will need one or two weeks in order to approve these documents and then write that into the contract.

If purchasing is part of the services which you are offering this client, you have to spell out your methodology. This includes their requirements for deposits *before* ordering and prepayment of the balance *before* delivery. Try not to leave any of your money at risk, and make that clear to the client in advance.

You have to state clearly how your fee is determined. It is fairly clear when you have a fixed fee. Some methods may have to be defined more than others. If you charge by the square foot, you should specify exactly how square feet are to be measured. Just to make the point, there are different measurements of area by architectural gross, zoning gross, rentable, BOMA rentable, REBNY rentable, assignable, and usable methods. Use whatever is in the client's lease, which is probably either BOMA or REBNY rentable square feet. (See the last chapter for an explanation of the differences between these methods.)

If you charge by the multiple method, you should specify that it is a multiple of X times the Direct Personnel Expense. The client may ask what percentage the fringes are that are added to the salary to get the DPE and you can include that. You should state that this multiple will be used on the DPE which is current for the time the job was actually being worked upon, and normal increases will be passed along when received.

Whatever means you are going to use to handle overtime required by the client should be specifically stated. (Usually firms charge their normal billing rate and only add on the additional overtime cost to them. See the chapter on financial management to understand how this affects a company's bottom line.)

If you are going to charge a standard hourly fee per job category, you should state when increases will normally occur and if there will be a surcharge for overtime.

If your fee will be a percentage of the cost of the job, you should carefully state what your percentage will be charged against. That should include all goods specified and accepted, as well as purchased. You should be protected against the client getting the furnishings elsewhere and avoiding your deserved fee.

You should also receive a fee for other tenant improvements, not just furnishings. You should get a percentage of all construction work that is built according to your construction documentation.

Some firms ask for, and get, a percentage of any savings they show if they come in under the design budget, or even their fee budget. This would be based on the approved preliminary budget and determined at the end of the job. While it could raise some suspicions on the part of some clients, if your share is small, between 10 and 25 percent, it could be incentive for good planning and efficient production.

Pricing design services based on a design fee plus a mark-up on furnishings occurs more regularly in the residential field. I would consider it a transitional phase for anyone getting into the contract field. If you use it, deal with it as mentioned above.

The contract also has to state how the billing will be rendered and how payment should be made. The most common method is billing the time costs monthly, plus expenses, up to the pre-agreed guaranteed maximum fee. It is also possible to bill fixed amounts per month, with the last month's payment adjusted for any descrepancy between total billing and the contract amount. If you are charging by the furniture mark-up method, that will take care of the methodology, except you may need a retainer to get going.

A retainer is extremely desirable for any firm. The cost of paying your staff to work on this assignment for a month or two before the first payment rolls in may be prohibitive. It is especially tough if you are marking-up purchases, since deposits for furniture should either be paid to the manufacturer or put in escrow. By getting a retainer and charging purchases against that, you maintain enough money, "working capital" in financial terms, so you can run your shop.

Your contract should specifically state when payment for a bill is to be made and what the overdue charge is. Some firms state that payment is to be made on demand, within fourteen days. That is more appropriate for residential work, since a company's billing cycle may be longer than that.

On the other hand, there is no excuse for any payment taking longer than thirty days, and a late payment charge should be levied. I would recommend the same percentage that Visa or MasterCard charges, since we are all used to that amount. If you like the carrot-and-stick approach you might also add a "2/10, net 30" clause that translates to giving a 2 percent discount for any payment within ten days of billing with the full amount due within thirty days.

All too often designers do not indicate when and how a contract might end. It should be stated specifically that the contract ends at a certain date or after move-in when the punch list has been *substantially completed*. This will avoid your final payment being held up for three years while a substitute foot is being sought for one piece of furniture.

Many designer contracts are written so that the client has the right to cancel. I would suggest that you write in a clause that allows *either* party to cancel upon five or ten days written notice, at which time all fees for work already completed will become due. Some firms add a penalty clause of 10 percent of the unpaid portion against a cancellation without cause. That is great, but hard to get a client to sign.

You can also write in a clause about the cost of being on an indefinite hold, or winding down and starting up, so the costs of keeping people available can be defrayed if the job schedule is radically changed.

If you are billing over a long period of time, if the job will take two or more years, you might build an inflation factor into the maximum fee.

It should be clearly stated that the designer owns the originals of the documents, and if the client wants to use any of that work for additional space or products outside the boundary of this job, the designer will be entitled to compensation. This is to stop a client from letting you design one store and then franchising that store design across the country. It may also give you production rights for any specific piece of furniture designed for the client.

The designer should also state that he has the right to photograph and publicize the project. The client may not allow it, or allow it only without attribution, but you would want to know that in advance.

Another clause that is important to include is an "arbitration clause" so that disagreements between you and the client can be resolved without expensive litigation. It might read, "Any claim or controversy arising out of or relating to this contract, or the breach thereof, shall be settled by arbitration in accordance with the Construction Industry Arbitration Rules of the American Arbitration Association. Judgment upon the award rendered by the arbitrator(s) may be entered in any court having jurisdiction thereof. The arbitration proceedings shall take place in the city in which our office is located unless another location is mutually agreed upon."

You should also consider adding a "hold harmless" clause which frees you of responsibility for the performance of any vendor, contractor, or workman, whether recommended by you or not, on the project.

Another entirely different approach to contracts is to use one of a series of prepared contracts available from the American Institute of Architects and the American Society of Interior Designers. They have created documents specifically for designers who are providing services in a variety of ways. They are available at extremely modest cost and protect you completely.

Unfortunately designers and clients find them so legalistic that they frighten a great many off. You can try to sell the client the idea that these have been created by two prestigious organizations working together, and are of the best pedigree. But it may not work. In any case, since they cost less than a dozen dollars all told, you should get a set, read them, and understand what they mean.

The available forms are:

ASID #401.   Professional Services/Stipulated Sum

ASID #402.   Professional Services/Hourly Rate

ASID #403.   Professional Services/Residential Long Form

ASID #404.   Professional Services/Residential Short Form

ASID #001.   Compensation Agreement/Presented Price

ASID #002.   Compensation Agreement/Hourly Rate

ASID #003.   Compensation Agreement/Fixed Fee

ASID #004.   Compensation Agreement/Percentage Cost

(Note: Forms 403 and 404 require one of forms 001-004)

ASID B171.   Standard Form of Agreement for Interior Design Services

ASID A271.   General Conditions of the Contract of Furniture, Furnishings, and Equipment

One other ploy that some clients have been known to use is copying these contracts almost exactly, leaving out only those clauses that protect the designer. Be careful about using contracts designed by your client.

To practice contract design, you must have a lawyer. Have him go over any contract offered to you. Don't be afraid to cross out items you don't like. Have your lawyer cross out items he doesn't like.

Write yourself a basic contract that you can be comfortable with. Make sure your lawyer approves. Understand all the ramifications of any changes, and make as few as possible.

And never go to work without one.

CONTRACT CHECKLIST

Client:	*M.D.C.*
Date:	*1/21/84*
Person Completing Checklist:	*A.T.*

Any contract should contain the following information:

- ☑ Who is doing the work — firm name: *T.I.D.*
- ☑ Who represents the design firm: *A.T.*

☑ Who work is being done for — firm name: *Mon Dieu Cosmetics, Inc.*	☑ Who accepts contract for client: *Issaac Epstein*
	Are they legal representatives? *Yes – CEO*

- ☑ When does the contract begin? *When signed*
- ☑ What is included by location, area, & department: *whole HQ — at 1flr 9393 Post Road*
- ☑ What is included (see Schedule of Possible Services): *attached*

☑ Exceptions:	☑ revisions after approvals:
	☑ tasks out of scope:
	☐ work on additional space:

- ☑ What is not included: */ STD BOILERPLATE*
- ☑ The Designer's responsibilities: *" "*
- ☑ The Client's responsibilities: *" "*
- ☑ Critical dates: *'LISTED*
- ☐ The Designer's methodology *STD BOILERPLATE*

☐ Purchasing Methodology:	☑ Fee or cost basis: *cost +15%*
	☐ Payment amounts and timing:
☐ How the fee is determined:	☑ guaranteed maximum based on one of the following
	☐ fixed total fee:
	☐ percentage of cost:
	☐ dollars per hour:
	☑ dollars per square foot *$2.15/☐ (RSF)*
	☐ multilple of DPE: *Billed out at 2.75 XDPE*
	☐ minimum cost of retail purchases *NONE*
	☐ design fee plus mark-up:
	☐ bonuses for coming in under budget:

- ☐ Cost of time spent when project "on hold":

☑ Plus reimbursables:	☑ reproduction:
	☑ presentation renderings/models:
	☑ travel:
	☑ telephone:
	☑ mail/messengers/express:
☑ How payment will be made:	☑ monthly billing of actual expenses:
	☐ monthly billing on portion of fixed fee:
	☐ initial retainer against future billings:
☑ When payment will be made:	☐ on billing:
	☑ within thirty days:
	☐ 2/10, Net 30:
	☐ delays of more than 30 days will cost 1.75%/mo.
☐ When does contract end naturally:	☐ when work is complete
	☑ after a certain time period
	☑ when client cancels & how:
	☑ when designer cancels & how

- ☐ Who owns original documents: *T.I.D.*
- ☐ Who holds design rights: *"*
- ☐ Are rights to photograph included: *Yes*
- ☐ Are rights to publicize included: *Yes*
- ☐ Arbitration clause: *Yes*
- ☐ Hold Harmless clause: *Yes*

8 Scheduling

No one likes to talk about, think about, or work on schedules. But our clients consider it to be one of the two most important aspects (along with budget) of the service we sell. We *have* to spend time and effort getting it right.

To be effective, a true schedule must include three attributes. *What* has to be done, the type of work and its extent in time, money, or output; *who* will do that task; and *when* it must be finished.

There are no scheduling tools that take away the drudgery of doing this task. It is labor-intensive and requires your attention, or that of a senior person in charge of production, to keep pushing, day in and day out. It has to be done at the least on a monthly basis. And you have to do it for both big and little projects, because all the little projects usually add up to a whopping big one. Finally, you can't stop doing it. You have to keep it up.

In this modern age, computers can do some of the work. But they can't do the important work. They won't make those pesky entries every month. You can buy a program for about $500, but simple forms will really accomplish the same thing for you for a lot less, and you don't have to buy the $5,000 computer to run the program.

The larger the firm, the more important scheduling becomes. Small firms don't spend a lot of effort on scheduling because some overtime usually gets them out of trouble and they can hire contract labor to do a lot of that. They also don't get many large jobs which require major scheduling efforts. But that does not mean they turn out a lot of high-quality work on time. When a firm is rushed, and produces work in a last ditch *charrette,** mistakes slip through. A hurried job is not a good job.

The opposite side of the coin is that good scheduling produces good work at a profit. The reason is that your people know how much time they should put into actually performing their tasks. People work far more efficiently under those conditions than they would if they were just trying to solve a problem in as much time as it takes. Being told to do the layout in forty hours of effort will produce a good job in forty hours. Just trying to do a layout may take fifty and be no better. Your staff should design to your budget, not to perfection, and produce good quality work at a steady planned profit.

*CHARRETTE, from the french *en charrette*. At the Ecole de Beaux Arts, student projects were collected for grading on a cart — a charrette. Students desperately working to finish at the last moment would get on the cart —*en charrette,* and continue to work. Charrette now means desperate work to finish a project at the last minute before a deadline.

Even small firms should schedule three things closely: the principal's time, the critical dates of all jobs being designed, and the work on hand. Bigger firms should be able to convert fee remaining in a job with man-hours left to finish the job and then schedule all employees' efforts to do so. There are forms in this chapter for doing nearly all of that.

But there are some simple things you should do as well. If you are a principal, you have to make sure the demands of selling your services, overseeing the work, and making sure client presentations don't overlap. You probably also need good backup for how you charge your time, and you have the most complicated schedule to remember. The principal, and all other important folks in the firm, should keep a detailed diary.

If you are not used to any other, go out and get one of the DayTimer series of executive diaries. They come in all sizes and types. It is the one your client is most likely to have when you pull out diaries to search for the next good time to meet. Keep it up to date, always keep it with you, and let your secretary copy it regularly so the office will know where you are. At the end of each day, charge your time off to all the projects you worked on. (A major loss of profit in many medium to large firms is the principal's time which is not charged to a project simply because he is too busy to record it.)

There are certain critical dates for every project you work on. Some are important just because the principal should be there. Some are important because no matter how well paced your work has been, the last week or couple of days is always a *charrette* to get the work out, such as the construction documents issuing date. And some are important because if the client misses them, your project will never be done on time.

A **Critical Date Scheduling Form** is provided for you to keep all of these dates together. The point of getting them on one sheet is to make obvious possible future conflicts in terms of demand for time. It may also prompt you to keep your employees up to snuff, or even more likely, the client up to the schedule.

The dates I would consider critical, and you can redesign this form to include fewer or more dates, are start-up, program approval, layout approval, design/budget presentation, design/budget approval, construction documents issued, construction details issued, and move-in. All the "approval" dates are prompts for the client. The other dates are prompts for you.

Now look down the columns and see if any of the major work dates are close to any other. This would signal a possible disaster in the future if, for instance, you had two construction document sets to be issued the same week, or three design and budget presentations within a fortnight. Being forewarned, you should be able to handle it by starting overtime early, getting some contract help, or rescheduling a presentation.

When you have these dates filled out on the **Critical Date Scheduling Form**, you should also put those dates critical to the firm on the principal's **DayTimer** and the **Firm Calendar**.

Every firm should have one huge "composite" calendar mounted on a wall, showing three months at all times. It should have all the critical dates for all the jobs, holidays, personnel vacations, and so on. It's amazing how much information can be put on a 30" × 42" sheet of paper. It keeps everyone reminded of important priorities. It minimizes surprises and keeps you from promising too much. And the **Firm Calendar** will promote a great deal of communication at all levels which will help everyone.

The amount of work-on-hand is also important to know for anyone managing a design firm. Knowing that can help you plan both your marketing and your scheduling. Knowing how much work-on-hand in total you have will help you decide how much effort to put into prospecting for new business to keep everyone productively employed and to make your strategic planning/ marketing/profit goals for the year. Knowing how much work on hand you have for each job will fine-tune your scheduling and guarantee your profit for each job. Of course, we have a form to do both of those things, the **Work-On-Hand Worksheet**.

This worksheet looks much more complicated than it really is. Once you've gone through the process for the first job or two, you should be able to do another one in less than a minute. Start off by noting your firm's Multiple on Salary, the *average* weekly salary you pay all billable employees, and your yearly capacity in terms of working man-weeks (just take your total number of billable employees and multiply by fifty).

Fill in the contract name and the total fee in the contract. Write down the amount of fee which has already been billed and subtract that to find out how much fee is left in the contract. If you divide the remaining fee by the original fee, you will see what percentage of fee remains to be billed. Estimate what proportion of work remains to be completed. How well do these last two figures compare?

If you have a smaller percentage of fee left than you have of work left, you could be in trouble. Is it possible that you have expended more already because of revision work that you should have billed separately? Perhaps you should go on record with that now, before you exceed your fee and get in trouble. Perhaps you just have to carefully control the process of this job through the rest of the contract. At least you know before you are in trouble.

Dividing the fee left by your multiple, you will have the salary left that should be applied to the job. If you divide that salary left by the average salary of the firm, you will have how many more man-weeks of work are left in the salary to complete the job. If you have already determined that this job will be tough to complete since the percentage of salary left is less than the percentage of work left, you now have an excellent tool to complete the assignment. You know exactly how many weeks you can pay for to finish up while making your planned profit. If you assign good people and control them carefully, let them know the limits of their work to complete the contract, you may still finish on time and on schedule.

CRITICAL DATE SCHEDULING WORKSHEET

Company:	T.I.D.
Date:	1/26/83 + A.T.
Person Filling Out Worksheet:	

Dates should be filled out for each project from the Project Analysis Form.

Responsibilities:	Both	Client	Client	Firm	Client	Client	Firm	Firm
A CONTRACT NAME	B Start Up	C Program Approval	D Layout Approval	E Design & Budget Presentat'n	F Budget Approval	G Purchase Order Approval	H Construct'n Documents Issued	I Move-in
JWS&B	10/15/82	12/15/82	2/1/83	3/1/83	3/15/83	4/1/83	4/1/83	9/15/83
TCBC-1	11/1/82	1/1/83	2/15/83	3/15/83	4/1/83	4/1/83	5/15/83	11/15/83
F&M	12/1/82	2/1/83	3/15/83	4/1/83	4/15/83	5/1/83	6/1/83	11/15/83
GG&G	12/1/82	2/1/83	3/1/83	4/1/83	4/15/83	5/1/83	6/1/83	1/4/83
TCBC-2	1/1/83	3/1/83	4/15/83	5/15/83	6/1/83	6/15/83	7/1/83	1/30/84
PPP&S	4/1/83	4/21/83	ON HOLD	—	—	—	—	—
J&K	4/15/83	6/1/83	7/15/83	9/1/83	9/15/83	10/1/83	11/15/83	3/15/84
TCBC-3	6/15/83	8/1/83	9/1/83	10/15/83	11/1/83	11/15/83	2/1/84	5/30/84
MDC	10/1/83	11/1/83	12/15/83	12/15/83	1/1/84	1/15/84	1/15/84	4/15/84
PPP&S	1/1/84	2/1/84	3/15/84	4/15/84	5/1/84	5/15/84	6/1/84	8/1/84

Alternatively, you may be able to talk to the client, discover the reason why you are behind schedule, and perhaps get an additional fee to cover the remaining work. It is usually far easier to do this before the fact than after.

The last column shows what percent of your yearly capacity each project will take up. This serves two purposes. You can check your total dependence on any contract or client by adding up what percent of your yearly income depends on that client. Or you can add up all the numbers in that column to see how much of your yearly output is already sold. If you deduct any amount for the following year, you will know what amount of your available time and talent is spoken for this year and how much remains to yet be sold. You'll be able to plan the amount of effort worthwhile to see the remaining time...or, of course, whether you should consider hiring additional staff to handle the work already on hand.

If you want to plan your schedules on a much tighter basis, you can split each job on this form into its component phases. By applying your percentages of work by phase (or the 14-, 20-, 24-, 28-, and 14-percent rate that I suggested) you can do the whole process by phase and assign time for programming, design conceptualization, decoration, construction documentation, and supervision.

Now that you know how much time each project should have spent on it, how do you make sure your people actually put the time in on those projects and in that amount? I think the simplest thing to do is to tell them. People respond well to responsibility and if you tell your staff how much time a specific task should take, they will do it within that time. Occasionally they may not be satisfied and put in some more time. Occasionally they will do that and not bill it, benefiting you directly. Other times, you should bill it, understand why it took longer and either bill the client extra time because they caused the complication or simply eat the difference, try to make it up later, and know better next time.

There's an **Employee Scheduling Worksheet** that will help you let people know what you expect them to work on. It's rather trivial to understand. Just customize it for whatever month you are scheduling by crossing out the days of the month which are weekends and holidays. All remaining days are split into four sections. Assign each person his or her jobs for the week by writing in the job by the week or day. If you just split one week into two jobs, the employee knows how much time he should be putting in on each. The idea is not to know what job each employee will be working on in each quarter of the day. You should allow them to schedule themselves during the work week, but you have told them what the general allocation should be. They will work to that total number of hours, if not to that precise timing.

Some designers have been in the business for twenty-five years and understand all this stuff intuitively. The rest of us have to work harder to get smarter faster. The key to getting smarter is having usable information easily available. When you get a job, fill out the Project Information Form. When you finish a project

EMPLOYEE SCHEDULING WORKSHEET

Company: T.I.D.

Date: 10/28/83

Person Completing Worksheet: A.J.

Schedule Month Of: NOVEMBER, 1983

Instructions: Cross out weekends, assign work to employees by quarter, half, or whole days.

EMPLOYEE NAME	Day																														
	1	2	3	4	5	6	7	8	9	10	11	12	13	14	15	16	17	18	19	20	21	22	23	24	25	26	27	28	29	30	31
A.J.	SALES							SALES/MGMT							SALES/MGMT						S/M							S/M			
		MDC						MDC							MDC						MDC							MDC			
								TID							TID						TID							TID			
R.V.		MDC						MDC							MDC						MDC							MDC			
	TCBC3							TCBC3							TCBC 3						TCBC3							TCBC3			
	666/TC2																				J+K							J+K			
	J+K							J+K							J+K						666							666			
F.M.	MDC														666						666							666			
	666							666													J+K							J+K			
	J+K														J+K																
	PPP+S							J+K/PPP+S							PPP+S						MDC							MDC			
J.T.	MDC							MDC																							
	666							666																							
								PPP+S																							
J.S.	MDC							MDC	PPP+S						MDC						MDC										
									J+K						PPP+S																
	666							666							J+K						666										
															666																
	TCBC2							TCBC2							TCBC2						TCBC2							TCBC2			
M.L. (part-time)																															

complete the Project Information Form. Use it to analyze your work and your operation. It will be invaluable.

If you simply can't get yourself to do any of this tedious, dull, exacting, numbers work, make sure the number-two person on your staff likes it. In this business we need good management, and good management requires good information. Schedules are just one aspect of managers being in control. Information makes management possible. You can only manage by being in control of good information. Never forget it.

WORK-ON-HAND WORKSHEET

Company	T.I.D.
Date:	1/24/84
Person Completing Worksheet:	A.T.

Constants for use in this work sheet:

3.6 = Firm's "Multiple" on Salary
500 = Firm's Average Weekly Salary
275 = Firm's Yearly Capacity (billable employees 50)

Directions: Fill in boxes, A, B, and C. Box D equals B minus C. Box E equals Box D divided by Box B. Box F is an estimate of your progress to date. Box G is Box D divided by the Multiple listed above. Box H is the result of dividing Box G by the Average Weekly Salary Listed above. Box I is the result of dividing Box F by the Yearly Capacity listed above.

A CONTRACT NAME	B Total Fee in Contract	C Total Fee Billed	D Fee Left	E Per Cent Fee Left	F Per Cent Work Left	G Salary for Work Left	H Man-Weeks Work Left	I % Yearly Capacity
TWS&B	70K	70K	Ø	Ø	2%	Ø	1.	Ø
TCBC-1	40K	36K	4K	10%	10%	1100	2	1
F&M	60K	51K	9K	15%	15%	2500	5	2
GG&G	74K	63K	11K	15%	25%	3000	6(7)	2
TCBC-2	80K	60K	20K	25%	25%	5500	11	4
PPP&S	65K	20K	ON	HOLD	—	—	—	—
J&K	68K	34K	34K	50%	50%	9500	19	7
TCBC-3	84K	42K	42K	50%	55%	11500	23	8
MDC	39,000	0	39K	100%	100%	11000	22	8

Total Work On Hand:	89	32%
	Man Weeks	% Yearly Capacity

9 Purchasing

Depending on how *you* look at it, purchasing is either a super way to make lots of money very easily, or a terrible risk that may eat up your time and capital. It all sounds so easy when you consider buying a nice desk and credenza set for $6,000 with the option to resell them at any price between $6,600 and $10,000.

But contract clients may be different from the residential clients you started with. They might have their own purchasing department. They know the difference between list and cost and may be willing to pay it for the chairman's office but not for three floors of standard systems furniture.

There is more than a small element of risk in ordering contract merchandise. If a residential customer does not like the shade of lacquer on the custom coffee table, you may have to buy it and resell it at a $500 loss. If your contract client decides that they will convert much of their central records to microfiche, but didn't tell you until too late, what will you do with twenty-four custom gray file cabinets, each costing over $500? Yes, you can settle with the client and manufacturer, but you are not going to make any profit and it's going to take three weeks, fifteen phone calls, and five meetings to solve the problem.

Of course, sometimes a firm will want you to charge with a mark-up so your design fee will not appear on their records, in case the home office wouldn't approve of such frills as having a designer oversee the expenditure of thousands of dollars. You might just get to do the vice-presidents' offices …and two want to bring along their wives so you know you just lost an additional week of time.

My feeling is that you don't want to be paid your design fees through mark-ups on merchandise, but you have to know how to purchase furnishings for the client both as an accommodation and as a method of being paid a fee. And you deserve some sort of mark-up for any type of purchasing.

Alan Siegel, an attorney with many designer clients, says most legal problems he gets involved in are the result of purchasing. These problems include bad merchandise, incorrect or damaged; wrong deliveries, lost, wrong time, wrong date, after hours; wrong price; wrong field conditions for items; wrong appearance, actual or in "feeling"; bad design, either in measurements or fabrication; money, whether a bounced check, late payment, or too small a payment; warehousing costs, or anything else. This is a real case of Murphy's

Law: anything that can go wrong, will go wrong — at the worst possible moment.

Always protect yourself. Take no concrete actions until you are covered. Get approvals before you act. *Approvals are not oral. They are WRITTEN only.* This includes estimates or any other pre-ordering activity. Many times a client will not want to leave a trail of paper of all these approvals. They know, consciously or unconsciously, that they may want to back out. The appropriate method of handling that is to document all decisions reached in meeting in minutes of those meetings and send copies to the client as a matter of course. The fact that they don't reject these decisions will serve as a record of approval.

When you prepare presentation boards and the client approves them, have him sign each board along one edge. This may be tough to get done the first time, but after that the client will expect to do so, and may even remind you if you forget.

Only write specifications that include all costs and the delivery dates. Have these approved with a signature on each page.

Never buy anything without a signed purchase order, never.

In contract work, the designer usually adds a percentage mark-up to the lowest possible cost of the items, and that is normally specified in the contract between the designer and his client. That allows the designer to save the client money by bidding a package of standard office furnishings between manufacturers responding to the same performance specification or dealers responding to requirements for identical items. It can save a great deal of money, but it is also dangerous. Don't allow any firm to bid whom you don't feel is qualified, capable, or whom you don't feel comfortable with. And don't bid at all, if you don't feel comfortable with the process, the bidders, or your ability to control the client.

The danger here is the complication of purchases for office furnishings. A chair is not just a frame and a fabric. A secretarial chair has a model number, a frame finish, a specific base type and finish, a choice of casters, and specific upholstery fabric. And if you think that is complicated, consider all the different little widgets that go into the purchase of one little systems furniture work station.

Just buying a piece of furniture may not be the end of the complications. You may also have to pay for long distance transportation, interim-staging storage, final delivery, and installation, not counting sales tax.

If you understand all the complications, you are now ready to write a purchase order. Every P.O. must have:

- ☐ a unique P.O. number
- ☐ your company's name and address
- ☐ ordered from...

- ☐ date...
- ☐ for job name and address...
- ☐ installation location of this item, floor & room...
- ☐ deliver to...
- ☐ ship by date...
- ☐ number of each item
- ☐ finish
- ☐ accessories
- ☐ cost
- ☐ freight cost
- ☐ warehouse cost, if any
- ☐ delivery cost
- ☐ subtotal cost
- ☐ tax, if any*
- ☐ total cost
- ☐ space for client approval signature

*If you charge on a cost plus basis, your fee becomes part of the base price, and most states require the sales tax cover your fee as well. If you charge a "service fee" many states require tax on that as well, since it is not part of your "professional" services.

Every purchase order should also have some general conditions printed on the back of each and every page:

A. All labor to be covered by insurance for Workman's Compensation Acts and other claims for personal injury, death or other claims. (This prevents you from being sued by a workman employed by a contractor who is employed by you. Otherwise, he can sue up the ladder of contracts.)

B. All labor will be in harmony with existing job labor conditions. (It is up to the contractor to have non-union, union, or the right union labor working on your behalf.)

C. All work on the premises will be governed by work rules on the premises and the responsibility of the contractor, including but not limited to the timing of deliveries and the scheduling of the necessary elevator services. (On a job in a new building, the use of the elevators may be scheduled weeks in advance to get the building equipment and components in. Many buildings have rules about the timing of deliveries, before or after work or at a lunch period.)

D. All work to be completed in compliance with municipal and state building insurance laws and the standards of the Bureau of Fire Underwriters. Certificates of approval to be provided where required. (Again, you want to be covered against suits based on insurance claims of all types, especially possible fire claims.)

E. All work shall be completed in a timely manner with as many workmen employed as are necessary, yet not so many as to impede the progress of any other contractor. (You want the contractor to meet his deadline no matter what his cost. You also do not want him screwing up the other trades with too many people. Let him use overtime if he's really late.)

F. In the event of unreasonable delay, this order can be cancelled without penalty by notice to the contractor, unless satisfactory explanation is provided by the contractor within three days of notification. (You don't want to be held up by a late item without recourse to a replacement item.)

G. All materials and workmanship provided under this purchase order will be guaranteed free from any kind of defects for one year from installation or delivery, unless the normal guarantee is longer in which case that longer guarantee will apply. (This avoids the problem of not guaranteeing "custom" items, or parts of other items.)

H. (Your design firm) is in no way responsible for the products or services of any contractor, vendor, or dealer responding to this purchase order. (The real agreement you want stressed is between the contractor and the client, with you out from the middle.)

These clauses are not the ones that should be on your purchase order. Those should be written by your attorney. These are a guide for him to write ones that are legally appropriate to you and your circumstances.

Of course your attorney should look over your entire purchase order form, front and back. Your accountant should also look over the form to make sure it is appropriate for his needs. In particular, he might decide how many copies you will need and how the paper flow through your books will proceed.

At the very least, you need five copies of each form:

1. The client gets to keep one copy for his or her records.

2. The client signs a copy, returns it to the designer, who files it in the master file.

3. The vendor gets to keep one copy for his or her records.

4. The vendor signs a copy and returns it to the designer who sends it through the accounting procedure.

5. The project director should have one for his or her files.

Some firms try to prevent the client going direct to the vendor by blanking out the vendor's name on the client's two copies. They may also try to prevent the vendor from trying to sell other items direct to the client by blanking out the client's names on both copies sent to the vendor. You can follow the same procedure if you want, but perhaps you should just cross off any vendor who does that, even once. Any client who tries to chisel you out of your commission will probably do even worse things in the future, and maybe you should avoid them in the future too.

Purchasing is a very complicated process, and every firm should probably work out its own sequence. But the following sequence may help you think through how you could do it.

One:	An approved quotation is received from the vendor.
Two:	The purchase order is sent to, signed, and returned from the client, along with a 50 percent deposit.
Three:	The purchase order is sent to the vendor, who sends back an invoice and may require a 50 percent deposit. If not, the client's deposit is put in escrow. At this point, the purchase order requires the design firm to buy the merchandise from the vendor and the client to buy the merchandise from the design firm. Any change would invalidate the contract, unless signed off by all three parties, so don't change it! Cancel it and reissue it if you have to.
Four:	Before delivery the vendor demands final payment from the design firm and the design firm demands final payment from the client. When all moneys have changed hands, the transaction is complete.

The bigger you get and the bigger your clients and their orders are, the less likely it will be that you will follow this method. For the really big jobs, the client pays the vendor in full at the end of the job.

Whichever way you are working, make sure it is spelled out in detail in the contract in which you start your relationship. Remember, you are putting yourself at substantial risk, considering the value of the goods involved in most contract work.

It is also worthwhile understanding the sales process in terms of who owns what when. Legally, we are discussing who has *title* to the goods at what point in time.

When produced, the manufacturer has the title and responsibility for the goods.

Normally the manufacturer sells goods *F.O.B. F.O.B.* means *Free On Board,* or the manufacturer is free of responsibility once they are placed on board a shipper. While being shipped, the shipper has the responsibility, although not the title.

When delivered, the dealer or distributor has both title and responsibility. When being delivered to the client, the dealer or distributor's shipper has responsibility, although title is still with the dealer.

PURCHASE ORDER FORM

Your Company Name:	T.I.D.
Address:	81415 Post Road
	Hotford, CT
Telephone Number:	(203) 240-5300

P.O.#:	84-193
Date:	1/25/84
Page:	1 of: 1

Vendor Name:	Posh Seating Inc
Address:	77 Sunset Blvd
	Hollywood, CA 94111
Telephone Number:	(800) 879-4449

Deliver to Name:	MDC
Address:	9292 Post Road
	Hotford, CT 06000
Telephone Number:	(203) 765-4321

Location:	Quantity:	Deliver:	Description:	Unit Cost:	Total Cost:
Pres. Office 3rd Flr	1	4/10 – 4/15/84	#747 Exec. Chair	3,975.00	3,975
			#DC7 Base	n/c	
			Finish - BL	n/c	
			Fabric - Leather color C-46	1,000	1,000
			Castors F-1		

Notify	K.D.
of (design office) immmediately of any exception to this order	

Estimate Date:	11/15
Client Accepted:	1/26
Client Paid:	1/26
Order Date:	1/26

Total:	4,975.00
Purchase Fee:	746.00
Sales Tax:	286.06
Delivery:	35.00
Installation:	—

TOTAL:	6,042.31

Client Name:	Mon Dieu Cosmetics
Address:	37 Post Road
	Hotford, CT
Accepted for:	
Accepted for:	MDC
By:	[signature]
Date:	1/26/84
Title:	Pres

This purchase order is subject to the terms and conditions stated on the reverse side.

It is the client's responsibility to define where the goods have to be delivered to. If you specify a street address, as soon as the goods are taken off the truck, they are the client's responsibility and title has been transferred to the client. If you specify delivery to a floor or room, that is where title and responsibility are transferred. Be careful, you do want to make sure the "site" as defined is the right floor and area.

All this purchasing business requires lots of time and energy. You deserve a fee just for handling purchasing. The standard in the industry is between 10 percent and 15 percent, and that is certainly reasonable. You should decide whether this is to be a cost center or a profit center to your firm, and treat it accordingly.

10 Construction Documentation

It is not the function of this book to teach you the professional aspects of interior design, whether or not related to the contract world. But there are two aspects of the professional construction documentation task that have a very direct impact on your bottom line. Nearly one third of your cost is normally spent on creating those documents. So a great deal of your profits are based on efficient production of these documents. And mistakes or omissions cause changes which, at best, cost more and, at worst, make all or part of your design dysfunctional. Correcting those mistakes costs you more money and profit.

It is a fact that some contractors have been known to base some or all of their fee on the size of the bid set they were handed. And the less work you have to put into the drawings, the more time you have left for the other, more enjoyable parts of your job.

Balancing the desire to spend as little time as possible on creating your construction set is the liability for them if they are inconsistent, cause incorrect dimensioning of pre-constructed items, damage the building, result in unforeseen delays, and so on. This suggests you should put a great deal of effort into making those documents accurate.

The most important thing to say is that your documents must be as good as they should be. You have to decide on the appropriate effort to put into them. They should be accurate, consistent, easy to read, clean, and as simple as you can make them.

The best way to do so is to establish a set of standards for drawing methodology, details, symbols, and everything else you can think of. The trick is to match the complexity of the job with the complexity of the drawings, and then simplify them as much as possible. This is an art and a science that practice will help you improve. Knowing when to stop drawing is a critical skill in this business.

If you have not done much contract work before, we should start by going through the information that should be contained on a full set of drawings.

The base information that you start with is your own firm name, address, and telephone number as well as that of the client. Each drawing should have your project account number, a north arrow, a scale, a date, a floor number, a drawing number, and page number if more than one is involved ("2 or 4").

This should, of course, match your corporate graphic image and be on standard size paper. Each sheet should have a place for the client to "sign-off" and accept the document.

If you don't have a set of accurate drawings (and I can almost guarantee that you don't unless the building is presently under construction) you have to create a drawing with the building outline. You can take an architectural, dimensioned drawing, if you have one, as a starting point and do a physical field survey.

Use the inside of the window glass as the fixed point to begin. Measure the convector, the drapery pocket, and the height of the existing ceiling. Note all the existing plumbing, including wet columns, along with the core facilities. Verify all the dimensions. If the columns are not labeled, do so with numbers in one direction and letters in the other (column A-1, A-2, C-4, etc.). Draw it all up on the Building Outline Sheet, along with labeling the streets outside the walls for orientation purposes.

Use the building outline to create your Partition Master drawing. Show all the ceiling height partitions as well as lower ones. Draw the built-in cabinet work, counters, closets (including types, like clothes, storage, electrical, janitor, etc.), water cooler locations, and new stair locations.

Use this as the basis for your Final Layout drawing by having a sepia or mylar made. This will show all furniture, including size and type; files, including type, dimension, and number of drawers; storage cabinets; steel shelving; future personnel locations; telephones, including their locations and types, such as call directors, etc.; and the names and limits of departments.

Label all the non-obvious items. Use that drawing to create your HVAC schedule and equipment schedule.

Use the final layout drawing as the basis, also, for the construction plan drawing. This will describe the types of partitions, in addition to their locations. Drywall partitions should be noted as extending either to the ceiling or to the slab, with or without sound proofing. Block walls might be described as having a drywall or plaster finish, etc. This plan should show the flooring, plumbing lines, water coolers, counters, cabinet work, and where specific construction should meet building code requirements. Also located on this plan should be the symbols that show where elevations, details, sections, and larger scale plans are keyed to.

If you have a reverse sepia or mylar made of the final layout drawing, you can create the reflected ceiling plan on it. This should show the size, types, and starting points of the ceiling tiles; lighting locations, types, and switching; exit signs; air diffusers, registers, or other returns; changes in ceiling heights; the possible location of the electrical/telephone ceiling tray (if used); and drapery track, perhaps with details or sections.

Another sepia or mylar should be the basis of the electrical telephone plan. That will show the outlets, all types, locations, and heights; the cellular deck system, if one is used; all telephone outlets, locations, and types; knock out

CONSTRUCTION
DOCUMENTATION CHECKLIST

Company:

Date:

Person Completing Checklist:

Use Stock Paper Sizes:
- ☐ 8.5 × 11
- ☐ 11 × 17
- ☐ 20 × 30
- ☐ 24 × 42
- ☐ 30 × 48
- ☐ 36 × 56

Leave room for:
- ☐ Design Firm name, address and telephone
- ☐ Client Firm name, address, and telephone
- ☐ Account Number
- ☐ North Arrow
- ☐ Scale
- ☐ Date
- ☐ Floor Number
- ☐ Drawing Number
- ☐ Set stat (#   of #   )

Start with the BUILDING OUTLINE
Based on architectural dimensioned drawing
Plus a physical field survey
- ☐ Use peripheral window as fixed point
- ☐ Measure convector and drapery pocket
- ☐ Measure height of existing ceiling
- ☐ Note existing plumbing
- ☐ Verify all dimensions for bldg outline
- ☐ Label all columns with Numbers/Letters
- ☐ Draw outline, windows, convector, core
- ☐ Show streets outside
- ☐ Label all core facilities

Use outline to do PARTITION MASTER drawing
- ☐ Ceiling height partitions
- ☐ Lower height partitions
- ☐ Built-in cabinet work or counters
- ☐ Closets (types—coats, storage, etc.)
- ☐ Water cooler locations
- ☐ Use stair locations

Use as basis for:
- ☐ FINAL LAYOUT drawing
- ☐ All furniture (size, type), including:
- ☐ Files (type, number of drawers)
- ☐ Over file storage cabinets
- ☐ Steel shelving
- ☐ Future positions
- ☐ Telephones (location, call directors)
- ☐ Departmental names
- ☐ Label all non-obvious items
- ☐ HVAC schedule
- ☐ Equipment Schedule
- ☐ CONSTRUCTION PLAN drawing
- ☐ Types of partitions

Drywall ☐ to ceiling
             ☐ to slab
             ☐ with/without sound batts

Block   ☐ gypsum
             ☐ plaster or drywall finish
             ☐ other

- ☐ Flooring
- ☐ Plumbing lines
- ☐ Elevation targets
- ☐ Details/sections marks
- ☐ Building Code (state requirements)
- ☐ Counter/cabinet work locations
- ☐ Larger scale plans
- ☐ Water coolers (spec. in legend)
- ☐ REFLECTED CEILING PLAN
- ☐ Ceiling tile starting points
- ☐ Size of ceiling tile
- ☐ Types of ceiling materials
- ☐ Lighting types (bldg. std. or special)
- ☐ Switching
- ☐ Exit signs
- ☐ Diffusers and Registers (std. or special)
- ☐ Drapery track detail section
- ☐ Changes of ceiling heights
- ☐ ELECTRICAL/TELEPHONE PLAN
- ☐ Cellular floor system
- ☐ Outlets (all locations and heights)
- ☐ Knock-out panels in convectors
- ☐ Special Requirements (conduit sizes, etc)
- ☐ Telephones (all locations and types)

The Preliminary Issue for Engineering is the above set of four drawings

---

DOOR & HARDWARE SCHEDULE
- ☐ Style of hardware (bldg std or special)
- ☐ Location of locks and closers
- ☐ Finish of hardware
- ☐ Fireproof self closing doors
- ☐ Special door and buck details

DOOR SCHEDULE DETAILS
- ☐ Hollow metal door and buck types
- ☐ Jamb details
- ☐ Saddle details
- ☐ Hardware specs and manufacturer

DRAPERY SCHEDULE
- ☐ Coordinate with track details in RCP
- ☐ Refer to drapery legend

COLOR SCHEDULE
- ☐ Coordinate with CP elevations & CWD
- ☐ Refer to color schedule

FLOOR COVERING SCHEDULE
- ☐ Coordinate dif flr mtls with saddles
- ☐ Refer to floor covering legend

CABINET WORK DETAILS & ELEVATIONS
- ☐ Done by cabinet contractor
- ☐ Coordinate with all drawings, RC & ET.
- ☐ Convey your message, do not assume
- ☐ Don't over detail (shop drawing will be provided by woodworker
- ☐ Always provide scale for each detail

CONSTRUCTION DETAILS
(by General Contractor)
- ☐ Include elevations with descriptors
- ☐ Show sections for details

SEE OTHER NOTES
- ☐ Other:
- ☐ Other:
- ☐ Other:

panels in convectors; and all special requirements, such as conduit sizes, Dwyer units, copy machines, CRT's, etc.

The last four drawings mentioned above make up the package known as the preliminary issue for engineering. You give this to the structural and mechanical/electrical engineers so they can plan for any special requirements created by your design. Their drawings should be returned in time to modify any of your work which must be in accord with their changes. Their drawings are normally part of the construction document set which you issue.

A series of schedules make up the second part of the construction documentation set. The door and hardware schedule shows the style of hardware (building standard or otherwise), the locations of locks and closers (right or left hand), the finishes of all the hardware, the types and requirements for fireproof and/or self closing doors, and special door and buck details.

If you have a separate door schedule details sheet, it will show the hollow metal door and buck types, jamb details, saddle details, and the hardware specifications along with the manufacturer.

If you have a drapery schedule, it is coordinated with the reflected ceiling plan track details and the cabinet work details.

The cabinet work details and elevations should not be totally detailed. You will be getting back "shop drawings" from the cabinet contractor showing how he will actually build the items. You should draw enough to convey exactly what you want to see, the quality level, and any hidden components which will affect the performance of the item. Convey your message, and never assume anything. No contractor can ever see a corner without cutting it. Coordinate the cabinetwork with the electrical/telephone plan (is there any power, light, or air handling in these items?). Always provide a scale for each detail.

Construction details should be provided by the general contractor. Make sure that it includes elevations with descriptors and sections with details.

There is a **Construction Documentation Checklist** provided so you can make sure you cover all the bases in a complex job. You should try to simplify the drawing process as much as possible. For instance, you should have many sheets of standard details already drawn up. To make them part of your set, all you have to do is photocopy them on 8½-by-11-inch special sheets, which take a copy on the transparent top layer that then peels off and can be placed directly on your drawing. This is available in many stationery and drafting supplies stores.

Anything to be typed should be on word processing so boilerplate specs and other documents can be reproduced easily. If you are too small to have a computer, and nearly no one is, at least have specs set up on easily reproduced and customized xeroxable paper.

You should also standardize your drawings to the greatest extent possible. Peter Pepe, who has headed up and straightened out many large firm's production departments, suggests that any drawing that leaves an office should look

| Company Name: |
| Date: |
| Person Completing Checklist: |

CONSTRUCTION DOCUMENTATION SYMBOLS CHECKLIST

Each drawing should have information, where needed, about each general and specific type of component which is mentioned below. It is also a good professional practice to have a separate and consistent symbol for each item and to use these in all your document sets. You may wish to put your symbol in the space provided.

Furniture Plan

☐ Space number
☐ Full height partion (any type)
☐ Low partition
☐ Moveable screen
☐ Moveable metal partition
☐ Moveable metal and glass partition
☐ Special partition—see detail
☐ Cabinet work (by cabinet contr'r)
☐ File cabinet—Legal/Corres/# dwrs
☐ Lateral file—Width (inches)/# dwrs
☐ Steel shelving (width & depth)
☐ Future equipment or furniture
☐ Miscellaneous equipment, news, etc.
☐ CRT/VDT
☐ Equipment item (see schedule)
☐ Desk telephone
☐ Wall telephone
☐ Call Director (# of buttons)
☐ Water cooler—wall mounted
☐ Water cooler—wall mtd. handicapped

Abbreviations
[AFF] Above Finished Floor
[BS] Building Standard
[TO] Trimmed Opening
☐ Other:

Construction Plan

☐ Space number
☐ Existing partition to remain
☐ Existing partition to be removed
☐ Drywall partition to slab above
☐ Drywall partition to above ceiling
☐ Drywall partition to ceiling
☐ Drywall partition—2 hr fire rating
☐ Drywall partition—1 hr fire rating
☐ Gypsum block partition ("thick")
☐ Low drywall partition
☐ Moveable metal partition
☐ Moveable metal & glass partit'n
Moveable part'ns need height, width, type
☐ Special partition (see detail   on)
☐ Door opening number (see schedule)
☐ Ceiling break line
☐ Closet (coat/storage/etc.)
☐ Elevation target (show letter/dwg #)
☐ Detail Section (show letter/dwg #)
Abbreviations (& elevat'n symbol if needed)
[G] Gypsum wall board ceiling
[M] Mineral tile ceiling
[P] Plaster ceiling
[SP] Special (see detail)
[CP] Carpet
[CT] Ceramic tile
[QT] Quarry Tile
[VAT] Vinyl Asbestos Tile
[WD] Wood
[FF] Finish to Finish
[NTS] Not To Scale
[OFS] Over File Storage
[C] Center Line
[CMP] Center Line Mullion & Partition
[EX] Existing
☐ Other:

Electrical/Telephone Plan

☐ Existing wall electrical outlet
☐ Existing telephone outlet
☐ Existing outlets to be capped
☐ New wall electrical outlet (double?)
☐ New telephone outlet
☐ Cell mtd electrical outlet (double?)
☐ Cell mtd telephone outlet (double?)
☐ Inactive floor electrical outlet
☐ Inactive floor telephone outlet
☐ Telephone call director
☐ New separate circuit outlet
☐ Water cooler outlet
☐ Clock hanger outlet
☐ Outlet on 5' flex conduit for cab wk
☐ Special—Quotron, Telex, Dow Jones, Reuters, Bunker Ramp—Show req'm'ts

Abbreviations
[CV] Standard telephone
[KV] Telephone with illuminated buttons
[MIB] Mounted in Base
[POC] Positioned Over Cell
[MIK] Mounted In (convector) Knock-out

Reflected Ceiling Plan
☐ Space number
☐ Ceiling break
☐ Ceiling tile starting point
☐ Light switch
☐ Three way light switch
☐ Gang switch
☐ Air conditioning clg diffuser (sup)
☐ Air conditioning clg register (ret)
☐ Ceiling tile pattern break
☐ Exit light—show illuminated faces
☐ Recessed 2' × 4' fluorescent fixture
☐ Recessed incandescent fixture
☐ Surface fluorescent
☐ Surface incandescent
☐ Special fluorescent (see   )
☐ Special incandescent (see   )
☐ Exposed sprinkler head
☐ Pop-out sprinkler head
☐ Other:

like any other drawing regardless of who drew it. This means you have to establish standard ways of showing everything.

Attached is a **Construction Drawings Symbols Checklist** that shows all the items Peter Pepe suggests should be standardized on your construction drawings. You should establish your own unique symbol for each item on the list. That way, you, your employees, or any hourly contractor you pick up for a job will produce similar drawings.

And, of course, you should understand what each means. If you haven't been exposed to much contract work, you should make sure you know what type of equipment each symbol refers to and when it is necessary. Remember, contract work is more specific and critical than most residential work.

The third part of a set of construction documents is the specifications. This is often very extensive and consists, in great part, of the design firm saying that no matter what happens, it is not the fault of the design firm. Your lawyer should help you write yours, but let us run down the sections and important paragraphs.

The specifications normally start with the schedule of drawings it goes with. It may state its general conditions, or state that the general conditions to be used are the current standard form of the AIA, unless specifically modified.

The general notes make up an important section, since it tries to absolve the designer of any problems. Sections state that work will comply with the National Board of Fire Underwriters, OSHA, the city building code, the specific building requirements, or whichever is most stringent.

Clauses will state that all design drawings are complementary, and any item present on one drawing is presumed present on all drawings. It is the contractor's responsibility to make sure the drawings are all complete and accurate and to notify the designer if he finds any discrepancies within the documents or with the actual field conditions. The contractor must visit the premises to make sure the work promised by the documents can be performed as shown.

It is the responsibility of the contractor to make sure all work can be performed on time, within the rules of the building. Deliveries will also be scheduled accordingly. The contractor will also remove all waste material from the floor and leave it clean.

The contractor must provide a schedule of his work before beginning that work. All correspondence to the client or to the designer will also be forwarded to the other. All shop drawings, equipment cuts, and "approved equal" requests will be submitted to the designer for approval.

The contractor will insure that his work causes no damage to other parts of the building. All existing parts of the space will be protected during the work, or restored afterwards. The contractor will protect his work until it is turned over to the client.

Exits will be posted, telephone numbers for hospitals, doctors, and ambu-

Client:	M.D.C.
Date:	1/28/89
Person Completing Checklist:	A.T.

Section 1: Drawings

☑ Schedule of Drawings

Section 2: General Conditions

☑ General Conditions (use AIA?)

Section 3: General Notes

All work will comply with:

☑ National Board of Fire Underwriters

☑ Occupational Safety & Health Act

☑ City Building Code

☑ Applicable Local Laws

☑ Building Requirements for Alterations

☑ The most stringent of the above   *Check about Local Laws 5/12/14/18*

☑ Woodwork to be fireproofed

☑ Drawings and Notes are complimentary, and anything left out is assumed there

☑ All work to complete this contract is included, except for: *hanging artwork*

☑ Contractor will still coordinate with other contractors and trades

☑ Notify designer immediately if a discrepancy exists

☑ Notify designer if field conditions differ, and request clarification

☑ Contractor will visit premises before starting work   *in company of T.I.D.*

☑ All correspondence to designer/tenant will also go to other party

☑ Contractor shall obey rules of building for construction and alteration

☑ Deliveries will be properly coordinated with building

☑ Building Conditions for deliveries will be checked in advance   *and confirmed with us*

☑ All extra charges for delivery will be paid by contractor   *ASAP*

☑ Contractor will show schedule for construction

☑ Contractor will furnish weekly field progress reports

☑ Contractor and subs are responsible for costs of defective work or merchandise

☑ Contractor shall clean up for self, and others

☑ "Equals" must be approved by designer   *send directly to J.T.*

☑ "Provided" means Contractor will provide

☑ "Cuts" of all fixtures and equipment will be provided to designer

☑ "Shop Drawings" must be approved by Designer   *send directly to J.T.*

☑ Contractor will prevent job from dirtying other areas

☑ Contractor will protect building and adjoining property or repair it promptly

☑ Contractor will protect his work until turned over to client

☑ Contractor will maintain a current and complete set of construction documents

☑ Contractor will supply, as needed:

☑ Building Certificate

☑ Electrical Certificate

☑ Plumbing Certificate

☑ Air Conditioning Certificate

☑ Fireproof Wood Test Report, if needed   *— a must for this job!*

☑ Exits will be safely maintained

☑ Emergency numbers will be posted

☑ Structural Engineer will certify structure to support maximum expected load

☑ Fire rated areas and walls will be maintained

☑ Fire extinguishers will be provided as needed, or as shown on drawings

☑ Contractor will provide "As Builts" of lighting and circuiting as installed

Continued

SPECIFICATION
CHECKLIST

Section 4: Demolition	
☐ Contractor will provide all labor and materials to complete demolition/removal	*none – new bldg*
☐ All demolition work to be done before or after building hours	
☑ Contractor will pay for needed overtime costs of labor and/or elevators	*still may need, as*
☑ Contractor will cap/flush off all unused plumbing, outlets, etc. to be abandoned	*plans change.*

Note: Specific details are not provided for in the following sections. You should determine the limitations and responsibilities you want to enforce on the contractor in your own particular circumstances, with the help of your attorney. These are more matters of design than business.

Section 5: Patching and Cutting	
Section 6: Partitions	
Section 7: Ceilings	
Section 8: Lighting	
Section 9: Electrical	
Section 10: Air Conditioning and HVAC Drawings	*A/C in Tel. switch rm. 2 wks early for connections*
Section 11: Plumbing	
Section 12: Doors, Bucks and Hardware	
Section 13: Cabinet Work	*This is very imporatant section for M.D.C.*
Section 14: Cleaning	
Section 15: Closets	
Section 16: Painting and Wall Covering	*Contractor weak here last job – make stronger*
Section 17: Floor	
Section 18: Changes in the Work	*Must document fully – who, when, why &*
Section 19: Claims for Extra Cost	*who approved changes here.*
Section 20: Transportation	
Section 21: Miscellaneous	*include section on requisitions here.*
Section 22: Client Rights	
Section 23: Insurance	
☑ Contractor will "hold harmless" the building owner, managing agent, etc.	
☑ Contractor will show proof of insurance, for himself and any subcontractors	
☑ Workman's Compensation	
☑ Comprehensive General Liability not less than:	
☑ $500,000 per person, Personal Injury	
☑ $2,500,000 per occurrence, Personal Injury	
☑ $500,000 per occurrence, Property Damage	
☑ $500,000 per aggregate	
☑ Comprehensive Automobile Liability Insurance	
☑ $250,000 per person, Bodily Injury	
☑ $750,000 per occurrence, Bodily Injury	
☑ $100,000 per occurrence, Property Damage	
☑ Contractor will show certificate of insurance acceptance before starting work	
☑ The insurance will not limit liabililty of contractor	

lances will be clearly shown. All fire requirements will be met. All structural requirements will be met.

The contractor will provide a set of complete plans showing how everything was actually built—the "As Built Drawings."

"Specs," as they are normally called, then have sections with specifics on demolition, patching and cutting, partitions, ceilings, lighting, electrical/telephone, air conditioning and HVAC drawings, plumbing, doors-bucks-hardware, cleaning, closets, painting, wall-covering, floor, changes, claims, transportation, miscellaneous, client's rights, and insurance.

The last section is very important. The contractor must agree to insure himself and his sub-contractors for Workman's Compensation, Comprehensive General Liability or personal injury ($500,000 per person, $2,500,000 per occurrence), property damage ($500,000 per occurrence and in aggregate), and comprehensive automobile insurance ($100/$300,000 personal injury plus $100,000 property damage) and to furnish evidence of same before they begin work.*

The above page or so of specifications is a summary of an actual document that fills over two dozen pages. There are plenty of books that go through the entire list in detail. My purpose in bringing the overall scope of them up in some detail is to make sure you are aware of the general coverage they offer and are convinced to get at least a short and long form to attach to the appropriate size job.

There are other specifications that should be part of your documents. The furniture specifications should simply list everything that will go on the purchase order when the client accepts the design and specifications. You may very well have carpet specifications, drapery specifications, etc.

I also don't believe that even a good designer knows everything, especially in some specific areas such as acoustics, lighting, security, or even planning art programs. Before you finish your construction documents, you should consult with any experts on any problem you feel may be beyond your expertise.

I don't believe that most in-house consultants know much. They are used to finding solutions to the common problems they face, and do not get to deal with enough different kinds of problems to have an open mind and the vast background an independent consultant does. They may be lower in the pecking order than the designer/principal and have to accept his solution, or they may simply have a few tried and true standard solutions that they apply to everything.

As you can tell from the accompanying chart on consultant involvement, consultants are used very frequently. They have another benefit, besides their greater expertise. They can often take the heat when you feel extra cost items are desired and sell your design when you shouldn't push too hard. Ask for their advice and then follow it.

*All dollar amounts are general examples and may not be appropriate for your goals, check with your attorney before using these figures.

CHART 9
Consultant Involvement

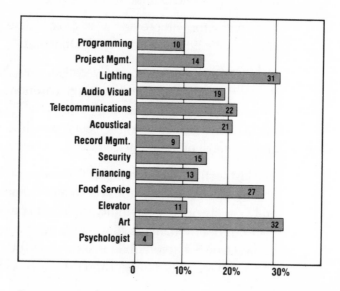

But try not to be their employer. The client should hire them directly and make you the coordinator of all the services being brought to bear on this project. If you are going to pay them and then charge the client, a mark-up of 10 percent is acceptable and done frequently. You are exposed to some risk by being in the middle of this kind of transaction, and thus deserve the fee. But I think the real reason for charging a fee for this pass-along is to convince the client it is better to hire direct.

Sometimes there is another alternative to hiring consultants. In occasional instances, the salespeople know as much or more than any consultants. Their advice may be all you need. To find out who those rare and wonderful people are, consult with your own support groups.

If you are going to bid a tenant improvement job and/or a set of furniture, your drawings, schedules, and specifications have to be in great shape. You should have the capability and right to qualify the bidders. You want to avoid low bidders who cannot produce the quality level of result you need. If the client wants you to include a bidder they have had experience with, make sure that they know there can be a real difference between the work of different contractors. Try to visit some job sites to convince them.

When the bids come in, make sure you check them closely.

Furniture bids, especially, have to match in a myriad of different ways (remember there were five different components in a simple secretarial chair) that require a great deal of time and effort on your part. You also have to monitor construction closely to make sure quality is not skipped to produce the profit which the low bid may have skimped on.

Remember, no matter who screws up on the job, the client will come to you. Make sure your best efforts are not sabotaged by poor dealers, contractors, or workmen. Make sure your documentation is up to the standards of your design, and the work is up to the standards of your documentation.

11 Job Supervision

It is amazing how designers fudge their responsibilities for job supervision in their contract descriptions. They will "monitor," "oversee," and usually "assist" others in supervising the construction. The designer contractually obligates himself to do hardly anything. In the context of the contract, that is the safest way to proceed. Promise as little as you can.

Notwithstanding the fact that you promised as little as you could, do as much as you can. You will be blamed or praised for the job that is built, not the job that was designed.

Your supervisory role consists of:

* Reviewing shop drawings, cuts, quotations, and contracts.

* Monitoring work in progress.

* Acting as "clerk of the works" to review work, recommend actions on invoices, and verify costs, discounts, rebates, etc.

* Attempting to protect client against defects, deficiencies, incomplete work, sloppy craftsmanship, etc.

* Overseeing scheduling and reporting.

* Assisting in coordination of all parties.

* Assisting in negotiations between owner, tenant, manager, contractor, and civil authorities for building permit, inspections, and certificate of occupancy.

* Preparing a punchlist showing missing items and work needing corrective actions.

* Assisting in preparation for move-in.

* Assisting in move-in.

You must establish credibility with the contractor immediately. Set up a day and a time for a weekly meeting with the contractor and all his subcontractors. Contractors get up early. It would be best if you did. Meet him with coffee and donuts before eight in the morning, the same morning each week.

Demonstrate your authority at once. Don't let any poor quality work be accepted. Stop sloppy workmanship immediately. Don't compromise until you have the proper rapport with the contractor.

By the same token, do not try to set up an adversary relationship with him, unless you are forced to. If you are reading this chapter, you probably don't know as much about putting a job together as the contractor does, and he may be able to squeeze poor work by you, if he feels he has to, to make a profit. Or he can make you visit the site two or three times a week. Be strict but fair.

A **Field Inspection Report Form** is provided to help you keep track of progress and quality of the job. Most of it is fairly basic. It may be helpful for you or a junior member who may do interim field trips. Remember, the client deserves to be kept informed, and with a form like this, a simple copy can be sent to them weekly. You can also give a copy to the contractor to see if he agrees with your assessments.

For handling the furnishings part of the contract, it really pays to use a good dealer. He can handle the trans-shipping, warehousing, repairs, damage claims, and make your life much simpler. It is always easier to deal with a local businessperson whose future well-being can depend in part on you, than to deal with someone remote.

The only way you can make sure that what you designed gets built is to check everything. All shop drawings and cuts must be checked against your original set of working drawings. They don't have to match precisely, since the contractor may be able to do some things better and more simply based on his experience. But examine differences to see who benefits and why.

This is also a time when you can catch your own mistakes and have them corrected before the client ever finds out. That is another reason to keep the contractor on your side.

You are protecting your client and your design. It may not be fun, but it is usually very instructive. It is also extraordinarily important. Give it the time and effort it deserves.

FIELD INSPECTION
REPORT FORM

Project Name:	J & K
Project Location:	423 MAIN ST
Floor/Location/Space Number:	3rd Flr.

To:	File
From:	F.M.

Report Number:	#9
Date:	4/15/84
Time:	8 AM

CC:	Client
	A.T.

ITEM	% Complete	Remarks
Demolition	100%	
Stair opening(s)		Note- furniture report on separate sheets
Structural Reinforcing		
Sub-floor		
Partition studding		
Sheet metal duct work		
Black iron work for ceiling		
Electrical wiring of ceiling ltg		
Electrical cabling		
Communications cabling		
Plumbing roughing		
HVAC systems		
Finished partitioning		
Finished plumbing		
Switches		
Convenience outlets		
Telephone outlets		
Ceiling		
Lighting fixtures		
Ceiling diffusers—grills		
Access panels		
Convector enclosures	100%	
Hardware	90%	} Glass entrance doors not yet installed
Doors	90%	
Glazing	100%	
Paint		
Wall coverings		Sloppy work in lunch room by vending area
Base		Rip in vinyl on core wall near elev. #2
Carpet		
Vinyl Asbestos Tile		
Ceramic Tile		
Woodwork	100%	
Cabinet work	75%	Missing serving bar in Bd. Rm.
Drapery	50%	Tracks in, casements still on order.
Blinds	—	
Dog houses	100%	
Special equipment installation	80%	A/V in Bd. Rm.
General Comments	95%	Everything looks fine but Bd. Rm.

12 Management Issues

Macro-Management Issues

Now that we have covered all the ways you perform the *professional* tasks of running an interior design business, it is time to settle down and discuss the really hard part, performing the *business* tasks of running an interior design business.

This is called "management" and is one of the most difficult jobs in every business. The art of management requires that you match the goals of the client with those of the organization, its employees, and yourself.

If you are investing your own money, effort, hopes, and future into this business, then your goals should come first. Do you want to be rich, retired, famous, secure, head of a big/small organization, in charge of design/finance, and so on.

Obviously, some of these should be short-term goals and some should be long-term goals.

You then have to choose the right goals for the business. These goals might well be different from yours, but they should allow you to ultimately reach your personal goals. Within the business, it is your job to then establish the strategy, methods, and systems to reach both those sets of goals.

At the same time, you must make sure that your business meets the needs of the client base you seek to serve. If their needs will not be met, then yours won't either. Does that require a redefinition of the target market for your services? Is that market big enough, or sophisticated enough, to use your services in the magnitude you hope for. Do you have to refine your goals and definitions again? This is another part of your strategic planning cycle.

Once these three sets of goals are in alignment, you then have to establish the right organization to achieve them. This means choosing the right **form** for the organization, establishing **methods** that work for the client and the organization, and developing a **style** that will attract the right clients and employees, and that seems natural to you.

An extremely difficult next step is to populate your organization with the right people. You want individuals who will function well within the ground rules that have been established and who will identify with, and pursue, the same goals. If you establish your style early, it will be a flag that makes it easier to choose, and be chosen by, the right employees.

Management must lead the employees in pursuit of common goals, develop those employees so they feel they are bettering themselves while they loan their skills to you, reward success, resolve conflicts, punish unnecessary mistakes, and change failures into grounds for better efforts.

Management "manages" by:

Planning:	Choosing the right goals, methods, and systems, testing them, improving them, and retesting them.
Leading:	Giving goals to groups, along with the directions to achieve those goals.
Organizing:	Meshing the people with the systems and methods so that both function well.
Motivating:	Giving reasons for individuals and groups to strive for the goals defined by management.
Monitoring:	Measuring the results, interpreting the results meaningfully, and recalibrating the organization, methods, and systems as the result.
Delegating:	All tasks should be performed by the lowest-level employee capable of doing so, including management tasks.
Following-up:	Knowledge is useless without being acted upon.
Controlling:	All of the above has to be knowledgeably controlled by the manager.

All management starts from within. You have to decide what type of person you are and match that to your management style. In general, there are four main styles of management:

Autocratic:	The father-figure leads the firm and no one questions his leadership or decisions.
Bureaucratic:	Leadership is established by a group working through established hierarchies and rules.
Consultative:	The manager seeks advice but reserves the right to make all decisions by himself.
Participative:	The manager asks for advice and everyone helps to make the decision.

Choose one which suits you and use it. Keep in mind that you can gradually move away from the autocratic method, but you probably can't move back to it without firing all your employees and starting over. As the firm grows, management has to change, usually becoming more formalized.

Typically a person can only manage six to twelve people. As you grow beyond half-a-dozen employees, there is a tendency to install "middle management" people. As soon as that happens, you have to worry about the form of the organization. There are three primary forms of company organization:

A **pyramid organization**: When one person starts a firm and remains the strong principal, the company is usually one of these. It is easy to manage with good control, and maintain good quality-control as well, but it becomes dependent on that principal for marketing and management continuity. The firm will probably disappear in the absence of that principal since replacements are not generally nurtured within the organization.

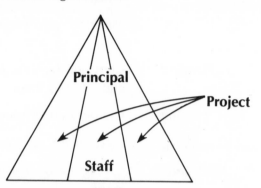

A **project-oriented organization**: When equal partners start firms, this tends to be the form they take. It is easy to expand with new partners, as long as they are all strong principals. Normally this produces strong client relationships and more than one marketing effort. This kind of firm is hard to manage well since there can be internal competition for resources and uneven quality control from team to team. It has questionable continuity, even with the partners alive and well. If there are two partners and one is a "marketeer" and one is the designer/manager, this firm will be more pyramidal than project-oriented.

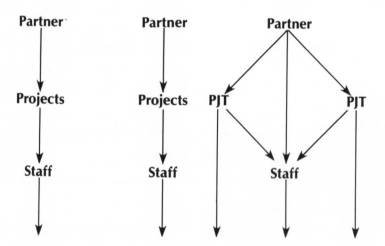

A **matrix firm**: This is typical of large firms and has excellent positive characteristics in that it offers excellent quality control, strong client relationships, good marketing, a solid base for growth or diversification, and good continuity. On the other hand, it needs at least two dozen people to work well, they should be specialists, it is somewhat inefficient in that it needs a lot of management, it works poorly on small jobs, and it may cause creative conflict.

Management

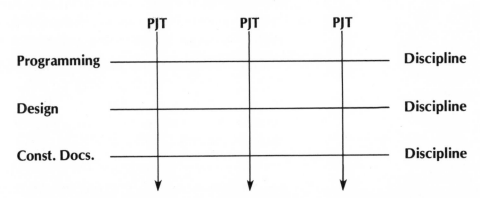

If you have an organizational form that makes sense for you and a management style that feels comfortable, you still have to motivate your employees to reach your goals. This is crucial, no matter what size your company is. And it isn't easy in this profession.

Unlike most professions, money doesn't seem to be a great motivator. As you can tell from the chart on salary ranges published much earlier in this book, this is a terribly underpaid profession. And it is also low in benefits as well. One reason is that most designers are young, well under forty (where do they go when they grow up?) and interested in disposable income.

But to understand designers' motivations better, we should review the famous explanation of why people work, Maslow's pyramid.

People work first to satisfy their basic physiological needs, such as food and shelter.

When these are satisfied, they work to achieve security.

When they have achieved that, they work for the sense of affiliation that comes from belonging to a group with like interests and desires.

When they belong to such a group, they then strive because of competition and achievement, feeding their ego and increasing their status.

And at the end, they work towards self-actualization, making themselves as much as they can be.

Frank Herzberg suggests that once you gratify a need, it no longer motivates you. In this field, money (above a certain relatively low level) motivates people least. Designers' needs are for responsibility, achievement, recognition and status, chance for advancement, and self-actualization.

So you will engender the most loyalty if you allow designers some autonomy and responsibility for doing part of the project. If you then allow the designers to present their work to the client, giving them both internal and external recognition, you will probably keep these designers a long time, especially if their assignments continue to grow in size and importance.

There are only two difficulties with this wonderful, loving picture. First, if you are naturally autocratic, you will find it difficult to watch someone produce work inferior to that which you could produce or direct. Second, if you desire that the previous delightful scenario should continue, your firm must grow and get increasingly better assignments for your employees sake as well as your own.

Not all people are so demanding of you. Most staff people are more interested in security and benefits. If they actually want to be designers, you probably don't want them. As soon as they master the skills you need, they will be bored and demand their transfer into design.

To keep the best people, you have to give them responsibility, recognition, learning/growing experiences, and advancement. Strangely enough, top salaries don't seem to matter that much, and good size bonuses are often cheaper over all but have a greater positive impact on the recipient.

A bonus should relate to individual performance. Don't tie it to Christmas, unless you're giving everyone a meaningless $100. Do not consider a bonus the same as a salary increase. It is definitely not a substitute for sitting down with an individual once a year and giving him or her a fair review. And it should relate to the fortunes of the firm and what the owner is taking out for himself. There are no secrets in a small firm.

If you have a top professional you want to keep, and you've already given him all of the above, maybe you should give him a little piece of the action, a small share of the firm. The ownership should be bought, not given as a gift. If you wish to create the next generation of firm management, you can sell the ownership in installments.

But remember one thing, both as majority partner or minority partner. Minority partners really have no rights. None. That's both good news for the majority partner and bad news for the minority partners. Which are you? Which do you want to be?

Micro-Management Issues

If you have never run a business, you should know some of the basics. Both law and good management techniques require good records. I feel that a basic form such as the **Project Analysis Form** should be filled out as soon as you get a job so that you can assign it a project number and then track the project through its life span. This form will automatically start your scheduling process, your personnel assignment process, and keep track of all the statistics you will need to analyze your operation, as well as submit to get on Interior Design's "Top 100" or "Second 100 list.

You have to keep track of receipts (money received) and disbursements (money paid out). A list of these is kept by category (called accounts, each with their own number, in the journal of accounts).

Since few firms keep accounts on a cash basis, you may also have books kept on an accrual basis (don't worry, we'll discuss these terms later).

You should have complete records on the time people spend on projects for billing purposes and later justification, if required. A sample **Time Report Form** is included. Every employee should fill one out weekly. No pay checks should be handed out without these being up to date for the employee. Each hour should be coded by phase, or provide the reason for being unbillable. Revisions should be so noted, as well as out of scope work. Revision work is, of course, work done on a task after client approval. If such work is requested, it should be done only after consultation with the project manager. A separate number can be assigned, if so desired. This sort of work must be closely kept track of in order to justify asking for additional fee, if that is later required.

You also need to keep track of all moneys spent by your employees, whether or not on behalf of a client. A sample **Expense Report Form** is included. This is fairly self explanatory. Normally any expense over $20 requires a receipt as well. Any guests or non-billable charge should be explained with the name of the contact, their position, their company, and the reason for the contact.

When you meet with anyone and make decisions, you should have backup for those decisions in your minutes. A sample **Meeting Minutes Form** is included.

When you send anything to anyone connected with a project, you should keep backup records of that. A sample **Transmittal Form** is included. Its use is obvious.

Whenever you issue a report, drawings, or revisions of either, a copy should be kept in files.

All correspondence, both sent and received, should be filed in the job file. Copies of your notes from meetings, programming interviews, write-ups, etc. should be kept in the files.

Files should be kept open and accessible so anyone associated with the project can find out any important information necessary to complete their task. The only private files should be employment, payroll, insurance, and financial records. Most documents should be kept for seven years, although they don't have to be on the premises.

One hint to make sure file folders don't get lost is to stamp all file documents in red with "File Copy." Since copies will show the stamp in black, no one should end up with the original. To keep file copies in order, place them in a labeled file folder and place that file folder in a similarly labeled "Pendaflex" hanging file, so removed folders will be returned to the right place.

The greatest waste of time in this business, or any business for that matter, is in meetings. Try to manage meetings well. Decide in advance if it is necessary and who should be there, trying to keep the number of people as low as possible. Make sure you know who called it and why. Decide on an agenda in advance and send every attendee a copy. Set a time limit and stick to it. We all work better under pressure.

In long meetings allow time for bathroom breaks and avoid boredom. I also think you should avoid wasting people's time by holding all but the most important telephone calls until the end of the meeting.

Send out minutes or a "call report." Show who attended, what was discussed, what decisions were reached, what actions are required, who will perform them by what time, who will review them, and when and where the next meeting is. A **Call Report Form** is included to make it simpler for you to keep people informed. I don't believe clean typing is required if, like most designers, your lettering is clean and regular. Even if it isn't, you can just hand the completed form to the typist for retyping on an identical form and quick and painless distribution.

Telephone calls should be handled a bit like a meeting. Bunch your calls at one time. Have an agenda so you cover everything. An ordinary writing pad is fine. Write down the answers on the agenda to make sure you don't forget. State your name and company right away along with the person you are calling, to get through quickly. Never have someone else place the call, do so yourself. I find it terribly annoying to be called by someone's secretary so they don't waste their time if I'm not there, but I waste my time if I am.

Make your staff aware of how to handle incoming calls. They should all answer properly, with a good telephone voice with a greeting, the name of the company, and a, "May I help you?". When transferring a call, the person doing it should never hang up until the transfer is completed. People should pick up their transferred calls by stating their name.

No phone should ring more than three times. Anyone should be able to take a message. If the desired party is on another call, the message should be given to him or her immediately, and not wait until they happen to pass the switchboard. Make sure messages are not lost, but are kept in a central area.

All staff should check in and check out. This should clearly *not* be a time clock, but simply initial themselves in and out, without noting the time, in the morning, at lunch, at night, or any other time they leave. If they are doing their work,

PROJECT ANALYSIS FORM

Company: **T.I.D.**
Date: **1/30/83**
Person Completing Form: **A.T.**

Account Name: **Mon Dieu Cosmetics**

Project Address: **1234 RST RD** Billing Address: **2345 Post Road**
Hotford, CT **Hotford, CT**
06555 **06556**

Contact Name: **IKE EPSTEIN** Telephone Number: **260-5600**

Submitted By: **A.T.** Floor Numbers: **#3**
Officer-In-Charge **A.T.** New Space **18,000**
Project Coordinator **R.D.** Renovated Space:

Project Description:
High Style reception, board room, &
president's office — rest is general
office space.

Project Number: **83-19**
Revision Letter: **—**
Date Submitted: **10/5/83**
Start-Up Date: **10/1/83**
Date Closed: **—**

Proposed Area: **18,000 RSF**
Budgeted Cost: **$1,000,000**
Fee: (Maximum) **$39,000**

Actual Area: **18,329 RSF**
Actual Cost: **$ 998,275**
Actual Fee: **$ 39,000**
Actual Hours: **943**
Cost/Sq. Ft.: **$ 54.56**
Fee/Sq. Ft.: **$ 2.13**
Fee/Cost: **3.9%**
Fee/Hour: **$ 41.35**

Date	SCHEDULED EVENT
10/1/83	Start-Up
11/1/83	Program Approval
11/15/83	Allocation Approval
12/15/83	Layout Approval
12/15/83	Preliminary Budget Approval
12/15/83	Design Concept Meeting
1/15/84	Final Design & Budget Presentation
2/1/84	Final Design & Budget Approval
1/1/84	Preliminary Issue for Engineering
2/1/84	Engineering Drawings Returned
2/1/84	Purchase Order Approval
2/1/84	Construction Documents Issued
2/1/84	Start of Construction
2/15/84	Construction Details Issued
5/1/84	Move-In
5/31/84	Punch List Completed

BUDGET	Person Days Allocated		
Task Assignment	Skill Level	Hours Prop	Actual
A Survey		20	18
B Programming		100	105
C Lease Negotiation		—	—
D Design	HIGH!	125	148
E Budgeting		50	48
F Decorative Design	HIGH!	95	140
G Furnishings Specifications & P.O.		25	30
H General Construction Drawings		185	199
I Construction Details		90	87
J Construction Specifications		25	26
K Bidding/Contractor Negotiation		20	20
L Field Supervision & Punch List		75	68
M Project Supervision		45	54
N General Office Work		50	61
Total:		855	943

TIME REPORT FORM

| Time Report Form For: | F. M. |
| Week Ending: | 12/18/83 |

Job Name / Job Number	Monday 12/12/83 hrs.	cd	Tuesday 12/13 hrs.	cd	Wednesday 12/14 hrs.	cd	Thursday 12/15 hrs.	cd	Friday 12/16 hrs.	cd	Weekend 12/17-18 hrs.	cd	JOB TOTAL
F&M 82-18	1	E			1	E							2
GG&G 82-23					2	D	2	D					4
TCBC-2 83-3	1	D			1	D	2	D	2	D			6
J&K 83-9			2	C	1	C	1	C					3
MDC 83-19	2	A/R											
	2	B	4	B	4	B	4	B	2	B			18
TCBC-3 83-10	2	B	2	B									4
T.I.D.									4	M			4
DAILY TOTALS	8		8		9		9		8				

EXPLANATIONS: MDC - 2A/R - revised program after change in D.P. equipment
T/D - 4M - work on new brochure

Signature: _____ Date: 12/19/83
Approved: _____ Date:

CODES:

Billable		Unbillable	
A	Phase 1	M	Marketing
B	Phase 2	H	Holiday
C	Phase 3	V	Vacation
D	Phase 4	S	Sick Leave
E	Phase 5	Z	Other
R	Revision	O	Out of Scope

EXPENSE REPORT FORM

Expense Report Form For:	A.T.
Week Ending:	12/10/83

CATEGORY Date	Sun 12/4/83	Mon /5/	Tues /6/	Wed /7/	Thur /8/	Fri /9/	Sat 12/10/83	TOTAL
City			Hatford					
City			NYC					
Job Name								
Job No.								
Job Name								
Job No.								
Lodging								
Auto @ _/mi			8					8
Taxi To			15					15
Air Fare			110					110
Prepaid?	☐ Yes ☐ No	☐ Yes ☐ No	☑ Yes ☐ No	☐ Yes ☐ No	☐ Yes ☐ No	☐ Yes ☐ No	☐ Yes ☐ No	
Rail Fare								
Prepaid?	☐ Yes ☐ No	☐ Yes ☐ No	☐ Yes ☐ No	☐ Yes ☐ No	☐ Yes ☐ No	☐ Yes ☐ No	☐ Yes ☐ No	
Bus Fare								
Prepaid?	☐ Yes ☐ No	☐ Yes ☐ No	☐ Yes ☐ No	☐ Yes ☐ No	☐ Yes ☐ No	☐ Yes ☐ No	☐ Yes ☐ No	
Taxi From			15					15
Local Taxi			4⁵⁰	5⁷⁵	4²⁵			
Local Taxi			3⁵⁰	6²⁵	4⁵⁰			32⁰⁰
Local Taxi			3⁷⁵					
Local Taxi								
Local Taxi								
Local Taxi								
Bkfast								
Guests?*	☐ Yes ☐ No	☐ Yes ☐ No	☐ Yes ☐ No	☐ Yes ☐ No	☐ Yes ☐ No	☐ Yes ☐ No	☐ Yes ☐ No	
Lunch			55	35	29			119
Guests?*	☐ Yes ☐ No	☐ Yes ☐ No	☑ Yes ☐ No	☑ Yes ☐ No	☑ Yes ☐ No	☐ Yes ☐ No	☐ Yes ☐ No	
Dinner						87		87
Guests?*	☐ Yes ☐ No	☐ Yes ☐ No	☐ Yes ☐ No	☐ Yes ☐ No	☐ Yes ☐ No	☑ Yes ☐ No	☐ Yes ☐ No	
Other								
Other								
Other								
Other								
Other								

*Explain Why and For Whom:		Bill Client	For		
12/6/83 I. Epstein/MDC		MDC 12/6	174⁷⁵		
12/7 Kay Tyke/Adds.					
12/8 Sam Malone/FPI					

Weekly Total:	406⁵⁰
Less Prepaid:	100
Less Advances:	100
Amount Due Employee:	196⁵⁰
or	
Amount Due Company:	

APPROVAL	
Signature	Date:
Supervisor	
Accounting	

MEETING MINUTES FORM

Company:	T.I.D.
Date:	2/4/84
Person Completing Form:	A.T.

Client Name:	M.D.C.
Date of Meeting:	2/4/84
Location of Meeting:	@ MDC
Purpose of Meeting:	EVALUATION OF EXECUTIVE FURNITURE

Attendees:
A.T. } T.I.D.
F.M. }
J. James — ESD Dealers
Ike Epstein — M.D.C.
L. M. Drake — MDC

CC Also:
File

Discussion:	Decisions/Actions Date to be done by, Responsibility of:
1. Showed I.E. three alternatives to unavailable green olive wood — he chose finish CC3T on laurel wood	— ORDER Desk as designed — in Laurel - CC3T
2. Must now re-examine leather chosen for exec. & visitor chairs.	— HOLD UP P.O. for chairs until further review
3. Reviewed progress to date — * I.E. said he just got a JCN personal computer + Qene printer — Design separate "sub-desk" for computer- Match main desk — (sub-desk on wheels?)	— Design computer "sub-desk" pronto!

Next Meeting Day:	2/11/84
Time:	8 AM
Place:	MDC

TRANSMITTAL FORM

Date:	2/4/84

FROM:

Company:	Top Interior Design
Address:	14285 Post Road
	Tertiary, CT 05432
Tel. #	(203) 879-4944
By:	A.T.

TO:

Company:	Wood Smooth
Address:	29 Spruce Lane
	Hotspur, CT 06432
Tel. #	(203) 841-2221
Att:	Rich Smithe

RE:

Client:	Mon Dieu Cosmetics
Address:	187 Post Road

Job:	M.D.C.
Job #:	83-27
Address:	200 Post Road
	Eighth Floor

Material is being sent to you:	by:	the following: # sheets 3	for:
☑ enclosed	☐ mail	☐ original dwgs	☐ approval
☐ under separate cover	☐ messenger	☑ prints	☐ revisions
☐	☐ telecopier	☐ specifications	☐ your information
	☑ Ephemeral Express	☐ specifications	☑ estimate
		☐ photostats	☐ bid
		☐ samples	☐
		☐ other	

Drawing #	Revision Date	# of Copies	Description
C.D. 1-2-3	2/4/84	1 each	New computer desk for M.D.C. (for Mr. Epstein, President!)

you don't care that they are responsible for their own time. You just want to make sure no messages are lost or not taken care of properly.

Managing people is really much tougher than following all these silly rules and regulations. You have to be a very accomplished listener. Listen to what people say. Observe what they actually do. Deal with the differences between them.

Provide good examples. People work long hours if the head of the office does. People take long lunches if their boss does. People are perfectionists if the principal is. People care, if you do.

You should really care about your people. You are probably with each other more than with your families. They become another family and if you think of them that way, they will think of you that way. You can still be autocratic, perfectionist, hard-working, or whatever, but be fair and care.

13 Types of Business Organizations

When you decide to enter business, you must choose in which legal form your business will be. The choices are **sole proprietorship**, **limited partnership**, **general partnership**, **corporation**, and "**Subchapter S**" corporation. A few professionals can also choose a professional corporation.

Each form varies in its characteristics in terms of organizational requirements, costs of start-up, costs of maintaining the organization, the personal liability of the owners, the continuity and transferability of the firm, the latitude management is allowed in running the firm, the ease of raising capital, and the taxation of profits.

If you form any organization with a partner (except, obviously, the sole proprietorship), you will need an agreement. That agreement should cover all four of the following areas.

The first part of the agreement should deal with the capital it will take to start and run the firm. Who will put in what amount of capital? Will it all be in cash? If not, how will the value of the other input be assessed? How will additional capital be raised from external sources initially? How will it be raised from other sources in the future? What initial stock or percentage of ownership goes to whom? How will that be changed in the future for more capital or more partners? How can more stock be issued?

The second part of the agreement has to deal with the management of the firm. Who will have the power to make decisions? What kinds of decisions will require what percentage of the ownership to agree? Who will attend to the day-to-day running of the firm? Who will make the longer-term decisions? How can they be challenged or changed? What responsibilities does each owner have day-to-day? Long term? Who will measure performance and how will it be measured?

The distribution of moneys and profits must also be considered before you enter into any agreement. What will the salaries or draws be? How will they change in the future? How will profits be distributed? How can that be changed? What insurance and pension plans will be installed? How will they be protected?

Lastly, the concept of ownership must be defined. Can the ownership be sold or transferred? Are there limits on that? As shareholders' equity or the value of the firm changes, how will it be distributed? Who can end the agreement; how;

and what happens then? How many people will it take to do so? What happens with the death or retirement of one or more owners?

All these issues must be addressed in the formal agreement that starts the company. The agreement must be in writing and signed by all parties. Each should be represented by an attorney. If you can't agree about an issue, don't form the company. If the agreement is too hard to agree to, perhaps the company would end up similarly contentious and unworkable.

Let's look more closely at the different alternatives you have.

The *Sole Proprietorship* is the simplest to set up. All you have to do is register the name your firm will do business under with the county clerk for the main office location. There are no more organizational requirements or costs, except those your attorney may suggest. The income of the firm can be distributed or used in any way the owner wishes. Profits, if any, will be taxed as personal income. It can be sheltered only in the same ways that individuals can try to shelter their own income.

The owner has unlimited personal liability for the actions of his company. In the event of a catastrophe not covered by insurance, personal bankruptcy laws would be followed. Since there is almost no protection for investors, it is difficult to raise capital for a sole proprietorship. You can raise money as an individual, based on your talent, connections, and assets, but it is easier to get a loan based on your assets, such as your home.

The company ends with the death or retirement of the proprietor. He is also totally free to sell or transfer the firm, but in a service business such as this, there is very little to sell or transfer.

The *General Partnership* form of business entity is a common one in this field. All partners should have signed an agreement covering capital, management, profit distribution, and changes of ownership before joining the partnership. Legally, there are few organizational requirements or costs. At least one general partner has to exist and the name of the firm and partnership papers should be registered with the county clerk.

As in the sole proprietorship, the task of raising capital is difficult since an investor has relatively little protection. If he becomes a partner, he becomes fully liable for the actions of all the other partners. If he doesn't, there is relatively little he could sue for in a service business.

The distribution of profits and assets is done in any way the partners agree to, since profits have already been taxed individually as personal income for each partner as per the initial agreement.

Each owner has unlimited personal liability not only for his own actions, but for the actions of his partners as well. Personal bankruptcy is the only protection, besides ample insurance, that ultimately protects the partners.

Management of this kind of firm is usually done by the partner or partners with the majority interest. There is some small amount of legal regulation.

The general partnership is dissolved by the death of any partner unless there is an agreement that specifies some other result. Usually, too, the transfer of any partner's ownership can be accomplished with the consent of all of the other partners, unless a previous agreement specifies some other way of handling it.

The *Limited Partnership* is very popular in real estate, but not very popular in service businesses. Depending on the state, a written financial and partnership agreement may be required. (If a public offering is involved, which would not happen in this field, the requirements are far more complex and stringent.) There must be at least one general partner and one limited partner.

Because the limited partners liability is limited to the amount they have invested or have agreed to invest, the ease of the general partners raising capital is greatly improved. The general partner(s) have unlimited personal liability.

Only general partners manage the firm, usually by majority rule, although there are some legal regulations protecting limited partners. All profits and losses are taxed as personal income. General partners decide, usually by majority rule although sometimes by previous agreement, on the distribution of profits and assets.

The continuity and transferability of the firm is the same as it is for general partnerships, except that limited partners always have the right to sell their partnership share.

The *Corporation* is the most complex and expensive type of organization to form. You would need to have articles of incorporation, and pay legal and filing fees based on the corporate structure. You can incorporate in almost any state, regardless of your residence, and some states such as Delaware offer cost advantages. If you are interested in this, you need competent legal advice.

The corporation, in various forms, is one of the most attractive forms of a company to raise capital with. The liability of each investor is limited to his investment. Officers and directors have personal liability only for any criminal actions they might perform. Ownership is through the owning of stock. Any amount can be issued and there can be more than one class of stock, each of which has different rights, within legal limits.

The management of a corporation is done by the board of directors as elected by the stockholders. This has the most legal requirements of any form of firm.

Corporate profits are usually taxed when earned by the corporation. They are also taxed when distributed as dividends to the stockholders. Thus the primary drawback of corporations is often referred to as "double taxation."

There are some ways around this. Profits of the corporation can be kept by the company as "retained earnings," and distributed later or not at all. (The IRS monitors this and will not allow a company to keep "excess" retained earnings over a certain limit.) If the stock increases in value because of retained earnings, operating profits, or anything else, and is sold at a profit, it is usually taxed

TYPES OF BUSINESS ENTERPRISES

This chart was developed to explain to my students the variety of business enterprises available to interior designers, and the characteristics, including both the advantages and disadvantages of each type. If you are starting up a new business, this information may help you to decide on the form your business should be. Although the data have been checked by three lawyers, I do not guarantee their applicability to any particular situation.

CHARACTERISTICS / TYPE OF ORGANIZATION	ORGANIZATIONAL REQUIREMENTS AND COSTS	EASE OF RAISING CAPITAL	LIABILITY OF OWNERS
SOLE PROPRIETORSHIP	Nominal organizational requirements and costs. Must register tradename with county clerk responsible for main office locale.	Difficult because no protection for investor. Based on individuals' talents, assets, connections and character.	Unlimited personal liability.
GENERAL PARTNERSHIP	Should have predetermined agreements covering all other characteristics. Nominal costs. Need at least 1 G.P. Trade name and partnership papers registered as above.	Difficult because no protection for interest. Based on individuals' talents, assets, connections and character.	Unlimited personal liability. Each partner is also liable for any other partner's actions.
LIMITED PARTNERSHIP	Written agreement and financial statement may be required. Slightly more expensive than General Partnership, but handled the same. However, totally different if public offering is involved.	Limited liability of limited partners improves on general partners ability to raise capital.	General partners have unlimited personal liability. Limited partners' liability limited to amount invested or agreed to invest.
CORPORATION	Need articles of incorporation, pay legal fees and filing fees based on corporate structure. The most expensive organization.	One of the most attractive forms.	Liability limited to amounts invested by each individual, except of officer's and director's liability resulting from criminal actions.
SUBCHAPTER "S" CORPORATION	Same as corporation. Status must be chosen at moment of incorporation.	May be more attractive than corp. as losses can shelter personal income and earnings can be distributed as capital gains.	Same as corporation.

When it comes time to consult a lawyer, choose one from personal reference and reputation within your field. Avoid friends and relatives and spend as much as is necessary to get the best. In the long run, expensive good advice costs less than inexpensive mediocre advice. And finally, choose someone you feel comfortable speaking with. The best legal talent in the world does you little good if you can't relax enough to discuss issues in whatever depth you need to. You must be able to ask dumb questions, and challenge smart assumptions or quick answers in order to get the service you need and deserve.

But remember the cardinal rule of small business: *No one cares as much about your business as you do.* So before you seek advice on any issue, learn as much about it as you can. After all, you may be hiring all those high-priced experts for their advice, but you must make the final decision on each issue.

MANAGEMENT LATITUDE	TAXATION (overly simplified)	DISTRIBUTION OF PROFITS AND ASSETS	CONTINUITY AND TRANSFERABILITY OF FIRM
Complete latitude with minimal legal regulation.	Company profit or loss is taxed as personal income when earned.	As desired by individual. These have already been taxed.	Company ends with death of proprietor. He is also totally free to sell or transfer.
Usually managed by majority of interests with some legal regulation.	Company profit or loss is taxed as personal income when earned.	As agreed by the partners. Usually majority of interests rules. No rules on distribution of profits as they have already been taxed.	Dissolved by death of any partner unless continued by previous agreement. Can be transferred by consent of all partners unless otherwise agreed.
Only general partners manage, majority required, some legal regulation.	Partnership profit and loss is taxed as personal income.	As desired by the general partners. Usually majority rule is sufficient. These have already been taxed.	Same as General Partnership except limited partners always have right to sell. Transfer is by consent of all General Partners unless otherwise agreed.
Management by Board of Directors as elected and therefore influenced by the stockholders. Has the most legal regulations.	Corporate profits are taxed at the corporate level when earned and taxed again when distributed to the individual as dividends. Some taxes can be minimized.	Sales of stock are usually capital gains. Section 1244 stock allows losses to be personal income losses and not capital losses.	Continues regardless of death, sale or withdrawal of any managing stockholder. Transferred by stock, assets, assigned income, etc.
Same as corporation.	Corporate profits are considered as distributed to the investors each year and taxed as such, just as in a general partnership.	Profits and losses have already been taxed. Any additional profits from dissolution are taxed as personal income also.	Same as corporation.

at the "capital gains" rate well below the personal income rate. And if stock is issued as "Section 1244" stock, losses of the corporation will be passed along directly to the investors as personal income losses rather than capital losses.

Corporations are treated as individuals by the law. Their life continues regardless of the death or withdrawal of any managing stockholder. Ownership can be transferred by sale of stock, assets, assigned income, etc.

There is another form of corporation available to people just starting a company. The *Subchapter "S" Corporation* must be chosen as the desired form at the moment of incorporation. You can not change to it later, although you can change from it to a regular corporation at any future time. The only way that it differs from a regular corporation, other than in the number of initial stockholders and other items of little importance, is that all income or losses of the firm are treated as ordinary income of the stockholders.

This avoids the penalty of double taxation and passes losses along at the full rate (a benefit as a tax shelter, although hopefully not for long). It thus becomes even more desirable as an investment, and a better way to raise capital, than a regular corporation, in the early years when losses or low profits are expected.

Another form of corporation is now possible, the *Professional Corporation*. This was created to allow *licensed* professionals, such as doctors and architects, to take advantage of certain pension plans. This is no longer very important since IRA's, Keogh Accounts, and other pension plans have become legal. The partners in a professional corporation are individually professionally liable for their own actions, but not for other partners' actions. Since it does not apply to most of us, I have not included it as an option.

This is just one aspect of the legal area you will get involved in. We will discuss the others in the next chapter.

14 Choosing Your Advisers

Every business needs good advice. The big companies have boards of directors composed of the most knowledgeable advisers they can get. You need the same thing, no matter how small your company is. Your board of advisers should consist of an attorney, an accountant, a banker, an insurance broker, and any other knowledgeable people you can get to give you good advice.

Even with the best advisers in the world, never forget the number one rule of small business: *No one cares as much about your business as you do.* Not your employees or investors, not your banker or accountant, not your lawyer or broker — not even your mother.

Professionals, even your best friends, or advisers, may not give your problems as much consideration as they deserve. Therefore you have to understand as much about all the issues as you can, so your questions will prompt people who know better to use their knowledge fully. They won't actually make any decisions. They will give you their best advice, and you will make the decisions.

Also remember, *there are no dumb questions, only dumb answers.* Ask whatever you want to. Never stop because you don't want to reveal your ignorance. You are hiring these "experts" to eliminate your ignorance. They can't do it if you won't give them your ignorance to eliminate!

The choice of an attorney is an extremely important one. Never use a personal friend and never, ever use a relative.

The interior design field is one of the most complicated fields around. It is a service business, but with many contracts involved with each client. Notwithstanding the service aspects, we produce products and deal with products of other corporations. We may have inventory and/or get involved with resale of items. Our product has both tangible and intangible results that might have to meet certain performance requirements.

Your first choice should be to try to get a specialist in this field, or at the very least someone familiar with some of the aspects of it. The best way to get an attorney is through references from other designers. Not only will he be familiar with the field, but those other designers may have paid for his education in interior design, making his services more efficient for you. If you don't know any attorneys or designers with good attorneys, look in the *Martindale-*

Hubbell Legal Directory which is available at most libraries. This lists lawyers, their clients, financial references, and rates general ability, although not related to this field in particular.

Interview prospective attorneys. You must feel comfortable with them and able to open up about your problems. You should also find an attorney who will give you his attention, not that of a junior member of the firm after you have hired the senior partner. Sometimes it works well, if all members of the firm are equally ignorant concerning the specifics of this field, to choose one of the junior partners. (A "partner" is an owner of the firm. An "associate" is an employee.) If anyone is going to have to research many of the questions you ask, it might as well be one of the cheapest bodies in the firm. And you will probably be one of his first clients, so he will be very interested in helping you and building up his own practice.

Try to work out an arrangement where you will not be nickeled and dimed to death. It is best to put the attorney on a retainer, so besides the big issues such as contracts, you can call up and ask a quick question at any time, without feeling that the clock is ticking away. It is psychologically easier to spend $1,000 at one time than lots of $20 bills on phone calls. Anything that encourages you to use your counsel whenever you think you might need it, before you become desperate, is worthwhile.

Once you have an attorney, he should help establish the firm, acting as a sounding board for your initial ideas. He should help you to choose the organizational form, write any necessary agreements, and handle the registrations of your name, stock, incorporation, and so on. He should review all your legal documents, including your letter of agreement or standard contract form, purchase order form, subcontracts, reporting requirements, and so on. He should review any contracts you enter into with anyone.

In contract design, you are working for other businesses. They usually have attorneys on retainer, and you should have one as well. Consider good legal representation an expense, like insurance. It seems like such a waste until you need it, and then it's a tragedy if you don't have the best possible.

The second person you need on your board of advisers is a good accountant. If you are like most designers, you dislike numbers and detest them when they appear in columns, as in your accounts payable. But businesses live, and die, strictly by their numbers. So you need a good numbers adviser.

There is an old story about how you should choose your accountant. Have all the applicants wait outside and invite them in one at a time. Ask each the simple question, "How much is two plus two?" If he answers "three," or "five" dismiss him as incompetent. If one answers "four," dismiss him as too literal. Keep interviewing until you get someone with the correct answer.

Oh yes, the correct answer is, "How much would you like it to be, Mr. Designer?" That is the accountant you want!

That is not illegal or silly. There is a great deal of leeway in accounting principles and the tax codes about almost all accounting issues. You want to hire someone who understands those issues and can help you make the decisions about such matters as when to recognize income or how to set up your profit-sharing plan.

Of course, just as with lawyers, you are better off with someone recommended by another designer or with experience in this field. Usually you are better off with a CPA, (Certified Public Accountant) than just a bookkeeper. You may use a bookkeeper to maintain your records and deal with daily issues, but you need someone to help you set up your accounting procedure as well as for important advice.

When you interview for accounts, you need to look for the same qualities you looked for in an attorney. The individual should either be knowledgeable about the field or able and willing to learn, approachable and easy to speak with, sympathetic, helpful, and someone you feel comfortable with.

Once you get an accountant, he or she will be responsible for seeing that you set up your book of accounts properly, establish a standard billing and payment procedure, and so on. More importantly, you should seek the advice of your accountant on formulating reasonable monetary goals for the firm and for yourself. He should help formulate strategies for you to use to make the firm's goals coincide with your goals.

You should be able to use his advice, and the money-making machine you create, to control your income to the level which balances taxes and yearly uses of funds. The rest of your income can be deployed for future recovery at lower tax rates or saved for your ultimate retirement, or even controlled for estate-planning purposes.

You should set up a mechanism so you both know where you stand on at least a monthly basis. You can save a fortune with the right advice, so don't be cheap. Get the best you can.

Bankers are a little harder to get on your team. Normally you need to have quite a bit of capital, or alternatively be in debt up to your eyeballs, before one takes an interest in you. In this day of megabanks with automated teller machines handling most transactions, it is hard to even meet a teller, let alone an officer.

You should make the effort. If you are starting out, you probably need at least $50,000 capital just to set up an office with a secretary and a drafter for half a year. If you have half of that in cash and want to know what to do with it until you spend it, someone at the bank would like to help you make that decision, and perhaps give you a clock-radio for your interest.

The point is you have to have money to start a business, and it may be enough to establish a relationship with a bank. As soon as you can, wave a big check in front of an officer, talk about your business, have letterhead and cards all ready to hand to him or her, and start to talk about what else you might need.

A line of credit is a great way to get them interested. This is a pre-approved loan up to a certain limit that you can take out as you need it. In order to get it, the loan is paid for both in interest after you start "drawing down" the loan and in the need to keep a "compensating balance" of some amount in a specific kind of account. In other words, if you have money the bank will loan you more money.

There are several benefits to having a banker on your "board."

First, when you need money, it is more likely that you will get funds from a bank than an investor. Having a friend at a bank may get you funds when they are scarce and at a better price than might be available elsewhere. And bankers have a vast supply of friends and contacts in the business world. They all may need interior design services sometime in the future. When they think of funding the changes, or new leases, or new building programs, and come talk to your friendly banker, he might mention the services of another one of his clients — you.

The fourth specific professional you might want to have as an adviser is an insurance broker. This is hardly as important as any of the other three, but there are two good reasons for having one.

Just like the banker and the attorney, the insurance broker has many other clients in the business community and can provide you with contacts and names of firms needing insurance for new space, buildings, etc. Also, you will need certain types of insurance, both by law and by prudent business practices. And as long as you will be paying these fees one way or the other, why not try to get the best person on your team as you can? Get someone you can communicate with easily. Find someone who knows as much about the insurance field as possible, including all companies and all types of coverage. This means you want an independent agent, not a specific insurance company's broker.

The insurance you must have is workman's compensation, if you have even one employee. If you operate a vehicle for the business, whether yours, the business's, or an employee's, you must have automobile insurance including both property and personal injury.

Most firms have some group health insurance including major medical, hospitalization, and disability, although they may split the cost with the employees. You may want to add group life insurance as well.

In terms of business insurance, you should have fire and theft insurance, general liability, and personal injury insurance. You may also want to have insurance for your valuable papers, accounts receivable, and so on.

All of this adds up to a pretty penny. You might as well get as much as you can for your money and get as good an insurance adviser as you can.

Of course, you should have any number of advisers for both the business aspects and the interior design aspects of your firm. If you find interested people who are willing to offer good advice for the price of a lunch or dinner, make use of them.

Established furniture dealers, contractors, realtors, and so on are all worth having on your Board. A funny thing happens to people when they give you advice. They tend to become partisans, interested in your success. Keep them informed and keep asking for help. You win both ways.

When you have a board of advisers with at least an attorney, an accountant, a banker, and an insurance broker, you have possible entre into four of the main professions in the business community who use your services the most, and all have other clients. Here is your chance to write articles for their professional journals, address their professional meetings, and get lists of firms in each field who might need your services.

None of this is sneaky. This is just good clean marketing. And if you have something to offer, you will be doing people a favor. Remember that marketing is the lifeblood of your organization. You should never forget that. Never decide that you can work on design or business aspects without considering marketing. The best designers are always marketing themselves. You should too.

15 Financial Management

You may work for the pleasure of designing, but you run a business for the pleasure of counting profits. To do that regularly, you have to understand some of the basic concepts of financial management.

An absolutely key management concept is that of **Working Capital**. In a nutshell, working capital is the money it takes to keep running a business while you are earning your fees that won't be paid until later.

After you sign a design contract, you usually agree to bill monthly for services rendered. Let us assume you have a contract that requires that one employee work fulltime for one year to complete it. After he has worked one month, you pay him one month's salary along with checks to the landlord, the electric company, the phone company, the blueprint company, and so on (ad nauseum).

You also have the great pleasure of sending a bill to the client for roughly three times that designer's salary that will cover all those other bills and leave a little more left over as profit for you.

Your client receives your bill, puts it into the monthly billing cycle, and issues you a check for the full amount on the last day of the second month. Of course by that time you have worked *another* month, and had to pay a second month of salary, rent, utilities, and so on.

In order not to go bankrupt, you have to have at least two months of money in order to keep working to earn your fees. That money is *working capital*. In this example, which is really an optimistic view of the world, you had to have the value of two months total expenses in working capital to keep your business going. In the real world, clients tend to be even slower at paying their bills, and you probably need three months expenses of working capital in order to stay afloat.

If you start up a business and run it at a steady pace for a while, the 20 percent profit you make (with luck) on each and every billing because it is built into your multiple, will eventually wipe out your need for working capital and let you build up a tidy cash profit. If we assume that your designer costs you $2,000 per month, your expenses run $3,000 per month, and your profit should be another $1,000 per month, your multiple will be 3 on salary. We can look at Example 1 and see how your profit finally wipes out your working capital need at the end of the twelfth month. The next year you would start to build up a capital surplus.

Now let us look at a much tougher problem. Let us suppose that all that we just proposed takes place for each design project you sell. Let us also suppose that the projects each last one year and, great news, you are able to sell a new one each of the first six months of the year. Given that you are a typical design firm, you hire people only when you need them and let them go when the work is over.

As you can see from Example 2, building a business demands an enormous amount of working capital. In this little example, your cash on hand has gotten down to -$45,000. You can easily go bankrupt by being exceptionally successful!

There are two more related concepts you should know about that go hand in glove with these examples. These are the accounting principles of measuring profits on the **Cash Basis** and on the **Accrual Basis**.

The cash basis for accounting is easy to understand. We count (recognize, in accounting language) expenditures when we pay them and income when we get paid. If we imagine the "little tin box" made famous in the musical "Fiorello," whatever goes out is an expenditure and whatever comes in is income. However much we have on December 31st compared to what we started with on January 1st is our profit.

That works well in a cash economy, which does not exist any more. Accountants started asking when would we recognize the expenditure or receipt of funds when checks are involved. Do we actually earn our fee when we sign the contract, perform the work, bill for services, receive the check, deposit the check, or when that check clears? The usual test is when is our income actually *assured*. In this field income is usually *recognized* either when the work is completed or the bill is sent. This is accounting on the accrual basis.

It would not be so important, except that the IRS normally expects to tax you on your profits as measured on the accrual basis. If we assume that your "paper profits" based on the accrual method are based on income recognized on the date of billing, and apply that to the two previous examples, look at what we come up with.

In our first example, we finally broke even in the last month. But on the accrual basis, we would have had a "paper profit" of $12,000. While that is all in our Accounts Receivable, we don't have any of it yet. But the IRS will expect you to pay your taxes on that "profit" even though you have not yet received it. You need even more working capital!

Now if you compare your successful expansion effort on the Cash Basis in Example 2 with the same successful effort on the Accrual Basis in Example 5, you will see an even more dramatic difference. On a cash basis, your taxable profits are actually a loss of $15,000 while on the accrual basis, your taxable

===

EXAMPLE 1: One Job, Cash Accounting, Year One

===

	JAN	FEB	MAR	APR	MAY	JUN	JUL	AUG	SEP	OCT	NOV	DEC	YR END TOTAL
Number of Jobs.........	1	1	1	1	1	1	1	1	1	1	1	1	
Salary for Job.........	2000	2000	2000	2000	2000	2000	2000	2000	2000	2000	2000	2000	24000
Overhead..............	3000	3000	3000	3000	3000	3000	3000	3000	3000	3000	3000	3000	36000
Fee Billed............	6000	6000	6000	6000	6000	6000	6000	6000	6000	6000	6000	6000	72000
Cash Received.........	0	0	6000	6000	6000	6000	6000	6000	6000	6000	6000	6000	60000
Cash on Hand..........	-5000	-10000	-9000	-8000	-7000	-6000	-5000	-4000	-3000	-2000	-1000	0	0
Taxable Profits.......	-5000	-10000	-9000	-8000	-7000	-6000	-5000	-4000	-3000	-2000	-1000	0	0
Accounts Receivable....	6000	12000	12000	12000	12000	12000	12000	12000	12000	12000	12000	12000	12000

===

example2

===

EXAMPLE 2: One to Six Jobs, Cash Accounting, Year One

===

	JAN	FEB	MAR	APR	MAY	JUN	JUL	AUG	SEP	OCT	NOV	DEC	YR END TOTAL
Number of Jobs.........	1	2	3	4	5	6	6	6	6	6	6	6	
Salary for Job.........	2000	4000	6000	8000	10000	12000	12000	12000	12000	12000	12000	12000	114000
Overhead..............	3000	6000	9000	12000	15000	18000	18000	18000	18000	18000	18000	18000	171000
Fee Billed............	6000	12000	18000	24000	30000	36000	36000	36000	36000	36000	36000	36000	342000
Cash Received.........	0	0	6000	12000	18000	24000	30000	36000	36000	36000	36000	36000	270000
Cash on Hand..........	-5000	-15000	-24000	-32000	-39000	-45000	-45000	-39000	-33000	-27000	-21000	-15000	-15000
Taxable Profits.......	-5000	-15000	-24000	-32000	-39000	-45000	-45000	-39000	-33000	-27000	-21000	-15000	-15000
Accounts Receivable....	6000	18000	30000	42000	54000	66000	72000	72000	72000	72000	72000	72000	72000

===

example3

===

EXAMPLE 3: Six Jobs, Cash Accounting, Year Two

===

	JAN	FEB	MAR	APR	MAY	JUN	JUL	AUG	SEP	OCT	NOV	DEC	YR END TOTAL
Number of Jobs.........	6	6	6	6	6	6	6	6	6	6	6	6	
Salary for Job.........	12000	12000	12000	12000	12000	12000	12000	12000	12000	12000	12000	12000	144000
Overhead..............	18000	18000	18000	18000	18000	18000	18000	18000	18000	18000	18000	18000	216000
Fee Billed............	36000	36000	36000	36000	36000	36000	36000	36000	36000	36000	36000	36000	432000
Cash Received.........	36000	36000	36000	36000	36000	36000	36000	36000	36000	36000	36000	36000	432000
Cash on Hand..........	-9000	-3000	3000	9000	15000	21000	27000	33000	39000	45000	51000	57000	57000
Taxable Profits.......	-9000	-3000	3000	9000	15000	21000	27000	33000	39000	45000	51000	57000	57000
Accounts Receivable....	72000	72000	72000	72000	72000	72000	72000	72000	72000	72000	72000	72000	72000

===

profits are $57,000. And you have $15,000 less than zero to pay your taxes on your profits which you have not yet seen.

This seems grossly unfair. However once you run at a steady pace for a while, there is actually no difference between the two methods. We can see from Examples 3 and 6, which are the results of running the firms a second year at the six job level, that they are very close. In the third year each would show a $72,000 profit and $72,000 in accounts receivable.

So the real difference occurs as you start up a firm, or if you grow aggressively and successfully. I doubt that the results would be as dramatic as the examples, since few firms sextuple in six months. But keep the principles in mind. And now you should have a better understanding of why you need good financial advice.

You should also know the basic accounting documents that will summarize your yearly performance. All companies use an **Income Statement** and a **Balance Sheet**. Another accounting summary sheet used by some companies is the **Sources and Uses of Funds**. All three of these sheets are done at least every year, usually every quarter, and for some firms, every month.

The Income Statement is simple to understand. It starts off with your income for the year or period being described. From that figure you subtract the costs of producing that income. In this industry that is almost all labor. Then you subtract the operating expenses which constitute your overhead. The result so far is your profit before taxes. You then subtract your taxes to show your profit after taxes.

The Sources and Uses of Funds document pinpoints where funds were generated and where they were expended. It is very useful if your design practice is part of a bigger operation, such as a dealership or an architectural practice, and both fees and sales are part of your income statement.

I feel you should separate all the parts of your business so you can view each as either a profit center or a marketing effort loss leader. In either case, you should know the exact profits or losses in order to judge the success or failure of each operation.

The Balance Sheet is more complicated to explain. Instead of looking at your operation over the course of a period, it looks at it in one moment in time, usually the last day of your fiscal year. It splits everything you have into *Assets* and *Liabilities*.

Your assets are items of value, such as inventory, cash, stocks, fixtures and fixed assets like desks and chairs, and your account receivables (which are, after all, IOU's to pay you money).

Your liabilities are items you may have to make good on in the future. This includes your account payables, your short and/or long term loans, the stock-holders equity (if you are incorporated), your retained earnings and net worth.

The assets and the liabilities are by definition always equal.

If you have more than one office, it may pay to run these documents through for each office. If you properly allocate the home office overhead, you may find that branch offices are less profitable than they seem to be.

You can also perform that kind of operation with separate projects run by different partners. It may pinpoint inequalities in either sources or uses of profits.

If you have understood this chapter so far, you are ready for the financial planning both for the firm and for yourself. It is similar to strategic planning and should mesh well with it. But in this case we are looking more closely at the planned and actual flow of money through the firm and ultimately into your pockets.

You should set budgets for profits, sales, expenses, and efficiencies in the production of your service product. These should all be monitored regularly and corrected as needed. People should know how well they are performing in meeting your goals and rewarded accordingly. Concentrate on what you think is important. The survival of the firm depends on money, not design, so watch your bottom line. And remember, *no one cares as much about your firm as you do*.

Set the budget for the profit of the firm to match your income needs. As you recall, you get compensated in three different ways:

First, you get compensated directly with salary and dividends. You can also compensate yourself indirectly by hiring your family. It may be better for taxes, but the IRS frowns on family members who get compensated for no work whatsoever. They should actually do some work.

Second, you get indirect compensation through benefits, such as insurance, pension plans, and so on. In a small firm, these should be tailored to your needs. If you have a big family, go heavily into the insurance aspects. If you are using this firm as your retirement plan, and you intend to do so, set up a good retirement plan, heavily biased towards staff with longevity. You can do this by setting a "vesting" procedure (the manner in which people who earn deferred benefits actually get to partake in them) that works well for you.

It is legal to "vest" people with 10 percent of their benefits per year of service, or, in an extreme case, give them nothing at all until they have been with the firm for ten years (this is called a "cliff" vestment). You can bias either a pension plan or a profit sharing plan to people with long tenure, but not both. Plan whatever works well for you...and whichever will keep the more valuable staff people involved. Usually the profit sharing plans are fairly short vesting periods while the pension plans are much longer. But how much of the firm's money is placed in which type of benefit is a management decision that you can make for your own benefit.

Third, you get compensated with "perks" (short for perquisites). This can be a

===

EXAMPLE 4: One Job, Accrual Accounting, Year One

===

	JAN	FEB	MAR	APR	MAY	JUN	JUL	AUG	SEP	OCT	NOV	DEC	YR END TOTAL
Number of Jobs.........	1	1	1	1	1	1	1	1	1	1	1	1	
Salary for Job.........	2000	2000	2000	2000	2000	2000	2000	2000	2000	2000	2000	2000	24000
Overhead...............	3000	3000	3000	3000	3000	3000	3000	3000	3000	3000	3000	3000	36000
Fee Billed.............	6000	6000	6000	6000	6000	6000	6000	6000	6000	6000	6000	6000	72000
Cash Received..........	0	0	6000	6000	6000	6000	6000	6000	6000	6000	6000	6000	60000
Cash on Hand...........	-5000	-10000	-9000	-8000	-7000	-6000	-5000	-4000	-3000	-2000	-1000	0	0
Taxable Profits........	1000	1000	1000	1000	1000	1000	1000	1000	1000	1000	1000	1000	12000
Accounts Receivable....	6000	12000	12000	12000	12000	12000	12000	12000	12000	12000	12000	12000	12000

===

example5

===

EXAMPLE 5: One to Six Jobs, Accrual Accounting, Year One

===

	JAN	FEB	MAR	APR	MAY	JUN	JUL	AUG	SEP	OCT	NOV	DEC	YR END TOTAL
Number of Jobs.........	1	2	3	4	5	6	6	6	6	6	6	6	
Salary for Job.........	2000	4000	6000	8000	10000	12000	12000	12000	12000	12000	12000	12000	114000
Overhead...............	3000	6000	9000	12000	15000	18000	18000	18000	18000	18000	18000	18000	171000
Fee Billed.............	6000	12000	18000	24000	30000	36000	36000	36000	36000	36000	36000	36000	342000
Cash Received..........	0	0	6000	12000	18000	24000	30000	36000	36000	36000	36000	36000	270000
Cash on Hand...........	-5000	-15000	-24000	-32000	-39000	-45000	-45000	-39000	-33000	-27000	-21000	-15000	-15000
Taxable Profits........	1000	2000	3000	4000	5000	6000	6000	6000	6000	6000	6000	6000	57000
Accounts Receivable....	6000	18000	30000	42000	54000	66000	72000	72000	72000	72000	72000	72000	72000

===

example6

===

EXAMPLE 6: Six Jobs, Accrual Accounting, Year Two

===

	JAN	FEB	MAR	APR	MAY	JUN	JUL	AUG	SEP	OCT	NOV	DEC	YR END TOTAL
Number of Jobs.........	6	6	6	6	6	6	6	6	6	6	6	6	
Salary for Job.........	12000	12000	12000	12000	12000	12000	12000	12000	12000	12000	12000	12000	144000
Overhead...............	18000	18000	18000	18000	18000	18000	18000	18000	18000	18000	18000	18000	216000
Fee Billed.............	36000	36000	36000	36000	36000	36000	36000	36000	36000	36000	36000	36000	432000
Cash Received..........	36000	36000	36000	36000	36000	36000	36000	36000	36000	36000	36000	36000	432000
Cash on Hand...........	-9000	-3000	3000	9000	15000	21000	27000	33000	39000	45000	51000	57000	57000
Taxable Profits........	6000	6000	6000	6000	6000	6000	6000	6000	6000	6000	6000	6000	72000
Accounts Receivable....	72000	72000	72000	72000	72000	72000	72000	72000	72000	72000	72000	72000	72000

===

company car, credit cards, expense accounts, travel and entertainment, and so on. If you are successful, you can have a chauffeur-driven limo, a private chef, and more. Ostensibly, these all have to be used to benefit the company in some form, usually marketing and sales. Only your accountant knows for sure.

You should be considering how to expand your private net worth and the company's net worth. Your accountant will be able to give you good advice on how to use your firm as a retirement plan and an estate plan. Of course this all depends on your running it like a business, not simply a design atelier or studio.

Once you've set your profit goals, you should automatically know your sales goals. If you are aiming for the standard 20 percent before taxes profit, your sales goal is five times that.

If you have a sales goal, you can check that out with your staff size. The Interior Design "Top 100" and "Second 100" articles give average efficiencies for different size firms and firms which specialize in different areas. If you are more efficient, all is well and good. If you are relatively inefficient, you should try to determine the reason. If you have complicated, difficult clients, perhaps you deserve more fee and should try to get it. (You can compare your fees per

CHART 10
Volume per Professional
As Support Staff Grows
(In Office Planning Firms)

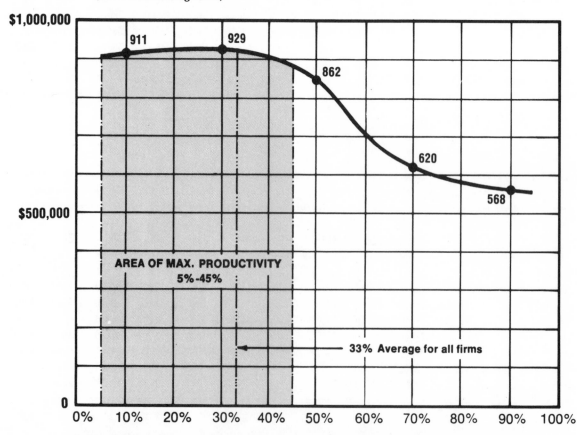

PERCENTAGE OF TOTAL STAFF ENGAGED IN SUPPORT FUNCTIONS

employee and per professional with the national averages in the same articles.) If you don't see any other reasons for your inefficiency, do you, perhaps, have to try to install some of the systems mentioned in the Construction Documentation chapter? Do you have too many or too few support people (see Chart10)? Do you need a skilled production manager to whip your people into shape? Perhaps you just have low paid, low-skilled workers. Is that appropriate to your clients? See if it is a problem or just part of your system.

Are you efficient or inefficient at getting paid? Check your statistics against the averages. Perhaps you need to bill more of the principal's time. Too often that is lost in the shuffle. Is your staff billing at least 85 percent of their time? If not, that is a correctible problem.

Are your reimbursables not getting billed? Any additional billing in that area, or any neglected area, goes straight to the bottom line as profits.

A real area of lost profit is running over the budget and not being able to bill for time spent. Is it a fault of the client, and should he be billed for revisions? Or do you have too many perfectionists on your staff who take as much time as you give them to complete a task, instead of the budgeted or appropriate amount of time? You must give them tasks with budgeted time limits to complete the job.

How much of your profit comes from overtime? Many design firms are overly profitable when they are busy because of this phenomenon, so when normal or slow times hit, profits plummet. Consider the basic situation during normal work hours. You pay an employee $1.00, overhead costs $1.50, and you bill the client $3.00, netting a $ .50 profit. Consider the standard overtime situation, with the employee making $1.50, there is *no more overhead*, and you bill the same $3.00, netting a $1.50 profit, *three times what you made during normal working hours*. If that employee is a salaried employee, not making the 50 percent bonus for overtime, *your profits are four times your normal profits*. And if you get to charge your multiple times the overhead rate, the $1.50 employee bills out at $4.50, costs are still just $1.50, and you make $3.00, *or six times your normal profits*.

It is not surprising that a busy firm can make tremendous profits. But if you were earning low profits to start, then this overtime bonanza is simply masking endemic problems that may crush you the moment work slows down. Look closely at your operation and balance it for profitable operation at normal work loads.

Manage your firm to make sure the expectation of the client, the owner, and the employee coincide. Set goals and be generous in rewarding staff for meeting those goals. Perhaps you should give 1 percent of a repeat contract right off the top to the people who did the previous work. Perhaps each employee should know that they will share 5 percent of the profits of any profitable job, as soon as it is finished. Perhaps you should give a cash bonus to the designers of any work that gets published.

The point of setting up the firm to benefit yourself is to remember that it only functions well when you also satisfy the needs of the other members of the firm.

Some firms are very generous with bonuses, but they put them into a fund that pays out a weekly bonus check along with each paycheck in the next year. So the bonus is for past performance but you get it for current attendance.

There are many ways to reward employees. Choose those that work well for you. Don't be greedy, just well informed, well planned, and a good manager. Keep the various aspects of managing your firm consistent. Let your employees know where you stand and where they stand. You should all profit together.

16 Computers

If sixth graders are using computers now, can you afford not to in your business? There are certainly any number of important business tasks that can be done more quickly and more easily by computer.

If you are writing new boiler-plate proposals by hand to each prospective client, you could save a lot of time by using **Word Processing**.

If you are sending out announcements to dozens or hundreds of past, present, and hopefully future clients by hand, you could use word processing with a **Mail Merge** feature to write and address each letter automatically once you write the first one.

If you want to send out hundreds of announcements and save money by grouping them by zip codes before mailing, you need a **Mailing List** program.

If your reports always seem to have at least one embarrassing typo, you could use word processing with a **Spelling and Grammar Checker** to make sure they are perfect.

If you are doing programming for a large, complicated client and the number of people in different standards doesn't ever seem to add up to the square footage you expect, you could be more accurate with a **Spreadsheet** program.

If a client calls up with a facilities management change and wants to see its ramifications in graphic form later that same day, you need a spreadsheet program with a **Graphics** package.

If you want to look at the efficiency your office has shown in producing work over the last decade and how that trend is changing in order to plan your rate structure, you need a spreadsheet program with a **Statistical** package.

If you wish to keep perfect track of all your customers, their purchases, their relative price ranges, their locations, their taste level, the names of their senior managers and the names of your people who take care of them, you need a **Database Management** program.

If you wish to know exactly what your accounts payable and receivable are, you need **Financial Programs** that would include your general ledger as well.

If you want to keep track of all the antiques you've purchased for eventual resale to future clients, you could add an **Inventory** program to the other financial programs.

If you want to do your own taxes, starting on April 14th, and keep a dinner date the next day, you need a **Tax Package**.

Nearly anything you could think of doing can now be done relatively inexpensively with computers. A very complete system to handle all the needs of a small business should cost less than $15,000 for both hardware and software.

But you need to be well prepared for such a change in the manner in which you do business. Far more harm than good can come from computerizing a system that is working less than perfectly now.

This chapter should help you understand what computers are, how they work, what software is available, and the costs of some computer systems you might consider. This is far from a complete guide, but it may help you start to understand this "Brave New World" of computers we are all moving into. The more you know, the better equipped you will be to deal with it.

First some general advice: Definition: *Computer — A box of electronic parts that normally sits on a desk. Its primary input is MONEY.*

No matter what you budget for computerization, even with the best of knowledge, you will be led into spending more. Each successful job you perform on a computer indicates another task that could be done better if you just added another little gizmo.

Another old computer saying is *GIGO!* (Garbage In, Garbage Out.) Do not attempt to computerize any system you don't fully understand and control already. The disaster will be complete.

To begin with, the world of computers is divided into two major areas, *hardware* and *software*. Hardware consists of things you can actually touch, such as the keyboard, the monitor, the diskettes, the printer, and so on. Software (also known as *programs*) is the set of instructions that make the hardware do what you want it to do. Even though you cannot hear, see, feel, or smell the software, it is probably more important than the hardware and can cost as much, or even more than those pretty beige boxes of electronic parts.

Buying a computer system is an important decision because of the overall price and the ways that it can change how you actually do your business. Like everything else, you have to know as much as you can. This chapter will discuss what kinds of software are available, how a computer actually works, and what computers are presently available.

The reason for this order, which may seem strange at first, is that this is the order you should consider your purchase. All experts agree that you should first decide what you need done, which software would be best to do it, and then what machine can most easily and effectively handle that software.

These things change so quickly, it is not clear that anything mentioned at this writing will be absolutely accurate in three months, let alone a year. So try to understand the concepts rather than locking onto any particulars.

COMPUTER USAGE
INTERNAL
FORM

Before you attempt to choose your computer hardware and software, it will be most helpful to think carefully about your present needs and future uses.

Application	% of Use	Comments
Word Processing—letters, memos, original work	65%	How many people should know how to work the word processor? 2 Very Well - Everyone slightly -
Spelling Checking—how important is perfect copy to you	Very	How good is your current secretarial staff Hard working- but bad spellers!
Word Processing—boiler plate like specs, proposals, etc.	15%	How many pages must be easily accessible? At least 175 pages
Mail Merge—mailing personalized letters, minutes, etc.	2%	Is there a lot of this Not yet...
Mailing List—regular mailings to large numbers of people	–	How many names are on your master list? Do you ever sort them? Should we consider this for mktg?
Data Base Management—for mailing list or other item management	–	How many names/categories/addresses/other information do you keep on your list? Just simple stuff
Inventory—do you track a large amount of inventory?	–	How many items/categories/prices/ do you track? None, yet.
Spread Sheet Programs—do you do programming or financial forecasting	10%	For internal or external use? 50/50 Programming/T.I.D. Mgmt.
Accounting Package—will you put your accounting on line?	–	How well organized is it now? Very well.
Graphics—do you need drawings or graphs and diagrams?	?	Drafting quality or sketch quality? Might be nice Color or black and white? to differentiate us from our competition.

Will you need letter, correspondence, or draft quality written output?	Letter and Draft.
Will output be limited to letter size, legal size, or larger?	Letter size only.
How many people will have to use the computer? At what hours?	5 ppl - 8AM to 8PM
How well organized are the functions you wish to computerize?	Quite well

In order to make your purchase more methodical, I've included a **Computer Usage Internal Survey Form** for you to fill out. Any salesperson will be able to serve you far better if you are able to tell him or her as much as you can about the ways you expect to use the equipment. This should help you quite a bit.

As a neophyte in the computer world, always get the simplest system that does what you need done today. The "learning curve" in computers is almost as steep as the "price curve." In other words, the cost of computers has been dropping about 10 percent every year. Even if you know what you might need in the future, it will be cheaper to buy it then than now.

Speaking of cheap, it is possible to save as much as 30 percent by buying equipment and software by mail order. That is a very poor bargain unless you are already an expert. Most people need the hand-holding that comes from knowledgeable sales people in a good store. So shop around both for equipment and the store-support you will need to learn to use it.

The benefits of using computers are overwhelming, but the many pitfalls could overwhelm you. Prepare by reading, walking into stores and playing, and just immersing yourself in the subject. Don't let someone else do it for you. The computer can change how you do *your* business for the better. But you have to understand it and control it. That is not a task you can give to another. You have to do it.

A Market Survey of Available Software Types

In this section we will describe some of the types of programs available to help you do your work.

Before beginning, though, you should be happy to hear that we will not mention anything that requires you to understand "programming," or computer-talk such as Basic, Cobol, Fortran, Pascal, etc. Computers have reached the delightful state where nearly any common business task can be done on one or another readily available pre-written program.

The real problem is that you have to know *EXACTLY* what you want the program to do before you purchase it. Be sure what type of input you will use, what the program should do with it, and what type of output you need. Many programs promise the world, but deliver Rhode Island. Only buy something that you can practice on in the store to guarantee you know what it does and how it will work for you.

Business programs come in an infinite variety, but they can be subdivided into about six major categories. There are accounting, word processing, data base management, spread sheets, statistical-graphics packages, and programs that combine several of these skills.

Perhaps the simplest types of programs to understand are the *Financial Programs*. You can get programs to keep your general ledger, keep track of your accounts payable and receiveable, payroll, cash receipts and disbursements, inventory, etc. These are not simple in the manner in which they work, or their costs ($500 to $1,000 for a complete system), but they should be simple to buy since you, or your accountant, should know the precise accounting system you now use. I would suggest you only try to computerize your present system, as a first step. Later, as you become familiar with the capabilities of the computerized system, you can seek to improve it.

But look for those future capabilities before you buy any system, since the data you enter into that system would probably have to be re-entered into any other system you might want to change to. This is true of all programs, not just accounting ones and is something to be wary of.

And remember that cardinal rule of computerization: *GIGO!* (Garbage In-Garbage Out!). If your accounting system isn't in fine shape before you put it on the computer, don't. First make sure your system works well for you or fix it so it does. Next, see how you might want to improve that in the future. Then get a financial package that can start with your present system with as little change as possible. See how close it can come to meeting your perceived needs for the future. Buy for your present needs first, then for your future needs.

Word Processing programs are the most common programs used in American business. Since some are built into specific machines that can do nothing else, you might not recognize that you are using a program, rather than a very sophisticated typewriter. All word-processing programs use certain features which make typing a delight. For instance, any decent word processor uses *word-wrapping*. This means that you never type a "return" until the end of a paragraph. You just keep typing sentences and the computer knows when to move the text to the next line.

When mistakes occur, you can either *write over* a mistake, *insert* new letters or words, or *delete* whatever you don't like anywhere in the document. While the paragraph may look strange after these operations, using a *format* or *align* command will reform the entire document into perfect paragraphs within any margins you decide. These margins can be changed after the document is finished and you can see how it looks in any format. Most word processors will also *justify* the right margin, making all lines end in an even, instead of a ragged edge.

Word-processing programs can also automatically number pages or produce titles or consecutively numbered footnotes properly at the bottom of the page. It is also possible to *block move* words, phrases, sentences, or paragraphs anywhere in the document. You can also bring in whole paragraphs from other files, so as to create appropriate documents from boilerplate. The *universal search and replace* command can go through an entire document finding each reference to a specific word or phrase and replacing it with any other word or phrase desired.

Other common commands include printing in *boldface* or *double strike*, *automatic hyphenation*, and *change of pitch* (characters per inch). In some programs it is difficult or impossible to underscore, produce superscript or subscript. In other cases it is the printer that restricts some aspects of the program, such as proportional spacing, boldface, or doublestrike, so check out how the combination of computer, program, and printer works together.

There are now adjunct programs available for word processing that will check your *spelling* against a dictionary of 50,000 to 100,000 words, or a *mail merge* program that will allow form letters to be written with specific references to the person addressed, produce mailing labels, or address envelopes. Other programs can even check your grammar for mistakes, cliches, and poor usage.

Word-processing programs cost between $150 and $500 and the subsidiary programs cost about $100 each. The best known word processing program for microcomputers is called WordStar, which does nearly everything one could wish, but is also relatively old (old in this field is over three years) and somewhat cumbersome to use. On the other hand, at this point it may be the only word-processing program many "temps" know. Many other word-processing programs are now available, but they may be available only for specific machines so we won't mention them here.

Don't forget that IBM, Wang, Xerox and others sell machines and programs "bundled" together as complete word-processing systems. But they can do little else. Some of the better micro-computers are equally competent at word processing and do much more as well.

Database Management Programs are designed to manipulate large amounts of data. If the data is the entire phone book, a database system could search for everyone living on the same street and print them out, in alphabetical order or in numerical street address order. If you wish to examine your client list on the basis of who owes you the most, or who bought the most last year, you can do it with one of these systems. These programs do their work by organizing all information (data) into *records* (a personal check, for instance) and *fields* (the payee, payer, amount, date, bank account number, and check number are all fields of information).

If you search through all your checks (those records) looking for the ones made out to your liquor store (that particular field) and bring them out together, you have created a file. Files are collections of records with similar fields.

When you use a database, you have to input information. This can be done most readily by using easily created *forms* on which you put the information you wish to keep track of. Some programs will check to make sure the forms are completely filled out. Then you can look for information by *sorting* (looking for the specific information you want and re-ordering it in a more useable form), *merging* that information with other information, and printing it out. It is also important to be able to modify the database as future changes in your business alter what you want to do with your assembled and soon-to-be-assembled data.

Database management systems are among the most complex and difficult programs to deal with. They cost anywhere from $150 to $1,000. And even more expense may come later in providing enough memory so the program can access it all and function quickly.

The Spreadsheet Program is one of the major causes for the explosive growth of the computer industry. "Visicalc," the first spread sheet program, was invented by a couple of students in graduate school in Boston and was (and is) so versatile that this $200 program may have sold more $2000 computers than all the marketing campaigns of all the early computer companies combined.

A spreadsheet program consists of a grid of at least 65 columns (labeled A, B, C, D...BK) by 250 or more rows (labeled 1, 2, 3...250), like a very large sheet of accounting paper. Each *cell,,* a space defined by the intersection of any column and row (and labeled A1 or BK250) is a specific number of characters wide when printed or shown on a screen, but actually holds as many as fifty or so characters, which may not all be visible in the cell when it is printed out.

Each cell can either be a label (words and letters) or a number. The really fascinating extension comes when one substitutes a formula for an actual number. That formula can derive the value of that particular cell (say, F21) by multiplying (or adding, subtracting, or dividing) the value of another particular ceil (say, C23) by another cell (for instance, whatever cell is exactly to the right of it).

To use an appropriate example, one could label all the floors of a building (one to twenty-three), put their area in the cell (next to each floor number) and multiply it by the rent (the number in another cell) for the third column of numbers. Then, whenever you change the rental rate in that rental cell that each formula refers to, the rental total for each floor would be recalculated and the total for the building.

The spread-sheet programs normally have a large number of built in functions which will allow you to *sum* columns or rows or numbers, or *average* them, *count* them, *present value* them,. or use logarithms or trigonometric functions, or boolean logic.

The process is really too complicated to explain in a paragraph or two. But Visicalc set a standard for this type of program for ease of use that is astounding once you learn the basics. There are now many such programs, some of which offer marginal improvements, but they are not much different. Programs that are often now called "visiclones" cost between $50 and $400.

Visicalc and its competitors are another set of programs that lead you into the expensive chore of providing more memory to bigger and bigger jobs. We often do a net present value cost of rental in various locations, with various cost escalations for different components of occupancy costs and different rates of change during a twenty-five year period. Such an exercise easily eats up 64K (we'll define that later) of total memory, or even twice that in a complicated, twenty-five year real estate transaction. But one can decide to look at a what if... situation, such as different inflation rates: change one number in a spread sheet of a dozen columns and thirty rows, push a button, and the whole sheet recalculates in fifteen seconds.

Spread-sheet programs now have a variety of peripheral programs available as well. The most common allow you to graphically plot the numbers in a spread sheet, as bar charts, pie charts, trend charts, etc. Other programs allow you to statistically analyze data from spread sheets for leading/lagging indicators, regression analysis, etc.

We are just on the verge of an exciting new development in software. Companies are developing programs that combine word processing, database management, spread sheets, and graphics into one package. The first two out so far are 1-2-3 and the MBA. These cost between $500 and $700 for many functions but each is not really as good as any of the stand-alone programs. But Apple will have released "Lisa" by the time this book is published, which integrates the hardware with an already integrated software package. It costs only $10,000 for everything but a printer. VisiCorp will also have released VisiOn by that time, which will have similar performance, but on several different computers. These two developments will set the standards for software in the next two year generation. Stay tuned.

How Computers Work: The Hardware

Computers can do an incredible number of things. But it may help you to realize that they probably can't do anything you couldn't do with a pencil, paper, reference materials, and an infinite amount of time. The real limitation of computers is that they cannot systematize confusion, bring order to chaos, or clarify that which you already do not completely understand. GIGO.

In this description I will try to avoid as much jargon as possible. In most cases, it makes no difference to the user HOW a machine works, as long as you know how to use it. Few of the readers of this book care how their car's automatic transmission works as long as they don't grind gears or stall. In the same way, we will talk about computer equipment and software as "black box systems" — we will include what they do, what you have to do to make them work, and how you measure performance.

The heart of the computer hardware is the *Central Processing Unit* — the *CPU*. This is what actually does the computing in a computer. For most personal computers and small word processors, the CPU costs anywhere from $5 to $20. The reason you have to pay $2,000 to $10,000 for the total package comes from the need to provide the CPU with input, storage for the input while the CPU follows its software instructions, and mechanisms to make the output useful.

Input can be provided by a typewriter-like keyboard, information encoded on a magnetic media such as cassettes, tapes, disks, or diskettes; a light pen; or output from other computers. Some input is also stored in the computer in *ROM*, which stands for "Read Only Memory." This is a set of instructions to the computer on how to act when information is fed into it. As the name suggests, ROM cannot normally be changed.

The computer can temporarily store data and programs in *RAM* which stands for "Random Access Memory." The more RAM a computer has, the more complex work it can do quickly and simply. For present business purposes, the minimum acceptable RAM would be 64K. This means 64 "thousand (*KILO*) "bytes" of information. "Thousand" is in quotes because it is actually 2^{10} or 1,024. A *byte* is like a word to a computer and consists of 8 *bits*, each of which is just a timed electrical pulse which may be on or off.

You hear a lot about 8-and 16-bit computers today. This defines the number of lanes information can take into the central processing unit (CPU). It does not determine the speed a computer works, but it does determine the amount of RAM the CPU can easily address. An 8-bit CPU can easily access 64K, and a 16-bit CPU can easily access 1,024K. That's a sixteen-fold difference in information that can be directly manipulated at any one time.

The difference in the speed in which a computer performs its work is measured in calculations per second. The early personal computers did about 2,000 operations per second. This measurement is called the *Clock Speed* and current personal, or micro computers work at around 4,000 or 5,000 operations per second. If you care to invest a few million dollars in a Cray "supercomputer," you could perform several million operations per second.

The CPU, RAM, and ROM are all on *chips* created of silicon that have thousands of transisters, diodes, and other semiconductor devices on them. While they are often smaller than a quarter-inch square, they need to have all sorts of wires to get information in and out. When it is all put together, you have those little black centipedes with gold or copper legs that you can see in lots of computer ads.

Output can be through printers, plotters, or screens (VDT, or Video Display Terminal, or CRT, Cathode Ray Tube, or TVs). Printers come in two primary types. Almost all computers use a screen of some sort. For business purposes, it is important to get a screen that shows at least eighty characters (roughly the width of a typed page) by twenty-four lines. You also have to make sure letters are shown in both upper and lower case on the screen. While all good business computers do this, the smallest and cheapest personal computers do not. The letters, and graphics shown on a screen are composed of discrete dots called *pixels*. The more you spend, the more readable the characters on the screen will be.

There are several varieties of screens available. The most basic is a TV. No TV, black and white or color, can show eighty characters. A *monitor* is designed to show at least eighty columns. These can come in white (or green or amber) and black or color. A color monitor can be a *composite* type or a *RGB* type. The former is cheaper, simpler, and less accurate in output. The latter is more expensive, more complex, more accurate in what it shows. But neither device will actually affect the accuracy of what the computer is doing.

The simplest system consists of a keyboard for inputing information, the CPU, a screen for showing you the output, and some sort of storage system, usually *diskette*. Disks are made of magnetic recording tape material, usually 5¼-inches or 8-inches in diameter, and are protected by square cardboard sleeves that have holes in them for the "read/write" head to contact the recording medium. Because they are flexible, they are often called "floppies." They work by being inserted into a *Disk Drive* unit. They can store information in various formats and each will store between about 100K and 1,000K bytes of information, depending on the format. An important thing to remember is that different computers read and write in different ways, so, with rare exceptions, disks (and the information they contain) cannot be transferred between different computers.

The least expensive type of storage is found in cassettes such as those you use to play music. These are too slow, cumbersome, and difficult to work with to be used for business purposes except as a back-up for another data storage system, such as *Hard Disk*. A hard disk system is very similar in concept to a floppy, but it works at least ten times faster, usually holds ten times more, and costs five times as much. It normally is permanently mounted in the disk-drive unit (although some removable ones have just been introduced). It has to store data elsewhere for back-up and to make more space for current projects as it fills up with older projects.

Once you have the basic system of keyboard, computer, screen, and one or more disk drives, you will probably become interested in other "peripherals." The first most people acquire is a printer. A *Dot Matrix* printer uses a large number of dots to form letters, much as the moveable news marquees that turn light bulbs on and off to spell out words. These types of printers are fairly inexpensive ($500- $1500), quick (they print 60 to 200 letters per *second*), and the quality of print varies from "draft quality" to "correspondence" quality. *Letter Quality Printers* use a "daisy-wheel" to produce print of the same quality as an office typewriter, or better, at 15 to 60 letters per second. These start at $800, but the better ones cost $2,000 and up.

Plotters can draw the output with accuracy of 1/100 to 1/1000 of an inch. They cost $1,000 and up. The low cost ones take quite a while to make an 8½-by-11-inch picture. For 100 times that, you can do your real drafting. Multiple color plotters are also available. A lower cost alternative for diagrams, not drafting, is using a dot-matrix printer in what is called a *graphics mode* to draw any figure by using discrete dots, just like the letters.

Any time you use a printer or a plotter for output, the result is called *hard copy*. That may be easier for you to use, but you will also simultaneously use the floppy discs for storage of information. Even a small capacity disk will hold about one hundred typed pages.

Each computer has a *Disc-Operating System*, or DOS, which controls how it deals with discs, instructions, and many other things. Most computers cannot deal with other computers directly or through their discs. They can talk through electronic means via phone lines. They do this through *Modems*, (MOdulator-DEModulator) which translate the electronic pulses into a common electronic form for most computers.

A General Market Survey of Hardware

This brief survey will describe some of the computers and peripherals that are available and appropriate to use in an interior design business. But we will not get into the very sophistocated equipment available for prices over $15,000. If you're aiming for that kind of system, get expert consulting help early on and make sure top management is involved in the selection since such systems can actually change how you do your business.

We are going to stick to the basics here. The simplist business system consists of a computer, monitor, floppy-disk drive, and correspondence-quality printer. Common extensions of that system include a letter quality printer, modem, hard disk, and more memory.

The computer field is growing and changing so rapidly that a five-year-old piece of equipment is obsolete. Anything you can think of doing *can* be done *if* you can pay for it... and you can keep equipment current with better software or newer peripherals. All it takes is money.

Computers

The computer itself is often the least expensive part of a data-processing system. This happens naturally, since the part of the computer that actually does the computing costs only about $5 to $25, even when the computer costs as much as $2,000.

It will be easier to discuss computers within certain broad categories. I classify them as educational computers, basic computers, and business computers.

The educational computer category includes many of the names you hear about most, such as all Atari computers, the Vic 20 and 64, the Sinclair/Timex, Texas Instruments 99/4A, and the Radio Shack Color Computer and Model III. These are fine machines for learning about computers, computing, and games. They are not really suitable for business applications.

The basic computer category includes machines adequate for business applications. It requires that they have a decent quality keyboard for inputting information, at least one disk drive for storage of information, a display that shows 80 characters (the rough width of a typed page) and their normal memory is at least 64K (64,000 bytes or characters, enough to hold both a software program and useful application in the memory without needing to access disk storage).

The business computer category improves upon the basic machines by having access to at least twice as much memory (128K), improved keyboards for better word processing, better displays for less tiring viewing, and usually two disk drives. They don't actually "compute" better, just more conveniently.

Basic Computers

This category includes the Apple IIE, Radio Shack TRS II, Commodore PET and CBM, NEC PC8OOOA, Franklin Ace 1000, Heath/Zenith 89, and others. These are all "8-bit" machines (which means they get information in groups of eight bits and can easily deal with 64K of information), and all but the TRS II use 5¼-inch disks with storage capacity between 100K and 300K. None of the keyboards are equal to the standard set by the IBM typewriters, so none is really good for full-time word processing. Their screens vary from just adequate to as good as you can afford. Most of these units have *expansion slots* for additional *boards* that can upgrade or expand their capabilities.

There is a great deal of similarity between many of these machines because the real CPU (Central Processing Unit) they use, which is what actually does the "computing" in the total system, is either a Z80, a Z80A, a 6502, or another look-alike microprocessor. Since those "chips" cost only about 1 percent of the total system cost, the real differences occur in the input and output functions.

A basic system consists of the computer with 64 kilobytes of memory (it can remember 64,000 characters), keyboard, monochrome monitor, and one disk drive. The total cost for such a system ranges from $2,000 to about $4,000.

Business Computers

This category includes machines such as the IBM Personal Computer, the DEC Rainbow and DECmate, the Radio Shack TRS 12 and 16, the Victor 9000, and many others. At this time, an extraordinary number of "IBM compatible" machines are being released from firms such as Texas Instruments, Columbia Data Products, and so on. This indicates that the IBM "PC" will set the new standard for microcomputers as the Apple did for the last five years.

Even if the machines in this category are not "IBM compatible," there is still a great deal of similarity between them since most also share one of three microprocessors. They use either the Intel 8088 (IBM's), the Intel 8086, or the Motorola MC 68000. For our purposes, these are similar "16- bit" units. (The real advantage of "16-bit" machines over "8-bit" machines is their ability to easily deal with more than 1 megabyte of information instead of 64 kilobytes, a sixteen-fold increase. They can, therefore, deal with data and complicated programs more quickly and easily.) A few machines in this category use the same microprocessors as a basic computer, but with special hardware or software so they can access up to 512K.

A basic system in this category will include two disk drives, a minimum of 128K of memory, a monitor, main unit, and usually a separate keyboard. They cost from $3,500 to almost twice that.

These machines have far better keyboards, as a group, and most are detachable from the main unit. Their disk drives will store between 320K and four times that. Their standard monitors usually give better definition to text, if not necessarily to graphics. All of these machines can be expanded through the use of internal "expansion slots" and optional "boards" that can add capabilities, memory, or internal peripherals.

In general, these machines don't do too many operations better than the basic group. They are far better for intensive office use because they have better keyboards, screens, disk drives, and overall "feel." This is important for someone who may spend half the day working such a machine. Because of their greater memory potential, they can also handle larger database management jobs, such as inventory control or 25 year pro-forma analyses without the complications of changing disks, etc.

They are also the current "generation" of simple computers, while the basic category is, to some extent, already obsolete. The usual rule of purchasing computer equipment is to buy the *latest* with the *most software*. For the last five years, that meant buy the Apple. This year, that means buy the IBM. It isn't the cheapest or the best. It is the one everyone writes software for, creates peripherals for, and it will have the most likely "transferability" from one machine or office to another. At this writing, there are seven magazines currently being published devoted exclusively to the IBM PC.

Portable Computers

Another sub-category of computers is becoming quite common. These are portable computers that can fold up their central processing unit, keyboard, and screen into a small suitcase close in size to the airlines "carry-on" dimensions. The current brands include the Osborne, the KayPro, the Compaq, the Hyperion (and Hyperion Plus), and the Colby.

The first two are equivalent to the basic computer group and use CP/M as an operating system which makes them very compatible with some other computers — but you still can't switch disks between them and anyone else. Their real value is in pricing. Both cost under $2,000 with software for word processing and spreadsheeting. They offer the bargain entry into business capable computers.

The latter group mentioned are (supposedly) compatible with the IBM. Keep in mind that almost-compatible is like almost catching the train. These machines cost between $3,000 and $4,000 and may, or may not, come with some software. You can take these with you, but do you need to? Their biggest advantage may be the price advantage they offer... or their styling to this style conscious industry.

Peripherals

Printers

The first peripheral any business needs is a printer. Otherwise you will not be able to communicate your computer's results with anyone else. Printers come in two main categories: *Letter Quality* and *Correspondence Quality*.

Letter-Quality printers produce text, and text only, by using either a "daisy wheel" or a "thimble" to create letters in the same manner that any typewriter does, but with even more capabilities. Some printers can print titles or headings in "boldface" or "double strike" by going over the words two or more times or provide "true proportional spacing" with the "i" taking up less space than the "o." With true proportional spacing (which also requires control by an adequate word- processing program), you can have fully justified margins on both sides of the page and lettering that looks as if it were typeset.

These machines produce words at speeds between 12 and 60 letters per second. The slowest, such as the Smith Corona TP 1 and converted electronic typewriters, cost only $800 or so and do not offer boldface or proportional spacing. Others, like the NEC, the Diablo, and the Qume, offer more speed, more options, and cost between $2,000 and $4,000.

Correspondence Quality printers produce text (and sometimes graphics) by using dots arranged into the approximate shape of letters. The dots are printed by a swiftly moving printhead that has seven, eight, or nine wires arranged in a vertical row. They shoot out as needed to hit a ribbon onto the paper to make any shape out of dots. This is a fast method, producing letters at speeds of 40 to 200 per second. The more expensive of these machines can make even better-quality letters by going over each letter two, three, or even four times. That is still not the same quality as letter-quality printers, but would be quite presentable to most clients.

The most popular of this type of printer by far is the Epson line, which has been chosen by IBM, Hewlett Packard, and others to be sold under their label as well. They are moderately slow and sell for between $700 and $1,000. Other brands in this category are Okidata, Axiom, Centronics, and Anadex.

The higher priced, and better, letter-quality, dot matrix printer lines are IDS, Malibu, and some of the Centronics printers. They cost between $1,000 and $3,000.

Before you make a decision, you have to look carefully at what each printer can and can't do *with your computer and your word processing program*. It will vary significantly.

Monitors

If you choose a computer that does not come with a monitor, you will have to buy one. Even with certain computers, if you want graphics, you may have to buy another monitor. There are three main categories: *Monochrome, Composite Color,* and *RGB Color*.

Monochrome monitors produce signals in white, green, or amber on a black background. Like a TV, they come in screen sizes between 9 and 13 inches. The green or amber signals are easier to read than white and cost more. Monochrome monitors cost between $100 and $350. Some brand names in this area are NEC, Sanyo, Amdek, USI, BMC, etc.

Composite color monitors are actually just like TVs in the way they take signals and produce pictures. While they are good at graphics, with a few high-priced exceptions, they cannot reproduce eighty characters clearly, and thus should not be considered for business use.

RGB Monitors produce colored pictures with each of the three primary colors that make up all colors under separate control. They are usually 12 inches or 13 inches and cost between $700 and $1,000. The major brand names are NEC, Amdek, Electrohome, and Princeton Graphics. IBM now carries one for its PC.

Other Peripherals to Consider

Hard Disks: If you handle large amounts of data, such as a warehouse inventory or a building management program, you may wish to have information equal to ten or more floppy disks almost instantly available. A hard disk system does this by using an enclosed shell, more rigid material, and higher speed to record or read information from a spinning disk of magnetic media. These are available from a wide range of manufacturers in sizes from five to twenty "megabytes." The cost for such a system is between $2,000 and $4,000. But remember that this has to work with *your* system and can't just be purchased without making sure of its compatibility with both your hardware and software. IBM now makes a computer with the hard disk built in, and other manufacturers are doing the same.

Modems: If you want your computer to be able to transfer information with another computer, you will need a modem (from MOdulator-DEModulator). This device will transfer information over telephone lines. The speed is usually either 300 "Baud" (characters per second) or 1200 Baud. You pay extra for the extra speed. Each computer has to have compatible software and, in some cases, hardware. The popular modems cost between $400 and $1,000.

Plotters: Plotters will take graphics and produce good to excellent quality drawings. While the hardware starts at $1,000, the software will add substantially to that. This is an area you should explore only when you've already used your computer for quite a while.

If you are thinking of getting involved in Computer Aided Drafting and Design (CADD), just be aware that the cost of entry into that field has been diminishing...from half a million dollars to a tenth of that.

Glossary

BIT	From the term "Binary DigIT," the smallest piece of information a computer can recognize...it has only the attributes of on or off.
BYTE	A sequence of eight bits, which is like a computer word.
CADD	Computer Aided Drafting and Design.
CASSETTE	A plastic holder of a reel of tape for storage of data. It is slow to write on or read from, but can hold a large amount.
CENTRAL PROCESSING UNIT	The heart of the computer that actually does the computing.
CLOCK SPEED	The number of times each second the computer performs an operation.
COMPOSITE MONITOR	A less expensive form of color monitor that uses one set of instructions for all colors.
CPU	The Central Processing Unit.
CRT	(Cathode Ray Tube)-Another name for a monitor screen.
CURSOR	A flashing line or spot that shows where you are working on a screen.
CURSOR CONTROLS	The keys that control the position of the cursor. Better computers have four or more keys whose only function is to move the cursor.
DISK	A round device made of recording material kept in a protective cardboard cover, which can have data written on it, read from it, and erased from it.
DISK DRIVE	A device that reads and writes data on disks.
DISKETTE	Another name for a disk.
DISK OPERATING SYSTEM	The set of instructions built into a computer that determines how it deals with information on disks, and, in fact, how it operates internally.
DOS	The Disk Operating System.
DOT MATRIX PRINTER	An inexpensive printer that produces letters made up of small, discrete dots.
GRAPHICS	Producing any type of figure rather than predetermined shapes, such as letters, numbers, etc.

GRAPHICS MODE	The method of producing any shape desired, rather than predetermined character sets, usually from discrete dots. This term usually applies to a dot matrix printer.
K	The universal symbol for 1,000. When related to computers, it stands for 2^{10} or 1,024.
LETTER QUALITY PRINTER	A type of printer that uses fully formed letter hammer, usually arranged on spokes sticking out from a central hub (as in "daisy wheels" or "thimbles") to hit a ribbon to make the high-quality impression on the page.
MODEM	(MOdulator-DEModulator) A device for translating computer output to a form that can be carried on phone lines between computers.
MONITOR	A screen, like a TV, used for seeing the output of a computer.
PERIPHERAL	Any attachment to a computer for input or output.
PIXEL	The smallest subdivision on a screen.
PLOTTER	A device for producing graphics images with continuous lines, rather than dots.
PROGRAM	A set of instructions that tell a computer what to do and how to do it.
RAM	(Random Access Memory) Quickly accessible memory that is usually not stored when the power is turned off.
RGB	A type of screen that requires separate input for the different colors. The computer must have a specific form of output for it to be useful.
ROM	(Read Only Memory) Sets of instructions built into a computer that are difficult or impossible to change. They are kept whether or not power is on.
SCREEN	The TV-like output device for a computer.
SOFTWARE	The programs which make computer hardware do the tasks the user wants it to.
VDT	(Video Display Terminal) Another name for a screen output device.

Some Other Words of Wisdom

If you are just getting involved in computers, there are a few simple rules to follow.

Don't computerize anything which isn't working perfectly already. Remember, *GIGO!*

Get the most popular, newest equipment with the most software. This will allow you to avoid shakedown periods, specially developed software, and ending up with a dead end, obsolete system that is not supported in the future.

Get the simplest version that does what you need done today. Everyday hardware and software get better and cheaper, making yesterday's bargain obsolete. If it doesn't become obsolete, it will still be cheaper next year.

If you aren't sure what you are doing, shop around for a good store that will support you with introductory lessons, tutorials as needed, and repair facilities. You can buy almost anything mail order for 10 percent to 30 percent off. It is not worth it, if you don't know how to use it, or why it isn't working as it should, and can't ask someone.

Be prepared to spend lots more money than you budget for the immediate hardware and software requirements. Computers, once they are being used and understood well, keep suggesting new uses and new capabilities. Remember, their primary input is money.

And good luck!

17 The Business Plan and How To Use It

The **Business Plan** is a document that you can use to create and run your business on a theoretical basis. You start with realistic assumptions, stated plainly. You proceed by fiscal periods, such as months, quarters, and years through the use of income statements and balance sheets.

The business plan can discover issues that you may not have properly addressed and help you come up with tentative plans to deal with them. It can also help you formulate realistic operating assumptions that you can later use in running the firm. The plan might help you target your marketing. It will certainly help you to establish your true financial needs before they are actually necessary. It can help you actually start the company by acting as your initial operating plan. It will be your guide for future growth.

A well thought out business plan is required to get any investor to offer capital, to get any loan or line of credit from a bank, and may be necessary to get credit from trade sources.

A good business plan has five separate components. The *Business Statement* describes the business and its purpose. The *Starting Position* indicates how, where, and when the business will begin. The *Market Description* distinguishes the clients and services of the company. The *Competition Description* describes the competitive environment in this market. And the *Financial Pro-Formas* show your business operating for a three to five year period.

The Business Statement should succinctly state the purpose of the business, such as what needs it actually fulfills, how it will operate to fulfill those needs, what it will actually produce or do, and who will be involved in the business as the owners, employees, investors, and advisers.

You have to describe yourself and your background. How is that appropriate to what you are expecting to do? Explain what your involvement will be, your financial status, and how it will be intertwined with this business.

What are your projections for yearly growth? Include the possible ranges of success. What are the alternatives for termination of the enterprise? Can it be sold, or does it just close up? Is there any salvage value?

The Starting Position should be well defined. Explain if this is a new business, a buy-out, or a merger of existing practices. What are the terms? Include if there are any long-term existing relationships with clients, suppliers, leases, and so on, and how long these relationships have existed? What are the initial financial needs for both start-up funds and working capital?

Describe the start-up location and physical facilities. Who will be the initial personnel involved and how might you expand?

The Market Description should distinguish the characteristics of the market you hope to serve. List your prospective customers. How will you inform them of your existence and your services? Describe the services, in detail, you are actually selling. Why is this service needed? By whom? Show the characteristics of this market: standard types of contracts, standard fees, terms, etc.

The Competition Description should list your half-dozen or so nearest competitors, how well they are presently doing, and what their strengths and weaknesses are. You should also explain how you will be better than they are and describe what you have learned from looking at their operations and customer base.

The Financial Pro-Formas must show your cash-flow projections, working capital requirements, profits and losses, loan-repayment schedule through monthly or quarterly projections for at least three years. You should consider running these pro-formas under pessimistic, most likely, and optimistic conditions to show what all the possibilities are. You should use pro-forma income statements (a **Pro-Forma Cash Flow Form** is included here) and projected year end balance sheets to show how your net worth (assets minus liabilities) changes over time. I hope it goes up...quite a bit.

Only with a good business plan can you try to get financing. Investors will look closely at your organization and its appropriateness to your self-defined mission. They want you to have a true grasp of your strengths and weaknesses and how they relate to competitive strengths and weaknesses. Have you taken a realistic look at the total business concept? Do you have a truly possible perspective on the time it takes to get work and build up a firm?

If you are actually looking for financing, the business plan should be prepared as well as any professional presentation you make. It should be neat, well organized, graphically identifiable, and thoroughly businesslike. Investors will also want to see that you are well aware of the concepts of finance, marketing, and are truly and realistically profit-oriented. A **Business Plan Summary Checklist** is included to help you get organized.

Some investors will be looking for security and some will be looking for profit growth. To which is your presentation oriented? You have to be aware of that, and pitch your presentation accordingly.

If this whole idea of starting your firm is interesting to you, but you are not ready to take definite action, start now with your business plan. It will be wonderfully educational and give you an entirely new perspective on the work you are doing for others. If you are not sure how to start a plan, try doing the final paper I used in my Business Practices class at NYU.

BUSINESS PLAN SUMMARY CHECKLIST

Company:	21ˢᵗ Century Design
Date:	4/4/84
Person Completing Checklist:	A.L.

Check off the following items after you have researched the area, come to realistic conclusions about it, and written a concise summary of your findings in your business plan.

1. Market Description

- ☐ The following client needs have been targeted for this business to serve: high ratios - computers to people
- ☐ This service will provide solutions for those needs in the following manner: Corporate & I.D. knowledge
- ☐ The needs exist in the following groups of potential clients. high tech companies + publishing
- ☐ These potential clients will need services (products) in the following amounts over the next five years: HUGE amounts - Growing firms more very frequently — plan little ahead-
- ☐ These clients can be reached through the following means with my message: Trade articles
- ☐ Normal fees for these services are: $2.50/RSF
- ☐ Fees are normally paid by: Monthly billing of D.P.E. multiple

2. Competition in this Market

- ☑ My six most likely competitors will be: lots of regular designers - none w/high tech ability
- ☑ Their perceived images are: Decorator - designers
- ☑ Their present level of success appears to be: Decent - but know more about Prints - not Pascal
- ☑ Their apparent strengths and weaknesses are: Don't know the new clients
- ☑ I will do better work than they do, because: I know how these folks do their business
- ☑ I have learned the following from studying them: Be on time and on budget — AND BETTER!

3. Business Statement

- ☑ The purpose of my business will be: To create business offices integrated w/ Technology
- ☑ It will fill the following needs: Let people work comfortably w/ computers
- ☐ It's distinctive competence will be: all sizes of CRT's - pc's, micro's, mini's, wp's
- ☑ It will produce its service by the following methods: same as any ID firm
- ☐ My relevant background is: 5 years in DP, Arch. degree, 3 years in interiors
- ☑ My financial status is: Just OK, $25K in bank
- ☑ My involvement will be: Principal — 100%
- ☑ It will be lead by: me
- ☑ It will be managed by: me
- ☑ It will employ: at least 2-3 others
- ☑ It will be owned, in the manner described, by: Incorporated, Sub-Chapter "S", stock - 100% mine
- My pessimistic, likely, and optimistic projections for yearly growth are
- ☑ attached in the pro formas.
- ☑ The business's terminal value may be: LOTS, I hope

4. Starting Position

The business will begin in the following situation:
- ☑ Financially: $25K cash, $25K debt
- ☑ Personnel: 3 ppl
- ☑ Location: store front next to computer store
- ☑ The start-up funding requirement will be: $50K
- ☐ The first year's operating funding requirement will be: $125K

5. Financial Pro Formas

- ☑ Attached are three years of quarterly pro forma operating statements: Done
- ☑ and year end balance sheets: "
- ☑ Cash flow projections: " } All on Pro formas
- ☑ working capital requirements: "
- ☐ loan repayment schedules: "
- ☐ profits/losses: "

Business Plan Project

Poor Uncle Samuel has passed on, at the ripe age of 94. Because he always liked you, and because you did such a fine job brightening up his home in his final decade, he has left you a very nice legacy of $15,000. The attorney handling his will, your kind Uncle John, may be willing to loan you $45,000, at prime, for up to three years, if you can convince him you can run an effective, and profitable, firm.

Write a business plan for the start-up and first three years' operation of your new firm to convince him you can do it for $60,000... and do it well enough for him to get his interest and principal. Consider all financial, organizational, informational, personnel, and personal factors. Lawyers have a short attention span, so keep your plan under five typed pages. Be totally realistic.

The details are as follows. You have $15,000 in the bank, free and clear. You are getting, perhaps, $45,000 more, which you will pay interest on at the prime rate (the rate banks charge their best customers... or you could assume 10 percent). The principal will have to be repaid in full in three years, in a single balloon payment.

You need to take out $20,000 each year to live on. You will need another designer/drafter ($20,000 salary) and a secretary/receptionist ($15,000 salary) in order to open your doors as a real design firm. You pay time-and-a-half after forty hours to your employees, but not to yourself.

You have only one client who will come with you right away, and his work will continue to average $1,000 per month for at least a year.

You cannot expect your clients to pay you any faster than sixty days after billing. But because you are trying to establish good credit, all your bills will be paid promptly in thirty days.

You can try to grow as fast as you can, but be realistic. And consider there is a strong likelihood of a business slowdown occurring in one year and lasting a year.

The goal of this game is to pretend that you are running a firm. Be as accurate as you can. Find out how much it would cost to rent space, your deposit, the cost of furnishing it, the deposits you have to give the utility companies, and so on. Try to earn enough in three years to buy your apartment, which will be going co-op. This is actually a very tough assignment which you can have a lot of fun with. And you can't lose any money... yet.

Firm Name:	21st Century Design
Page	1 Of 6
Person Completing Form:	A.L.

Assumptions:
1. Salaries and other expenses paid in month accrued.
2. All other expenses paid within thirty days (A/R = 30 days).
3. All income received sixty days after billing (A/P = 60 days).
4. Bad debts average 1.5% of income.

Month of:	Jan. '85	Feb	Mar	April	May	June
Salaries paid:	$4,650	$4,650	$4,650	$4,650	$4,650	$4,650
Salaries billed:	1,500	2,000	2,500	3,000	3,500	3,500
Multiple:	3.5	3.5	3.5	3.5	3.5	3.5
Total A/R:	5,250	7,000	8750	10,500	12,250	12,250
CASH FLOW						
Cash on Hand:	50,000	31,800	21,600	16,650	13,450	12,000
Cash Received:						
For Prof. Svcs.	0	0	5,250	7,000	8,750	10,500
Deposits for Furn. (escrow)	0	0	0	0	0	0
Payments for Furn. (to mfr)	0	0	0	0	0	0
Svc. Fee for Furn.	0	0	0	0	0	0
Other:	0	0	0	0	0	0
Other:	0	0	0	0	0	0
Total Cash Income	0	0	0	0	0	0
Expenses						
Salaries	4,650					
Fringes	1,400					
Rent	850					
Telephone	250					
Legal	206					
Accounting	200					
Insurance, Errors & Om.	0					
Insurance, Fire & Theft	150					
Utilities	200					
Supplies	750	150				
Reproduction	200	200				
Agency/adv/hiring costs	0					
Postage	50	50				
Equip. svc. contracts	50					
Travel	500					
Promotion	1000					
Interest	225					
Capital Improvements	5000	100				
Other: Deposits	2000					
Other:	0					
Allowance for Taxes:	500					
Total Cash Outlays	18,200	10,200	10,200	10,200	10,200	10,200
Cash On Hand (end of Month)	31,800	21,600	16,650	13,450	12,000	12,300
Professionals Employed:	2					
Staff Employed:	1					
Contracts on Hand	2	2	2	3	3	3
Square Feet Completed					1,500	1,500
Cost of Work Completed					3,500	3,500

18 Starting a Firm

In America the odds against success in starting your own firm are nineteen to one. If that sounds frightening, it should. Starting your own firm is not an act to be taken lightly. You can shorten those odds tremendously by good solid preparation. Tailor your career so you get all the experience you need. Look for jobs that develop your capabilities, not just your bankroll.

Prepare a good business plan and spend time with it so you are comfortable with all the aspects of running your own business. Instead of doodling over the layout of your future office, play "what-if" financial games, think of marketing ploys, plan on public relations gambits, and most importantly, develop a *distinctive competence*.

Gather your board of advisers gradually. Whenever you see someone with good experience, knowledge, or advice to offer, try to get them interested in you. Do that by being interested in them. Help them where you can in small things, and perhaps they can help you in larger things later on.

Lay out your expenses. These are basically the same ones you need to include for figuring out your multiple. But in a start-up situation, you probably have to include some deposits as well. I think you should plan on six months overhead expenses, just to be safe. You may get work sooner, but clients may not pay you for another two months. Six months gives you a fair shake at becoming self-supporting.

A **Start-up Worksheet** may help you organize your requirements.

I believe you should start a business with at least one full-time employee. You sound much more business-like with a staff person answering the phone when you are not there. You can also spend more time in marketing, when you don't have to do all the "grunt" work in running the business. Ideally, you should start with one low-level professional and one secretary/receptionist.

An effective way of cutting some costs, is to rent an "executive suite." No, this is not a mid-day rendezvous location. It is an office that various professionals share. Usually each has a private office and shares a conference room, copying facilities, and the services of a common receptionist/secretary. It can be a very effective, inexpensive way to set up a high-class professional-looking operation. It will be more expensive than the typical loft space in which you can show your own design skills as well. But the image is totally different. It is a good option, well worth considering.

START-UP WORKSHEET

Date:	1/30/85
Person Completing Worksheet:	H.S.

BOARD OF ADVISORS:

☑ Attorney:	D.W. Nichols
☑ Accountant:	G.R. Gilbot
☑ Banker:	L.M. Drake — 1ˢᵗ Int'l Bank
☑ Insurance Broker:	N. Lieder

BUSINESS PLAN:

Business Statement:	To serve firms swamped by the new technology
Starting Position:	Three clients want me to do some work for them
Market Description:	Burgeoning need for any firm w/ large database
Competition:	No firm has targeted this market, many serve it (poorly!)
Pro-Formas:	Done — they look okay

☐ Approved by Board of Advisors

SIX MONTH EXPENSE PROJECTIONS:		SUGGESTED MINIMUM:
$ 15,000	Your Draw	$?
10,000	Professional's Salary	9000
7,000	Secretarial/Receptionist's Salary	6000
4,000	Fringes	7500
3,000	Legal Retainer	3000
2,500	Incorporation or Agreement Cost	2000
1,500	Accounting Fees	1500
5,000	Insurance	1000
1,000	Rent	6000
2,000	Rent (Deposit)	1000
1,000	Office Furnishings (rental)	3000
200	Utilities	500
200	Utilities (Deposit)	100
200	Telephone Rental	150
1,000	Telephone (Deposit)	100
1,000	Telephone Long Distance	250
2,000	Office Equipment (Rental/Cost) (rental)	1000
1,000	Cards & Letterhead	1000
1,000	Postage	500
1,000	Office Supplies	500
1,000	Promotion—Travel	500
1,000	Promotion—Entertainment	1000
2,000	Promotion—Mailings	500
1,000	Promotion—Brochures	1000
$ 64,000	Subtotal	$ 47100
6,000	Contingency	4710
$ 70,000	Total Expenses (Your Draw +)	51810
25,000	Income Committed or Pre-sold	(?)
$ 45,000	Total Capital Required	$ (?)

It would probably be foolhardy to try to start your business without some work already pre-sold. The more clients you have who are willing to go with you, the better. On the other hand, it is not really ethical to try to steal clients from where you may be employed. I think a fair approach is to ask clients with whom you have already established some sort of relationship for their advice about going into business for yourself. If they are interested in following you, let them broach the idea. You should not ask them any such thing directly. After you leave, you may send an announcement to any clients you have personally dealt with. Don't make any efforts more than that.

Initial clients will certainly reduce some of your fear of failure. But you should still plan on spending most of your time during the first six months marketing. You have to assure yourself of a steady stream of clients, not just a little initial work. Remember, you can't do any work until you sell a contract.

Marketing is your lifeblood.

19 Getting a Job

Perhaps you are not yet running your own firm, or even getting close to being able to consider it. Maybe you are just looking for your first job in the field of interior design, and it is tough to get one. Or you may have gotten your first or even your second job in this field, but you are looking to make a good move to a truly superior job. How do you get the job you want?

It is strange that this low-paying field has such a large number of intelligent, well-qualified people competing to get that first job or vying for the advanced positions. If you are part of that crowd, you have to differentiate yourself by being better prepared and having skills your potential employers need, whether they know it yet or not.

The first step in getting a job is to start thinking about it as early as possible. The first day of school is not too early to decide that your education has two aims, to make you the most qualified interior designer you can be and to make you the most useful employee possible. Your classmates will compete in the former category. Few students, or even employees, will compete with you in the latter category.

In school, and throughout your career, try to concentrate on working on realistic, useful projects. It is better to work on a branch bank than to do a project on remodeling a cruise ship. It is far better to get your instructor to provide a case that is an actual assignment in his or her shop, than a theoretical assignment that is fun to dream about.

Continue working on projects after juries if you are not satisfied with the results. No matter how good your grade was you can make the project into something very fine with the additional time and input. There is never enough time to do this with all your assignments, but just one per class per semester will give you a good portfolio later.

Develop the most professional basic skills you can. Drawing, drafting, lettering, and especially the conceptual work of *presenting* any assignment are critical skills for many reasons. If you can't present your ideas well, your ideas cannot be evaluated well. Employers tend not to be too concerned with their neophyte's ideas, but are much more concerned with their skill in presenting others' ideas. Being *useful* is much more important than being interesting.

Firms also need certain skills. If you can become both proficient and quick at rendering, for instance, many employers will consider that a truly worthwhile skill to bring on board. If you can become capable of programming, in the interior design sense, on a computer, they may find that useful as well.

Avoid the trap of becoming a specialist in one, very limited area. I had the misfortune to meet someone, once, who's first assignment after school was a complex elliptical stair. Having completed that with brilliance, he was, *seven years later,* the firm's expert stair designer.

As you develop your technical skills, try to become an expert in some useful client area. A vast amount of design work is done for banks, brokers, law firms, and energy companies. Very little is done for the style industries, such as cosmetics and clothing. Which would you rather work on in school? Which do you think employers would rather see in your resume and in your portfolio? Stores always need work. Museums are a lot like stores, in presenting visual displays, and may offer a different perspective, if you do both. But if you had to choose, which will be more useful? If you do both, you get the useful experience plus the interesting perspective.

The point is that you should be trying to develop at least one area of "distinctive competence." You need both a skill and an area of expertise to set you off from everyone else. Take your time to find those areas of competence, but don't wait until the last semester.

Develop a portfolio you will be proud to show people. Think carefully, as you learn the many techniques that are available to you, which will work well in a portfolio. As you proceed through your schooling, consider this as a constant project. You will assemble better raw material over several years than you would over the several months before graduation.

Learn the techniques professionals use, such as transfer lettering, making mat windows (actually professionals know about these, but they never have the time...but it sure looks great), and a standard format for all pertinent identification data on each board. Utilize standard drafting techniques and symbols for your documentation, such as those you find in *Time Savers Standards* and *Architectural Graphic Standards*.

Look up the checklist presented earlier in this book on portfolios. Your portfolio should sell your abilities just as a firm's would sell their abilities.

Create a resume that sells you. That means stressing what you can contribute, not what you learned or expect to learn. That is why you spent time and effort developing a distinctive competence, both in skills and in an area of client expertise. You probably won't be as advanced as you think, but you'll be way ahead of your competition.

Physically, a resume should be one page, neatly formatted, simple to follow, with perhaps one distinctive graphic quality. In one of my many past resumes, I put my name, address, and telephone number in a box made with asterisks. More than 75 percent of the people who interviewed me remembered my resume with the "stars." You can create boldface headings by going over the typing five or ten times. Bullets always look good and you can make them with

RESUME
CHECKLIST

Resumes Should Be:

- ☐ one page, if possible
- ☐ clear, neat, attractive
- ☐ well written, w/ active verbs
- ☐ targeted to your audience and their market
- ☐ just slightly distinctive

Resumes Should Have:

- ☐ name, address, telephone
- ☐ professional objective (opt)
- ☐ education, most recent, first
- ☐ dates, in years only
- ☐ degree, year, school, city, state
- ☐ concentration, honors, etc.
- ☐ experience, most recent, first
- ☐ dates, in years only
- ☐ firm name, city, state
- ☐ title, what you did
- ☐ accomplishments
- ☐ jobs published
- ☐ professional affiliations/recognition
- ☐ articles published
- ☐ awards

Employers Want to Know:

- ☐ what you can contribute now
- ☐ how you can grow and do more

Try to Get Many of the Following In:

Employers look for potential, shown by:
- ☐ excellence (awards, etc.)
- ☐ leadership
- ☐ initiative
- ☐ competitiveness

Firms look for basic skills:
- ☐ drafting
- ☐ rendering
- ☐ color sense
- ☐ furnishings knowledge
- ☐ construction knowledge
- ☐ computer skills
- ☐ knowledge of client business
- ☐ organizational knowledge

They also look for basic business skills
- ☐ writing

- ☐ oral communication
- ☐ quantitative skills

human relations skills
- ☐ social
- ☐ persuasive
- ☐ supervisory

management skills
- ☐ organization
- ☐ coordination
- ☐ motivation

They want experience
- ☐ real world school projects
- ☐ summer job experience
- ☐ work for other firms
- ☐ work for their clients

a lower case letter "o," with the center filled in later. Of course, you should be using an excellent typewriter with a carbon ribbon.

Usually your personal data is at the top, a job objective is optional, but would follow, and your education, experience and accomplishments come next in reverse chronological order. The dates would be in the margin on the left. You should retype your resume as many times as it takes to get a good-looking one. Consider it a graphics composition project. If yours is too big for one page, type it on larger paper and photostat it down to fit on normal paper. Typewriter type looks even better that way. It is not necessary to have it typeset. Offset print the good quality typewriter version onto high quality paper and get extra sheets for cover letters and matching envelopes as well.

When you graduate from school, you would normally start with your educational background, your accomplishments such as awards if you got any, and, last, your experience which is probably summer and part-time work. As you gain experience, that experience moves to the head of the list, with accomplishments and schooling following. Eventually, with lots of experience, your accomplishments should head the list, followed by your experience, with your education listed last. Accomplishments would be jobs of specific interest that won awards, or were published, as well as articles you may have written, professional societies you may be a member or an officer of, and so on.

When you describe what you have done, never use the word "I." Say, "won a Rhodes Scholarship...," not, "I won a Rhodes...." Always use active verbs to describe what you did. Never say, "I helped clean up the library..." when you could say, "organized all reference materials." A list of active verbs is attached to help you create these wonderful accomplishments.

Your resume should be targeted to the kind of work you want to do. If you are not sure, create more than one. And remember, all resumes are fiction, to some extent. If you can upgrade actions such as cleaning the library, do so. It is expected.

Employers look for four things: experience, basic design skills, basic business skills, and potential. Make sure your resume indicates as much of that as it can. A **Resume Checklist** is included to help you make sure that you present as strong a case as you can.

Be sure you know what you want to do. Are your portfolio and resume targeted to that sector? How much do you know about the firms you are mailing your resume to? Try to find out as much as you can. Ask professors, other practicing professionals you may know, and look at Interior Design's "Top 100" and "Second 100" articles that list 200 interior design firms, their clients, their employees by category, salaries, billing rates, and so on.

Find out to whom to send your resume by telephoning. Call them and say you

ACTIVE VERB LISTING
FOR RESUME

accomplished	edited	performed
accelerated	elected	planned
achieved	eliminated	prepared
administered	enlarged	presented
allocated	established	preserved
amended	evaluated	presided
amplified	examined	processed
analyzed	executed	produced
appointed	expanded	programmed
approved	extended	proposed
arbitrated		promoted
arranged	forecasted	published
assisted	formalized	purchased
attained	formulated	
augmented	fortified	qualified
audited	founded	
awarded		rectified
	gathered	recorded
broadened	guided	recruited
built	governed	reduced
	graphed	regulated
calculated		reinforced
catalogued	headed	researched
chose		restored
collected	implemented	resulted
commented	improved	revamped
communicated	increased	revised
compiled	initiated	reviewed
completed	issued	
computed	installed	scheduled
conceived	instituted	selected
conceptualized	interpreted	served
condensed	interviewed	serviced
conducted	introduced	strengthened
consolidated	invented	studied
constructed	investigated	suggested
contracted		summarized
contributed	launched	superceded
contrived	listed	supervised
controlled		systematized
convinced	maintained	
coordinated	managed	terminated
created	mapped	traced
cut	marketed	trained
	moderated	transferred
delegated	modified	translated
delivered	monitored	traveled
demonstrated	motivated	trimmed
designed		
determined	negotiated	uncovered
developed		unified
devised	offered	utilized
diagramed	opened	
directed	organized	widened
distributed	originated	won
documented	overhauled	wrote
drafted		

are sending them a resume and gush just a little bit about how much you would like to work there. Hang up before they can tell you there are no open positions. Send the resume, wait one week, and call up to see if they got it and would like to see you. This way, instead of their getting an unknown resume, you've made three contacts, which strengthens your impression substantially.

Since they will probably say no, turn back to the chapters on marketing and sales and use some of those techniques. Push them once or twice, just to make sure that they are sincere about having no positions. Ask them if they would be so kind as to offer a professional opinion as to the quality of your portfolio. The reason you are pushing here, is because the person you see is the person who will probably know what firms are busy and hiring. If you call up firm X and say Ms. Y at firm Z said you should call, you are coming in at a much higher level than most students.

If this all sounds familiar, we are just going over all the techniques mentioned in the marketing and sales chapters...except in this case you are selling yourself instead of design services.

Go through all your contacts to get names; professors, relatives in the business, relatives who have used designers. Go to speeches or presentations designers make. Go up afterwards, tell them how much you enjoyed their presentation, and ask if it is all right to mail them a resume. Do so and call them a week later. Again, you've made three contacts instead of one and created a much stronger impression.

At the interview, you are still selling yourself. Always dress for the position you aspire to. Be on time, or call to say you'll be late. Give a firm handshake. Make eye contact at least half the time.

Do your selling. Find out what his problems are and try to show how you can help in solving them. Know what your price should be and ask just a little bit more. It will make you seem like you are worth it. Never price yourself inexpensively, unless you want to be perceived as pricing yourself accurately.

Thank your interviewer for his time. Follow up with a thank-you letter which reiterates why you would love to work there, how you feel you could be of real value to the firm immediately, becoming more so through time. If you had a good interview and did not get an offer for an apparently valid reason, keep in touch. A call once a year, if you really want to work there, telling them what a success you are, is not a waste of time. They will remember you, and when the right time comes, you'll get the call.

If you are already employed for one year or many, if you need a job, you should follow the same methodology as I just described for the student.

Make sure you are always developing your overall competence and, if possible, a distinctive competence. Once a year, write up a new resume, whether you plan on using it or not. Compare it to last year's. If it's the same, you are in a rut and should get out. Try to move into a new role or greater responsibilities in your present firm or consider looking around. Don't wait for five or ten years to discover you have gone nowhere and have nowhere to go.

Try to dress and act as you would in the position you would like to move up to. Think like a manager, not a designer. Great design is a gift. You can only train yourself to be good, not great. Management is a skill you can learn, doubling your chances for success. Why not try to be a double threat?

One other thing. It is a sad but true fact that most people advance by changing firms. It is your responsibility to always have a job that balances your contribution and your reward. Your contribution is your best effort, long hours, and hard work. Your rewards should be decent pay, recognition, and education and training to allow you to become the best all around designer you can.

If your company is not providing you with that opportunity, look for one that does. Employees tend to feel a loyalty to a company which keeps them. But, in fact, they *owe* you. You work a week or half a month and then you get paid, after the fact. You should feel that there is an equality here. As an excellent book of the same title says, "Go Hire Yourself an Employer." Consider employment as a two way contract and negotiate from a feeling of quality and equality.

20 Additional Facts Professional Designers Should Know

Fact One: Square feet come in many sizes.

There are many different measurements of area that are applied to space within buildings. You should know roughly what they are and what the differences tend to be.

Architectural Gross is a measure of all space on all floors inside the outermost boundary of the walls. *Zoning Gross* is usually a measurement of all area above grade within the outermost boundary of the wall excluding any mechanical floors which are above grade. This measurement is often used in the *FAR*, or *Floor Area Ratio* measurement that compares the total zoning gross area of the building to the area of the site. This is usually a ratio, such as 8:1 or 14:1 which are then called simply by the first number, 8 or 14. City zoning codes will establish different FAR's for different parts of the city in order to control height and overall development density.

Rentable area is the square footage a tenant pays rent on. It is measured from the inside surface of the perimeter glass to the center of any demizing partition separating tenants, or tenants from public space, not including any floor penetrations, such as elevator shafts, stairs, chases, shafts, etc. It is also called BOMA Rentable Area since it was officially defined by the Building Owners and Managers Association.

REBNY Rentable expands the BOMA definition to include a pro-rated share of the mechanical space as well. Thus REBNY Rentable space has been expanded virtually back to the Architectural Gross measurement. In fact, during the recent scarcity of space in New York, building owners simply lied about the amount of space in a building in order to raise rents in a more subtle way. After all, it may seem cheaper to keep the rent at $35 per foot, but raise the square feet count per floor by 5 percent.

Net Usable area is the area inside the convector perimeter minus the core area. If you could call any part of a floor part of a department, like the elevator lobby on a full floor occupancy, it is part of the net usuable area.

Assignable area measures the total space on which you could put a desk. This eliminates the convector along the perimeter wall, the elevator lobby, the core, and the core access corridor along either side of the core.

In general, and very roughly, the following relationship holds true for fairly well designed buildings:

$$\text{Architectural Gross Square Feet} = 100 \text{ percent}$$

$$\text{REBNY Rentable Square Feet} = 95 \text{ percent}$$

$$\text{BOMA Rentable Square Feet} = 90 \text{ percent}$$

$$\text{Net Usable Square Feet} = 80 \text{ percent}$$

$$\text{Assignable Square Feet} = 70 \text{ percent}$$

All these numbers are approximate, but it does show what a difference a label can make. We can't tell about the zoning gross without knowing how many basements, and so on. The other relationships hold true in most well designed buildings, but a sloppy core can make a building far less efficient.

Fact Two: The Work Letter has a specific value.

The Work Letter is the part of a lease that describes what a landlord will provide for a tenant in the way of finished space. The landlord starts with the building shell and then promises to provide a ceiling, lighting fixtures, wall, doors, bucks, hardware, electrical and telephone outlets, flooring, wall finishes, and so on in order to provide a finished space for the tenant to move into.

This is all described both as to quality and quantity. The quantity is usually described as a number per square feet (whatever rentable square feet is defined in the lease). It could be one two tube flourescent fixture per fifty square feet, seven feet of partition, and so on.

This can also be priced out so the tenant can get a *Tenant Allowance* which he could then apply to the quality and type of interior he prefers. Any upgrading of the *Building Standard* interior (that which the work letter describes) as well as additional work the tenant may require, such as a new interfloor stair or reinforcing under a file room, is described as *Tenant Improvements*. All of this is frequently the subject of intense negotiation.

Fact Three: Open plan and systems furniture are not the same thing.

Too often designers are confusing *open plan* and *furniture systems*. "Open plan" really refers to desks placed in open space. "Office landscape" refers to desks surrounded by screens which do not extend to the ceiling. "Closed offices" or "closed plan" refers to offices surrounded by ceiling-height walls.

In point of fact, most "closed plan" offices are between one-sixth to one-half "open plan," in order to accommodate the necessary secretarial and clerical staff.

"Systems furniture" combines furniture components with walls of any height, including ceiling height demountable partitions.

Fact Four: Designers are involving themselves with many decisions which used to be the sole purview of the architect. This is a healthy and necessary trend.

If you remember, earlier in this book I mentioned that decorators used to just choose the furnishings and finishes in a room. Then interior designers came along and started controlling the shapes of the rooms for the benefit of the client's actual use, which they knew. Finally, what might be called interior architects are coming along to modify the building systems to create the entire environment the client requires to function properly.

Eighty percent of the cost of a building is in five primary systems. Foundation and structure, elevator, skin, and mechanical systems (or HVAC — Heating, Ventilation, and Air Conditioning) make up the vast bulk of the cost of the building.

Interior designers should have an impact on the module of the building, which affects the frame and core; the HVAC and convector decisions; and the skin/windows which have such a great impact on lighting and feeling inside.

Other systems that used to be within the design scope of the architect but which should be primarily designed by the interior designer are the ceiling and lighting system, the electrical, telephone, and signal distribution system, and flooring systems.

You are doing a great disservice to any client you have who is constructing his own building or becoming a prime tenant in another owner's structure if you do not learn his needs in these areas, study the options, and represent the client's interest to the architect who certainly does not understand the client's needs as well as you do.